A PEDDLER'S TALE

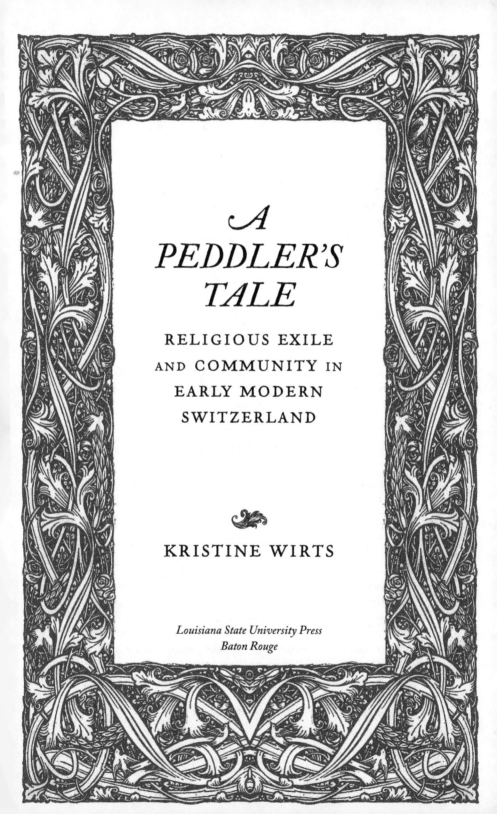

A
PEDDLER'S
TALE

RELIGIOUS EXILE
AND COMMUNITY IN
EARLY MODERN
SWITZERLAND

KRISTINE WIRTS

Louisiana State University Press
Baton Rouge

Published by Louisiana State University Press
lsupress.org

LSU PRESS PAPERBACK ORIGINAL

DESIGNER: Barbara Neely Bourgoyne
TYPEFACE: Adobe Caslon

Cover image courtesy iStock/Dinamiracle

Portions of this book were first published as "Keeping the Faith: The
Story of a Seventeenth-Century Peddler and his Protestant Community"
in *Proceedings of the Western Society for French History* (now the *Journal of
the Western Society for French History*) 42 (2014): 21-31.

Maps created by Mary Lee Eggart.

LIBRARY OF CONGRESS CATALOGING-IN-PUBLICATION DATA
Names: Wirts, Kristine, author.
Title: A peddler's tale : religious exile and community in early modern
 Switzerland / Kristine Wirts.
Description: Baton Rouge : Louisiana State University Press, [2024] |
 Includes bibliographical references and index.
Identifiers: LCCN 2023045548 (print) | LCCN 2023045549 (ebook) |
 ISBN 978-0-8071-8203-1 (paperback) | ISBN 978-0-8071-8253-6 (pdf) |
 ISBN 978-0-8071-8252-9 (epub)
Subjects: LCSH: Giraud, Jean, 1639–1708. | Huguenots—Switzerland—
 History—17th century. | Refugees—Switzerland—History—17th century. |
 Switzerland—History—1648–1789. | Freedom of religion—France—
 History—17th century. | Huguenots—France—History—17th century.
Classification: LCC DQ49.H77 W57 2024 (print) | LCC DQ49.H77 (ebook) |
 DDC 284/.5092 [B]—dc23/eng/20231220
LC record available at https://lccn.loc.gov/2023045548
LC ebook record available at https://lccn.loc.gov/2023045549

FOR MY PARENTS

CONTENTS

ILLUSTRATIONS

GRAPHS

MAPS

ACKNOWLEDGMENTS

Ever since my graduate years when Donna Bohanan introduced me to Carlo Ginzburg's story of the Italian miller, Menocchio, I have been interested in exploring the lives of ordinary people to understand how they made sense of their world. This book attempts to do that for a common seventeenth-century merchant-peddler, who has been an all-consuming but exciting part of my life these past few years. I thank Donna Bohanan and Frank Smith for helping me bring this project to completion: Donna for her invaluable and perceptive observations, and Frank for his thorough and meticulous review of my manuscript. Without both their encouragement and steadfast support this book would not have been realized.

If it takes a village to raise a child, it most certainly does to write a book. There are numerous family members, friends, colleagues, and former teachers who shared my journey in researching and writing this book. Family I wish to thank include Steve Wirts, Carla Repice, Lea Ann Crisp, Margi Tucker, Rick Tucker, Sharon Maestri, Dolores Stolfi-Dicks, Paul E. Dicks, Lisa Morrell (*Chef économique*), Efren Rodriguez, Neil Wirts, Judy Wirts, Charles Wirts, Martha Hopper, Kay Wirts, Lisa Marshall Cockrum, Theresa Marshall Bangert, Jeanine Marshall Peters, and Dan Peters. I would like to extend a special thanks to Kathleen Marshall, whose fruitful discussions regarding Jean Giraud over Chinese take-out and plum wine were a great inspiration for this book.

Friends, colleagues, and former teachers to be thanked include Gary Noll, Russ Skowronek, Dora Garcia Saavedra, Fred Ernst, Leslie Tuttle, Bob Miller, William E. Hammond, Meredith L. Adams, Sylvia Hoffert, Ginger Harris, Thomas Daniel Knight, Stella Behar, Robert Behar, Constance Elaine Goss, Carol Ann Vaughn Cross, Cliff Vaughn, Jennifer Mata, Amy Cummins, Shawn Thomson, Tamer Balci, Tania Han Balci, and Ayda and Ayla Han Balci. I am deeply indebted to Chris Miller for his critique of earlier drafts of this book and to Amanda Eurich for her critical comments and suggestions. Amy Hay kept me grounded and lifted my spirits during the research and revision phases of this book. I appreciate her many insights regarding religious and economic identity. I am profoundly grateful to Ruth Whelan, who befriended me at the "Women and Work across the Eighteenth-Century Francophone Globe" international conference and provided me with an impressive array of illuminating sources. I thank Christopher Tomlins, who read and furnished feedback on my book proposal, and Grigory Talalay, who freely offered his photos of Paul Monnet's *oignon* pocket watch. I am additionally indebted to my doctors, Azfar Malik, Rose Hiner, David L. Super, Olivier Casez, and Anne Cross, whose care ensured my health and enabled my research overseas.

I have benefited tremendously from the help of many French and Swiss archivists and historians. Danièle Tosato-Rigo at the Université de Lausanne provided constructive input and recommended important sources for this project. Lorraine Filippozzi of the Archives communales de Vevey was a wonderful resource and responded to all my inquiries and concerns, no matter how small. Fanny Abbott of the Musée historique de Vevey met with me and offered expert guidance, while Carole Laubscher, Raphaël Berthoud, Acacio Calisto, and Gilles Jeanmonod of the Archives cantonales vaudoises were a great help in answering my numerous questions and navigating me through the archives. Cristel Romera of the Archives départementales des Hautes-Alpes played a vital role in identifying crucial documents, and Hélène Viallet of the Archives départementales de l'Isère supplied indispensable research and direction on the various archival collections concerning the village of La Grave.

I am grateful to the University of Texas at Austin's Center for European Studies and to my host institution, the University of Texas–Rio Grande Valley, for their financial assistance. The University of Texas at Austin's Center for European Studies awarded me a grant to complete my research for this book, while the University of Texas–Rio Grande Valley subsidized my writing with a Faculty Development Leave.

I would like additionally to thank Louisiana State University Press. My anonymous reader furnished me with generous comments and precise suggestions for revisions that enabled me to clarify many points, making the book that much stronger, while my editor, Alisa Plant, showed patience, encouragement, and positive energy throughout the entire process. Alisa, whom I met many years ago at the Western Society for French History annual conference, believed in the merits of this project from its inception through its final stages. I am eternally grateful to her and the Press for their support.

Finally, to my mother, Toni Wirts, who nurtured my creative spirit and impressed upon me from an early age an appreciation for other cultures, and to my father, Ron Wirts, who instilled within me a passion for history and compassion for others; to both my parents, whose unwavering love and support enabled me to make this book a reality, I dedicate this book to you.

A PEDDLER'S TALE

Introduction

On August 25, 1685, French peddler Jean Giraud returned to his Alpine home in La Grave following a business trip to Lyon. The Huguenot merchant's arrival coincided with the sound of booming cannon, as companies of royal cavalry descended on the small towns and Protestant communities that dotted the valleys of the Hautes-Alpes. This military sweep anticipated the issuing of the Edict of Fontainebleau by Louis XIV, the King of France. By this mandate, the Edict of Nantes was revoked: henceforth Protestantism was officially banned in France. In the weeks and months that followed, provincial authorities enforced the king's decree by quartering dragoons in the homes of recalcitrant Protestants.

Jean Giraud recorded these harrowing events in his *livre de raison*, an account book that merchants typically maintained for record keeping. His contemporary reporting of arrests, book burnings, pillaging, and executions described the full and crushing power of the state and the resources brought to bear on local Huguenot communities. The Revocation and its violent aftermath resulted in the mass exodus of Dauphiné's Protestants, including every member of Giraud's church. Many émigrés were merchant families, who scattered throughout Europe and the Americas seeking refuge. Giraud and his family escaped to Geneva, carefully slipping undetected through the narrow Alpine passes. They were the lucky ones; others, caught in the attempt, were sent to the galleys or publicly hanged, their severed heads later placed on pikes for all to see. The merchant turned chronicler ensured that these events, too, found their way into his livre de raison.[1]

Jean Giraud belonged to a community of merchant-peddlers; many owned shops in nearby cities such as Lyon and Geneva, and maintained their homes in rural villages in the French Alps. Giraud's peddling business grew from marriage alliances and family networks that provided the social and economic foundation for his commercial enterprise. In France, Giraud built up an enterprise based on moneylending and the sale of textiles and books. Later, while in exile in Switzerland, he pursued sales of books, possibly watch tools and parts, and women's lace and accessories. In his livre de raison, Giraud detailed his experiences and that of fellow Huguenot villagers after the Revocation, transmitting his first-hand account of the persecution of other church members and their flight from France, including his own family's perilous journey across the Alps. Though not of great wealth, Giraud possessed sufficient resources to depart France and permanently resettle his family in Vevey, Switzerland.

Historically important as a contemporary narrative of events, Giraud's livre de raison also reveals the peddler's thoughts and activities as a father, church member, and cultural mediator. And, too, the rich corpus of commercial paperwork that made up a merchant's typical livre de raison tells us a great deal about the operations of family businesses. Aristocrats and merchants alike often recorded their business transactions in this fashion, information that consisted of account records in the form of lists, numbered columns, and in some cases, double-entry bookkeeping.[2] In addition, a livre de raison typically included records of family events: marriages, births, baptisms, and deaths. These dates were important for commercial purposes. Businesses were family enterprises built from financial alliances secured through arranged marriages and generational wealth.

Though often similar, livres de raison followed no single formula, and while the livre was not a diary in the modern sense, it might at times convey the personal thoughts and musings of its author. As historian Isabelle Luciana has noted, "men and women alike" were sometimes moved "to document their struggles with unequal social and cultural competencies." In this respect, the livre de raison offered a rare and intimate glimpse into the mindset and private concerns of the family patriarch, especially as he viewed and understood his society and community. Luciana notes additionally that livres de raison, written in the first person, permitted their authors the chance "to affirm themselves as subjects and reclaim their dignity—namely, the dignity to speak about the self."[3]

Though only one volume of Jean Giraud's livre de raison has survived, much can be gleaned from it regarding his life during a time that marked an important cultural and intellectual crossroads for western Europe.[4] Like other merchant account books, Giraud's *livre* detailed much of his routine business (mainly from the 1670s until his escape to Switzerland in 1686), along with family marriages, births, baptisms, and deaths. The account records and inventories that appear raise important questions regarding the wider implications of Giraud's role as Alpine peddler and cultural mediator. It was through peddlers like Giraud that an insular Alpine populace learned something of the outside world and were directed to new markets for their village goods. Beyond sharing a faith with fellow villagers, Giraud communicated an appreciation for art and music, proper standards of etiquette, and the importance of reading and learning.

Giraud's *livre* can be divided into six distinct sections, each revealing an important aspect of his life and the history of his community in La Grave. The first section represents Giraud's account records from the 1670s until his departure from France in 1686. Though somewhat fragmentary and sparse regarding information about the kinds of goods he trafficked, these records document the history of Giraud's commercial activities and provide data with respect to his business associates and the geographical extent of his peddling. Giraud traded in textiles and supplied buyers with regional resources like timber and wool; he also served Alpine communities by providing individuals credit. He operated a "healthy" business and extended credit to members of his church, fellow villagers, family, and numerous other Alpine merchants, at least forty-five of whom operated shops between Italy and Spain.[5] At the time of his departure from La Grave, forty-two individuals from his home village were indebted to him for a total of around 9,145 *livres*.[6] By furnishing credit in this manner, Giraud provided a service critical for the economic well-being of his family and community.

The second section of Giraud's livre de raison was written in Vevey following his immigration and consists of a list of books he possessed, an accounting of costs accumulated during a family illness, and inventories of watchmaker's tools and ladies' accessories for use in businesses run by Giraud or his relatives. This section provides important insight into Giraud's entrepreneurial activities following his departure from France and resettlement in Switzerland.

A third section of Giraud's livre de raison contains a lengthy and detailed inventory of personal possessions enumerated during the Huguenot persecutions, while Giraud still resided in La Grave. The inventory gives crucial information about Giraud's material life and provides insight into his role within his community, shedding light on the kinds of cultural artifacts that he valued and introduced to others who were part of his social circle and commercial network. This section also includes notes on belongings left behind with neighbors for safekeeping, anticipating their reclamation at some future date should a general amnesty be declared. The remaining sections four, five, and six narrate the details of the persecution itself as it unfolded in La Grave and the surrounding villages. Included here are a list of members and families of Giraud's church in La Grave and matters of personal family history.

Giraud's frequent travels connected him with groups outside his rural sphere. Peddlers like Giraud encountered international clients and co-religionists with shared interests and tastes, both politically and culturally, despite differences in language, ethnicity, and social class. Commentary on the material and religious culture of Alpine Protestants, especially as seen through the eyes of a well-traveled Dauphiné peddler, both during and after the Revocation, sheds light on the transnational nature of Huguenot commercial traffic and the cultural trends and political events, international as well as regional, shaping Huguenot identity. Though socially diverse, many Huguenots experienced a common economic paradigm: they increasingly derived their livelihood from new economic ties and social bonds that evolved with the appearance of nascent capitalism. Europe in the seventeenth century witnessed the emergence of new forms of commercial and capitalist activity, especially in the area of textiles, the manufacturing and marketing of which Huguenot artisans and merchants played a crucial role. One important aspect of the story of Jean Giraud is how it elucidates the economic ingenuity of a minority religious community.

A Peddler's Tale is organized into five chapters. Chapter 1 explores Jean Giraud's first-hand account of life in the French Alps during the seventeenth century. The village of La Grave, home to Giraud's church, was uniquely positioned at the intersection of commercial traffic for the book and textile trades that flourished between the cities of Lyon and Geneva and the rural mountain communities to the south. In Lyon, Giraud maintained a shop likely stocked with both textiles and books, which he obtained from the book dealer Jean Nicolas in Grenoble and from local printers. During this era of French religious conflict, Giraud undoubtedly supplied religious reading to members of his church and others he encountered along the backroads and rural mountain passages en route to and from La Grave. Also, the first chapter reveals that Giraud enjoyed music, art, games, and books. An inventory of his possessions taken at the time of the Revocation makes plain that Giraud lived comfortably and appreciated fine things.

Chapter 2 recounts Giraud's flight from France following the Revocation of the Edict of Nantes. According to Giraud, the persecutions his community experienced began following his return from Lyon in August of 1685, just a few months before Louis XIV revoked the Edict of Nantes. Braving threats of punishment, defiant Protestants fled La Grave. Giraud was carefully watched by authorities and kept under close guard because he was a known leader of his Protestant community. Several attempts to flee France with his family were aborted.

Giraud finally escaped with his wife and daughter in July of 1686. Giraud's family first arrived in Geneva, and settled finally in Vevey, Switzerland, in January 1687.

In chapter 3, the narrative follows the refugee community in Vevey, with analysis focusing on the early years of Huguenot immigration as refugee families struggled to obtain Swiss residency. After the Revocation, between 150,000 and 200,000 Huguenots departed France for destinations across Europe, the largest migration in early modern French history. Most went to England and Ireland, the Dutch Republic, Protestant German lands, and Switzerland. Giraud and other refugee families in Vevey received a mixed reception. The city of Bern set immigration policy for the region, and this oscillated frequently, reflecting the conflicting positions within Swiss leadership. Some in power sympathized with the refugees; others were not so benevolent and sought to expel the most needy. Faced with this regional ambivalence, the Huguenot community developed local social relations to its advantage. This emerged in marriages between Huguenot refugees and people outside that group, unions destined to foster social relations within the larger Swiss community. The distinction accorded godparenthood at the time also assisted Huguenot refugees to develop and extend their influence.

All this social bonding existed under the scrutiny of the local *consistory*, a regulatory body that, taking its cues from Bern, functioned to impose social order and discipline. The consistory had existed in France, too. But, in contrast to France, where local consistories operated without the support of the governing authorities, Bern directed and backed the authority of those institutions in Vaud. Refugee misbehavior noted by the consistory factored in decisions of residency status, though one's economic worth and social connections probably weighed more heavily in such decisions.

Chapter 4 examines Jean Giraud's family business and the economic developments that occurred in Vevey following his relocation. Giraud and other Huguenot refugees found Vevey commercially attractive because it was located outside the municipal jurisdiction of a larger city, and presumably free of the restrictions urban guilds imposed. Upon arrival, Giraud undoubtedly found himself in reduced circumstances. He had left behind home, land, livestock, and almost all of his personal belongings. But he survived, reestablished his business, and earned residency when others were compelled to leave.

Giraud's story was part of a larger economic transformation unfolding across Europe. Capitalist expansion in the seventeenth century led to advancements in manufacturing, commerce, and shipping and to the proliferation of lending houses, joint-stock companies, and stock markets. Within the context of these economic developments, one may conclude that Giraud was a minor figure in a larger movement of economic change, a progression that laid the foundation for a major economic transition in the next century. Vevey's death inventories, wills, and other legal documents provide valuable data on early modern capitalism, patterns of trade, and cultural values.

In addition, chapter 4 delves into Giraud's book peddling, an activity that he continued once in Vevey. Along with a large number of Bibles and other devotional texts, Giraud's book inventory included works of political and religious controversy. The presence of these titles speaks to the anguish of a community that sought understanding, renewed meaning, and political direction at a critical moment in its history. Giraud's literary inventory demonstrates the increasing cosmopolitanism and internationalism of the Huguenot movement as it acted to regroup and rebuild following the Revocation.

Chapter 5 concludes this odyssey with an intellectual journey into early modern concepts of time as they related to the larger, cosmologically significant events in Jean Giraud's life. Giraud kept a pocket watch which he used to help record the daily events in his life. His possession of works on prophecy and the apocalypse by such leading figures as Pierre du Moulin, Pierre Jurieu, Jacques Massard, and Michel Nostradamus complicates any interpretation of Jean Giraud's understanding of time. No scientific image was more prevalent in Huguenot religious texts than the concept of the *grande machine* or *machine ronde*, clocklike metaphors for God's universe. References to the clock, along with other mechanical images, were abundant in Huguenot sermons and intimated a confidence in the power of technology. Though Giraud valued technology and likely entertained mechanistic views, this did not discount the validity of miracles and apocalyptic premonitions. Like other Huguenot refugees and theologians, Jean Giraud sought explanations for the sufferings of his community. He likely accepted the argument that he lived in a cosmologically significant time—the Huguenots, tested by God, would prevail, and triumph at the time of Christ's second coming.

Jean Giraud was an ordinary peddler who did extraordinary things. He enjoyed his life and loved his family. He was a pious man who led and supported his community, recording its troubled experiences. He wrote during a period of significant change, as the king of France imposed extreme anti-Protestant measures in step with the Counter-Reformation. Concurrently, Protestant regions like Bern strove to fortify the gains of the Reformation. Huguenot refugees hoped their foreign sojourns would be temporary and that Louis XIV would one day grant them amnesty, allowing them to return to France. When this did not happen, the exiled learned to adapt. Giraud's family rebuilt its life by engaging in a new industry that portended the beginnings of the industrial economy of the eighteenth century. Jean Giraud's livre de raison, important yet incomplete, provides, with other contemporary documentation, notions of an early modern European world in the midst of change. In this one life, the larger forces of religious conflict and upheaval, state-building, and economic transformation come to bear.

ONE

✺✺

La Grave

Jean Giraud was born July 12, 1639, into a community of French Protestant merchants, many of whom owned shops in Lyon but maintained their church and homes in La Grave and its surrounding villages, a region high in the French Alps. Giraud's father, a village assemblyman and Lyon shopkeeper, prepared his son for life as an Alpine merchant, likely furnishing him the necessary apprenticeship and initial resources needed to establish his own peddling outfit. Over time, Giraud's enterprise grew, mainly from marriage alliances and family networks that served as his firm's financial and social foundation. At its height, Giraud's commercial operation reached as far west as Plaisance, southward to Rodès near Perpignan, and eastward to Turin in northern Italy.[1] Like his father before him, the younger Giraud had a shop in Lyon, while his family resided in Les Hières, where he owned a large four-story house. He also owned a smaller home in the neighboring village of Valfroide, along with thirty pieces of land, eight meadows, and four forests.[2] The focal point of Giraud's community was neighboring La Grave, where his church stood and village assemblies took place.

Jean Giraud was a courageous merchant living in troubled times. He was commercially successful but the encroaching power of the state threatened to upend this livelihood. In the latter part of the seventeenth century, Protestants living in France experienced a gradual ero-

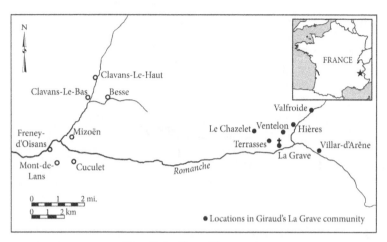

Giraud's La Grave Community

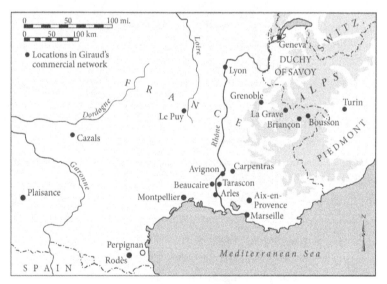

Geography of Giraud's Commercial Network

sion of religious freedoms. Giraud remained committed to his church and faith, but over time circumstances worsened, and he was faced with the painful decision of whether to remain in La Grave and denounce his faith or seek refuge and start a new life in another country.

To succeed as an Alpine merchant Giraud learned to navigate through mountainous terrain. La Grave was a rural village located in the Hautes-Alpes, a mountainous region of Dauphiné, where summits reach 3,900 meters. It divided topographically into three regions: the eastern mountains that were too cold for vineyards or wheat fields, the lower plains where the porous soil primarily yielded fruits and grains, and the fertile land east of the Rhône River, one third of which was cold and marshy swamp.[3] The mountainous eastern side of the province, La Grave's location, had fewer towns due to the terrain, while the western side was more urban.[4] Following the Black Death in the fourteenth century, increased demand for Alpine materials like wood, wool, and leather led to the growth of local fairs, which evolved to support trade between low and highland communities such as La Grave. Regions like the Hautes-Alpes that had been historically viewed as poor in resources due to low agricultural yields now grew through the development of local and regional trade networks. Those living in the elevated region depended on trade with lower lying areas for economic survival. Mountain villages depended on the lower valleys that supplied grain, wine, vegetables, and oil in exchange for timber and animal products like cheese, fur, hides, and meat.[5]

Giraud relied on the historic trade routes central to the region. La Grave was situated on a major trade artery connecting transnational traffic running parallel to the river Romanche. This road was "a major route in the sixteenth and seventeenth centuries used by preachers, itinerant workers, peddlers, merchants, and armies."[6] Meanwhile, fairs, like those in Briançon and especially Lyon, emerged in conjunction with wider trade circuits emanating from northwestern European cities.[7] Such fairs connected rural Alpine people with transnational trade. "Long mule trains [supplied] cargoes of silks, carpets, dyes, Indigo, gold, and silver thread along Alpine routes. . . . The more isolated the route, the more profitable it was, and even remote valleys saw the benefits of the growing traffic in luxury items."[8] These patterns continued into the seventeenth century, as the Alpine economy became more fixed on stock raising and the domestic economic activities associated with it. For the local mountain villages this meant a mixed economy of sheepherding, barter, peddling, and other forms of cottage industry. It also meant increasing monetization, as villagers, seeking ways to supplement domestic income, became increasingly dependent on commercial outlets and systems of credit for facilitating commercial traffic.

Dauphiné was also home to native artisanal trades that would have served Giraud's business relationships. The limitations of grain agriculture in the mountain regions encouraged the rise of workshops, where rural artisans, working outside the jurisdiction of larger cities and their urban guilds, manufactured products for local and regional markets.[9] Dating back to the fourteenth and fifteenth centuries, such workshops tended to be concentrated in rural mountain villages, where wood, wool, and other natural resources were most accessible. During the late Middle Ages, small mountain villages like La Grave boasted two or three trades, while larger communities possessed as many as ten. The growth in rural trades continued throughout the sixteenth and seventeenth centuries, with as many as one in ten Dauphiné peasants working as rural artisans by the close of the eighteenth century.[10]

The peddling enterprises of the Alps were multifaceted organizations operating around family networks that were "linked to migratory movements." Peddling organizations were well developed and hierarchical, yet flexible, structures. Sizable peddling firms operated by merchant-peddlers like Jean Giraud typically had three tiers of employees. At the head was the *commis*, a salaried employee who represented the firm at fairs, towns, and surrounding villages. Jean Monnet, Giraud's brother-in-law and early business partner, left the firm as one of its investors, but stayed on as its salaried *commis* following the company's reorganization in 1674. Within the firm's hierarchy, directly below the *commis* was a tier of apprentices, typically the sons of merchants or relatives, who served as packmen.[11] In his *livre* Giraud mentioned his nephew, Jean Masson, as one of his pupils. In all likelihood he served as an apprentice to Giraud until Masson's death in 1686. Although difficult to glean from the *livre*, there typically existed a third tier of peddlers beneath the apprentices, who also served the firm.

As a boy, Giraud presumably apprenticed with a merchant-peddler, possibly a relative, perhaps an uncle, who worked for the family business. Knowledge of reading, writing, and arithmetic was essential. As a youngster, Giraud probably had a tutor who taught him reading and composition. Later, he learned arithmetic and more difficult calculations, including the conversion of weights and measures and computation of interest and exchange rates. He was taught how to perform double-entry bookkeeping, manage an inventory, and calculate the value of different currencies, a skill called "reduction in coins."[12] Giraud's education required him to accompany a master merchant-peddler on trips and observe his dealings with clients. The instruction of a merchant-peddler was very practical; he was taught the rudiments of the trade. Once these various skills were mastered, a pupil might launch his own career as a packman, working at a lower level for a firm (likely the family firm) until he accumulated enough experience and sufficient capital to enter into a more lucrative arrangement. By the time Giraud reached his thirties, he had become a partner in his own firm.

Giraud's business in La Grave was supported by family-based arrangements that provided the capital to operate his firm. The undertaking pooled resources via a family banking system in which family members, including Jean Giraud's uncle and sister, pledged their personal fortunes. The uncle provided 6,000 *livres;* Giraud's sister surrendered her dowry and late husband's pension. Each investment partner shared in the start-up capital and profits, with earnings proportional to his or her investment. With the family banking system well established, the firm then arranged partnerships with different family firms. Giraud's partnerships generally lasted for four years, dissolving and reforming as needed with new financial terms and associations. The Giraud-Chicot-Grengent association, for example, was replaced in 1670 by the Giraud-Chicot-Monnet partnership, which was supplanted in 1674 by Giraud-Chicot.[13]

These partnerships were sealed with marriage alliances between merchant families. In the case of the Giraud, Chicot, and Monnet families, all hailed from the same Alpine village, La Grave. Family records show that Jean Giraud married twice. He wed his first wife, Madelaine Monnet, the sister of another La Grave merchant, in 1665; she was twenty and he twenty-six. They had one son, who was born in 1668 and died a year later from "flux de sang," or dysentery. Madelaine fell ill of dropsy not long after, dying in 1670 following a miscarriage. Whatever the cost in personal grief, the death did not threaten Giraud's business relations. His sister Marie married Madelaine's brother, Jean, and the brothers-in-law remained close, as both the Girauds and Monnets settled in Vevey following the Revocation of the Edict of Nantes.[14]

Giraud married a second time in 1672, wedding Magdelaine Chicot, the fifteen-year-old daughter of Jacques Chicot, a La Grave merchant originally from Chazelet. This was a match that Giraud had unsuccessfully sought at an earlier time. At fifteen, Magdelaine was literate, a fact illustrated by her elegant signature following Giraud's notation of the marriage on their wedding day.[15] The new marriage secured a business alliance between the Giraud and Chicot families, creating what Giraud referred to in his accounts as the "Giraud-Chicot Compagnie," a concern that lasted four years until its dissolution for reasons unspecified in 1674. Magdelaine was the offspring of two important merchant families, Chicot and Gravier, with connections to Switzerland (her father had a shop in Geneva), so the union portended well for the scope of Giraud's commercial enterprises. Previously, Giraud's business was backed with the financial support of close family members and his Monnet family in-laws.[16] Following the marriage to Magdelaine, Giraud was in a position to establish a firm foothold within the commercial scene in Geneva and to expand his operations beyond Lyon and the French Alps.

Worth noting is the importance of the role women played in these financial arrangements. In fact, French women possessed the legal standing and financial wherewithal to make investments, and did so, a clear indication that they had some participation in the conduct of business operations. This observation comports with one prominent study that found Alpine women in the early modern era exercised a

Signatures of Jean Giraud and Magdelaine Chicot.
Courtesy of the Archives cantonales vaudoises, CH-ACV PP 713/1.

"decision-making role" in financial affairs and "were expected to know about agricultural matters." They were not strictly relegated to the domestic realm. They owned property and acted as "estate managers," and, although their husbands exercised use rights, women maintained control over their own dowries.[17] Jean Giraud's sister was one obvious example of a woman exercising influence in the family's financial affairs when she contributed her dowry and late husband's pension to Giraud's peddling organization, thereby gaining a stake in the enterprise.[18]

Jean Giraud's livre de raison additionally suggests that his sister Anne may have served the company as a peddler herself. Giraud's business accounts disclose her numerous purchases. He provided her sugar, bread, serge, colored thread, silk, black ribbons, taffeta, guipure (a kind of imitation lace), Dutch camlet, Indian cloth, painted cloth, and a pair of shoes—all possibly procured for clients of her own. Another time she bought taffeta gloves, soap, more shoes, an ivory comb, a pair of Psalms, and paid on credit for trips to Lyon and Grenoble. She purchased or received on credit salt and bread that she sold. Anne also procured barley flour, cheese, butter, needles, and uncarded wool from Giraud's flock, and sold Giraud's sheep at La Grave's fair. She reciprocated as well, selling her brother oil, wool, candles, and lace.[19]

As with men, women maintained the right of testamentary disposition of property they owned. In her will, Marie David Philip, a relative of Giraud, left each of her children a sizable inheritance. Her daughters each received two hundred *livres* along with parcels of land they were to "take possession and enjoyment of from the day follow-ing [their mother's] demise and do with as they see fit." In addition, she left them all her "clothes, sheets, chests, rings, and other women's ornaments," including a gold ring mounted with three stones. It seems the mother bequeathed to her daughters all her personal possessions with the exception of one gold ring and a prayer book that she reserved for her sons, Jean and Samuel Giraud. Whether any property devised to the daughters became part of some commercial venture is not par-ticularly important. The consequential reality is that each had a sizable inheritance to wield as she wished. Philip's daughter Marie chose to use her inheritance for a dowry, not a typical business transaction, but a crucial investment in securing her future.[20]

Women who had their own money could invest it and buy property. Magdelaine Chicot, Giraud's young wife, purchased from the estate of her husband's deceased relative a number of personal items, and Jean Giraud did as well.[21] These were separate purchases, indicating that though married, each made his or her own financial decisions. Women family members often assisted in the financial upkeep of family farms and businesses, while their male counterparts were busy extending credit and hawking merchandise.

La Grave was home to numerous Protestants, many of them mer-chants. In the seventeenth century an estimated 800,000 Protestants lived in France, and Dauphiné's Protestants constituted around 8 percent of that total. Some 40,000 of Dauphiné's 64,000 Protes-tants lived in rural regions. For Dauphiné, this translated into nearly seventy-six Protestant churches, most found in rural villages.[22] Some 9,500 of these Protestants resided in the Hautes-Alpes, 4,000 in the diocese of Grenoble.[23] Of these, 1,500 occupied the mountain region of the Oisans, the eastern side.[24] The exact number of Protestants who attended the Huguenot churches of La Grave and its neighboring villages of Mizoën, Besse, Bourg d'Oisans, and Le Freney is unknown. La Grave's Protestant community made up a significant minority of the population, as was the case in Mont-de-Lans and Le Freney. Mizoën's population was completely Protestant.[25]

Apart from a few references in Huguenot synodal records from 1651 and 1658, little information exists on the life and history of La Grave's Huguenot Church.[26] In 1664 Protestant church leaders furnished the state written proof of religious services held in La Grave dating back to 1590, well before the Edict of Nantes.[27] The proof was accepted and the church remained operational. The neighboring villages of Chazelet, Terrasses, Ventelon, and Les Hières also provided written proof, but it was deemed insufficient in all instances, and those Huguenot villagers were ordered to demolish their temples and to cease holding religious services in private homes. This included the private homes of Samuel Giraud and Paul Chicot.[28] Records reveal that the church in La Grave was governed by its own consistory and maintained a cemetery.[29] It also had a hospital subsidized by the village and over which the local priests assumed control following the Revocation. Records also show that the consistory served as a bank for local Protestants seeking loans. An account book from 1701 discovered among the records of Grenoble's hospital indicated that members of La Grave's church, including Jean Giraud and his sister Anne, Jean Monnet, Félix Chicot, and Jean Masson, borrowed from the church consistory in the 1670s and 1680s.[30]

More is known of the Protestant community of neighboring Mizoën. Parish records of this Alpine church indicate its members honored baptismal and marital practices that Protestants exercised elsewhere in France.[31] Alpine consistory records reveal little regarding church enforcement of social discipline; they do imply a preoccupation with financial matters. Early modern Calvinist communities were known to extend loans and charity as a way of exercising social discipline.[32] Seventeenth-century church records for Mizoën indicate a careful, meticulous accounting of donations to the poor, weekly collections at the church door, and costs involved with the upkeep of Mizoën's hospital.[33] Records of obligations owed suggest that some church members, as in La Grave, considered the consistory a resident bank for financing various ventures. They also likely resorted to the consistory for settling personal financial matters.[34]

The La Grave Huguenots were accustomed to a local political culture of self-government, despite the expansion of state power during the Bourbon monarchies. Absorbed into the larger kingdom of France in 1349, Dauphiné continued to adhere to long-established traditions of representative government. The French Crown guaranteed the province's long-established provincial rights and liberties at the time it was annexed into the larger state, and the province's representative traditions continued to thrive, despite royal incursions during periods of economic strain. The province enjoyed privileges unknown in other parts of the kingdom. Few Dauphinois, especially those in the mountain region, were subject to the feudal assertions and claims exercised elsewhere in France. The lack of feudal oversight, in combination with regional economic, historical, and geographical characteristics, made for a society and political culture largely independent and self-reliant.

This representative culture found expression in the communal assemblies used by villages as a means to organize politically. Assemblies of La Grave's "commoners and habitants . . . both rich and poor," and representatives "of one religion as much as the other," met to discuss the selection of village councilors. A "plurality of voices" granted these consuls the powers to discharge community business.[35] Village assemblies also discussed matters concerning tax collection, road improvements, and agricultural affairs, as well as the maintenance of local churches.[36] Communal records indicate that in 1657 and 1660 La Grave approved payment for casting the bell intended for the Protestant church.[37] The community also paid for the repair and upkeep of the local priest's house and wardrobe.[38] The meetings of village assemblies could become quite heated, as with La Grave in the 1670s, when village gossip fueled quarrels and led to open conflict on occasion.[39] In the end, it was the responsibility of communal assemblies to defend the interests of the local community against the seigneur, which could mean identifying a syndic to represent the community's interests in court.[40] Alpine villages exercised a wide degree of autonomy and were accustomed to a village life that was, for its day, comparatively democratic.[41]

Although village politics impacted the lives of people living in the Hautes-Alpes, Giraud made no mention of them in his journal. Reading his *livre*, one gathers that his roles of father and paterfamilias were more important. Following common practice in *livres de raison*, Giraud assumed the responsibility of recording marriages, births, baptisms, and deaths of his family members, including in-laws and extended relations. Giraud's record of deaths, especially of his children, sadly illustrates the demographic realities of the time. During the seventeenth century, Europe's population growth remained stagnant. Death from famine, malnutrition, and disease was common. Those most vulnerable, of course, were the poor, who had few resources during times of dearth, a reality that made them more vulnerable to disease and death. Giraud was in a better economic position than most and could afford surgeons and doctors to care for his sick children (not that this helped very much).[42] His family was also better fed than most. He could afford meat, when others made do with gruel. Despite Giraud's privilege, there was no escape from the epidemics and scourges of the era. His sisters, Anne and Marie, died a year apart—Anne in Amsterdam in 1700 at the age of sixty-four from an intermittent fever; Marie in Erlangen, Germany in 1701 at fifty-nine from "dropsy." Giraud recorded the deaths of other family members who suffered from fever, the dropsy, or the flux. They died in nearby Lyon, Grenoble, or Geneva, and as far away as Cádiz, Turin, or "Carroline."[43]

Some of Giraud's in-laws were among the 30,000 Huguenot refugees who fled to London following the Revocation of the Edict of Nantes. The Chicot family first settled in Stepney, then moved to Soho, where they attended different French churches at Swallow Street and Leicester Fields.[44] Swallow Street Church was conformist and followed the Anglican liturgy, translated into French. The French church at Leicester Fields, by contrast, was nonconformist and adhered to the traditional worship of the French Reformed Church.[45] In all likelihood, most of the Chicot family died during the smallpox epidemic that swept through London in 1694. Jacques Chicot had expired in London one month after his arrival in 1686. Giraud's mother-in-law,

Marie Chicot, brother-in-law, Jacques, and sisters-in-law Manon, Anne, and Marie all died in 1694. These sudden passings prompted Giraud to depart for London where he assumed the responsibility of three minors—Jacques, Marq Henri, and Michel—left parentless by the epidemic. The decision to travel was a courageous and compassionate choice. Unfortunately, Giraud did not leave a description of his trip. He did record that all members of the Chicot family were interred in London's Church of St. Anne.[46]

The mortality rate for Giraud's family, especially his children, exceeded by far that found in standard demographic studies of the era.[47] Giraud recorded the birth and death of fifteen of his own children. Most succumbed to dropsy, the fever, or the flux. Others were stillborn or died shortly after birth. Few children of the time were named at birth so poor was the chance of survival beyond their first year. Only two of the boys to whom Magdelaine Giraud gave birth were named: Jean Giraud, who was baptized in 1678, and Jean Claude, baptized in 1689. The first son, Jean, died shortly after birth; the second, Jean Claude, lived only two years, dying in 1691. Jean was interred with five other siblings at Ventelon, France, his younger brother in the cemetery of St. Martin in Vevey, Switzerland.[48]

Other than dates of births, baptisms, and deaths, Giraud recorded little regarding his children. Even so, his writings reveal heartbreaking feelings of paternal hope, love, and devotion. Often Giraud closed his paragraph written at the birth or death of a child with a devotional remark reflecting hope or faith in God. Following the death of one son, Giraud wrote: "God's will be done, and give us the grace to live in His fear." On another occasion, he beseeched, "The good Lord be merciful to us poor sinners." Writing with hope after the birth of another son, he implored, "To whom God gives a good and long life and always in His fear." Yet no notation was more descriptive or moving than Giraud's final remarks regarding his daughter Suzon, who passed away in Vevey in 1695 at the age of fifteen after a long illness. When the family fled France in 1686, she had to leave behind a doll, not only a girl's toy, but also an indicator of a household that cultivated young females for their future roles as mothers and care-givers. Suzon was only six when she left La Grave. Once in Vevey, she blossomed into a lovely young woman. Giraud captured her nature and final words: "The memory of a pleasant person with beauty and a spirit will remain imprinted in our thoughts all our life. Her last words in the same moment she expired, she said to me—my father, I want to ask your pardon, I am far, farewell, farewell."[49] Despite his god-fearing character and implicit belief in the will of God coming to pass, such moments must have weighed heavily.

Life went on. Giraud was a father who loved his children, and he was also a merchant of cultivated and fashionable tastes—and one who was involved in widely varied enterprises. Giraud's business records reveal that he sold hats, books, shoes, ladies' accessories, and a broad range of textile products.[50] He also harvested wood, stocked materials for use in storing quantities of grain, and owned livestock. An inventory of his personal possessions at La Grave, drawn up not long after the Revocation, reflected his interests and personal habits. Giraud was a peddler, so it is no surprise that he possessed many chests, cabinets, and baskets, items useful for storing or transporting merchandise.[51] He owned plumes and pens, an inkstand and writing tables for maintaining records and correspondence, candlesticks, lamps, torches, and lanterns for late night reading and travel. Along with standard farm implements, Giraud's inventory lists a strange mix of odds and ends: rocking cradles, scrap metal, birdcages, multiple pairs of shoes, carpentry tools, country cloth and rolls of linen, blankets, a cabinet of "*diverses drogues et médicaments* (various drugs and medi-cations)," pommels, ladies' garments, carpets, tailor's scissors, sieves, hammers and files, animal hair for padding materials, and numerous cauldrons. Such a diversity conceivably reflected La Grave's regional trade and consumption patterns. Worth noting as well, Giraud also kept a *trébuchet*, a special scale with weights used for measuring the heaviness of different kinds of coins to determine their value. This device was especially useful for traveling merchants like Giraud who, in dealing with various international currencies, might be worried

Coin-weight (Trébuchet) by Guillaume de Neve, 1600–1654.
Copyright © The Trustees of the British Museum.

about their debasing. The size of Giraud's trébuchet is unknown, but many of these scales were small, portable, and easily carried in one's pocket, enabling the merchant to conduct transactions both at local markets and more distant ones.[52]

Giraud's entrepreneurial success afforded him material pleasures beyond the reach of most. In addition to the standard hearth *cré-maillère*, or pot hook, Giraud owned a rotisserie and roaster for cooking meat, and a copper *coquemar*, a kind of early modern kettle for boiling water.[53] As tokens of comfort and social refinement, Giraud owned several mattresses and two beds, one with red damask curtains, a patent sign of his wealth and rising status.[54] Giraud's collection of tableware was sizable and diverse. It consisted of one crystal and four tin cups, porridge bowls, dinner and soup plates (*assiettes creuses*), a

Painting of a Trébuchet, *The Moneylender and his Wife*,
oil on wood by Quentin Metsys, 1514.
Copyright © RMN-Grand Palais / Art Resource, NY, Musée du Louvre/Paris/France.

marmite, platters, vinegar and olive oil decanters, a salt container, knives, four forks, and over thirty spoons.[55] The variety of tableware indicates eating habits that entailed multiple-course meals, while tablecloths and napkins, along with table decorations, suggest a knowledge of and appreciation of table etiquette. A barber's basin, a large mirror, and cleaning brushes, together with his wardrobe, signal the importance of personal appearance and cleanliness to Giraud, which, along with table manners, had become an increasing preoccupation of European elites.[56]

Seventeenth-Century German Pot Hook (Crémaillère).
Copyright © Victoria and Albert Museum, London.

Various cultural artifacts in his possession suggest Giraud's curiosity and propensity for collection. Why else would a peddler own a pair of pocket pistols, fencing swords, and a halberd? The pistols might provide protection while traveling, but fencing swords were aristocratic arms and suited for one accustomed to resorting to ritualized codes for settling matters of personal or family honor.[57] The halberd, the medieval-style fighting axe of the Swiss, was by the seventeenth century, at least for a peddler, likely an ornamental showpiece and marker of masculine identity. The known weapon of the Swiss soldier, it also represented the freedom and independence historically associated with neighboring Swiss Protestant cities like Geneva. Giraud enjoyed games and was a collector of curiosities. He owned a set of checkers, "*dames damier,*" and two ostrich eggs, "the standard natural *exotica* of virtuoso cabinets at the time."[58] Giraud also enjoyed art and music and possessed several tableaux and stringed instruments. His stringed instruments included two violins, a vielle or precursor to the violin, and a trumpet marine, a kind of triangular wooden stringed instrument popular during the Renaissance and Baroque. Giraud preferred natural and historical over religious themes in art; his inventory lists three landscapes and seven pictures depicting the *Seven Wonders of the World.*[59]

Compared to that of Giraud, a more expansive catalogue of inventoried goods can be found in the property lists prepared by Pierre and Jacques Albert, fellow merchants who attended church with Giraud and served the region's Protestant and Catholic clientele.[60] Inventories from 1661 and 1663 indicate the Alberts sold everything from lace and tobacco to mustache lifters, Turkish padlocks, and eyeglasses. The brothers stocked both Catholic and Protestant texts, including in

Woman Attending Cooking Pot Held by a Crémaillère,
print by Boëtius Adamsz Bolswert, after Joos Goeimare, 1600–1620.
Copyright © The Trustees of the British Museum.

1663 sixty-six catechisms. The sizable number of alphabet books they sold—142 are listed in their inventories for 1663—suggests the Alberts may have assisted locally in the spread of literacy. They also sold paper and wax, and stocked 2,000 writing plumes. The inventories included braids or trim (some with the stitch of the cross of Malta) and buttons (some with the emblem of the Jerusalem cross). Numerous tools such as driving hammers, scissors, and a press for cutting baleen were likely bought by artisanal workers for making finished products. The

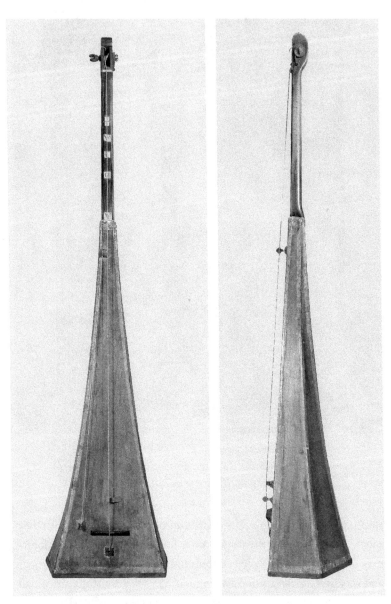

Tromba Marina (Trumpet Marine), Switzerland, ca. 1750, front and side view.
National Music Museum, The University of South Dakota, Bill Willroth Sr., photographer.

Alberts' clientele spanned a spectrum of artisans that included tailors, button makers, a pastry chef, saddlers, a locksmith, glove, spur, and pin makers, and a rosary maker. Many clients were connected to the courts as lawyers for the king; others were apothecaries, arquebusiers, notaries, messengers, a lieutenant, or other merchants. A number of single women and widows were clients, as were members of the clergy, including several priests.[61] Catholic clergy may have shown interest in purchasing the wooden or rocaille rosaries the Alberts stocked, while representatives of the military establishment may have sought the Maltese Cross, symbol of the king's musketeers. The inventory of the Alberts was illustrative of the versatility of Alpine commercial agents and their indisputable role in serving as a bridge between different faiths and social classes. Because they catered to the interests of both Protestant and Catholic clients, merchants like the Alberts and Giraud were important agents for keeping the peace in their community—at least until the 1680s, when strained relations between Catholics and Protestants gave way to open conflict.

Of all his possessions, Giraud treasured his books most and went to great lengths to protect them. On July 9, 1685, the king issued a royal order calling for the confiscation of Protestant religious works. Directed against printers and booksellers, the order's purpose was to proscribe the circulation and sale of Protestant publications.[62] Orders from the Count de Tessé appeared on La Grave's church doors instructing Protestants to hand over controversial works within twenty-four hours or face corporal punishment. Local priests, including the curé, Claude Planchet, began confiscating and publicly burning religious texts. Simultaneously, the priest of Mont-de-Lans collected and burned there, at Freney, Cuculet, and other villages "all the subjects at the parish known—Bibles, Testaments, prayers, sermons . . . and all sorts of books" of Huguenot faith. In response, Giraud hastened to safeguard works from local authorities by hiding "various printed books of our religion" behind the beam on the wall in the pavilion in his garden, and in the rising steps of his home's first room. He consigned forty books, along with a three-volume set of the "History of the Reformed Faith" and a copy of *Anatomie de la Messe* with Monsieur Louis Aymon, presumably a trusted neighbor.[63]

A vast book-trade network linking Alpine peddlers to urban booksellers in Lyon and Geneva emerged from the Alpine Briançonnais shortly after the Reformation. Giraud became an important dealer for Dauphiné's Protestant book market in the late seventeenth century, receiving most of his texts through contacts with Genevan publishers, who brokered sales with Dutch and German suppliers.[64] Regrettably, except for mention of a Bible and a book of Psalms he purchased for his niece, Giraud left no indication in his *livre* of the volume of books he trafficked, nor of the kinds of books he bought and sold. Of course, the great majority of titles he hid at the time of the Revocation were religious in nature. Books listed in Giraud's La Grave inventory include one historical dictionary, a three-volume history of Jacob Spon's *Voyage d'Italie, de Dalmatie, de Grèce, et du Levant,* Spon's *Histoire de Genève* (two volumes), a History of Alexander the Great, a History of Lyon, and four volumes of Guillaume de Salluste Du Bartas. None of the books listed, historical works mainly, was controversial, even though the Protestant Jacob Spon, a celebrated classicist and physician, sought refuge abroad for refusing to abjure his faith.[65]

Giraud was peddling books during the height of the Catholic Reformation. Royal decisions and policies touched daily life, as did Catholic educational initiatives. The well-traveled merchant was aware of the increasing presence of state officials, intendants, and other powerbrokers beholden to the crown in cities like Grenoble and Lyon. Giraud and other members of his religious community undoubtedly encountered zealous reformers embarked on educational projects and programs purposed to win back Protestants to the Roman faith. Historians have frequently characterized the time as an era of cold war. Religious violence between Catholics and Protestants subsided, but theological tensions and rivalries continued, finding outlet in the courts, and as propaganda and instructive campaigns. The Council of Trent (1545–63) issued new directives regarding the education of priests and the church laity. New educational initiatives resulted, with the Capuchins seeking out remote rural regions—the Jesuits did the same in the cities—to teach the rudiments of the Catholic doctrine. Books on devotion, the lives of the saints, catechisms, prayer books, and books on meditation rolled off presses, all intended for instruction in the Catholic faith.

Étienne Le Camus, bishop of the diocese of Grenoble, was an important figure of the Counter-Reformation. His jurisdiction included territory in Dauphiné and neighboring Savoy, and he confronted the formidable task of educating his parishioners in understanding the basic tenets of Catholic faith. According to historian Jean Delumeau, Catholicism remained unmodified until the evangelization movements of the early modern era, when educational reformers endeavored to change popular religion to a religion rooted in orthodox ideas.[66] The Catholic Reformation brought a new emphasis on interior faith, an "individual examination of conscience, dutiful participation in the sacraments, and a more exacting understanding of proper doctrine." Through pastoral visits, Le Camus sought to eliminate superstitious and popular practices tied to village religion, bring an end to unruly aspects of village festivals, and dictate proper devotion to acceptable saints and pilgrimages honoring the Virgin Mary.[67]

When Le Camus arrived in the diocese in 1671, he woefully denounced the general ignorance of the local population: "Can you believe that there are in this diocese entire villages where no one . . . has even heard of Jesus Christ?" Other painful truths included illiterate priests, drunken curés, clerical concubinage, and time spent "gambling, hunting, and in socializing with the Huguenots." With respect to the Protestants, Le Camus sought their conversion through persuasion rather than force. Still, he emphasized keeping boundaries between Protestants and Catholics. Catholic and Protestant children did not attend school together, and the dead were buried in separate cemeteries. In a visit to Chazelet, he ordered a halt to Protestant participation in village assemblies. Despite these measures, Le Camus's rapport with Protestants in the province overall was civil. Once, while speaking in the village of Besse, he gave a sermon that impressed Protestants for its scriptural accuracy. In his effort to persuade, Le Camus, "had . . . spoken on polemical matters [but] in a gentle way."[68]

While Le Camus was seeking converts and stamping out superstition in the province, Catholic renewal efforts were also undertaken by the laity. One example was the revival of confraternities, voluntary organizations staffed by lay people with the aim of promoting charity and good works. One confraternity, the Congregation for the Propagation of the Faith, spread across France, taking root in Grenoble in 1647. The Propagation's fervent desire to convert Protestants to Catholicism reflected the general enthusiasm of Catholic renewal that swept across Dauphiné during the seventeenth century. Grenoble's Propagation of Faith focused its greatest energies on winning back poor Protestants in the rural areas of the province, a formidable undertaking since more Protestants lived in Dauphiné's rural than its urban regions. Working with Catholic villagers, local priests, and seigneurs, the Propagation acted on information it gathered from around the province: "From their headquarters on the Rue St. Jacques, they deposed village notaries, intervened in family disputes, manipulated local tribunals, and kept a close watch on Protestant ministers from Pont-en-Royans to Chateau-Dauphin."[69]

As the church and Catholic lay groups pursued persuasion, Protestant writers contended with a more coercive entity when dealing with Louis XIV's provincial courts. As the Counter-Reformation spread its influence across the province, Grenoble's court sought to curtail the work of Protestant authors and printers through acts of censorship. The state's pursuit of censorship and expurgation increased steadily over the course of the seventeenth century as royal powers grew and religious tensions became more intense. In 1644 Grenoble's court condemned the publication of the book *Marseilles without Miracles*. The author, a pastor named Hugues Rollin, disputed the legend that Mary Magdalene and the risen Lazarus had actually visited Provence in biblical times. He asserted as well that all miracles associated with relics and images of saints were spurious.[70] What further actions beyond condemnation were taken against Rollin for his blatantly heretical notions is unknown, but the case surely served as a caveat and forewarning to Protestant authors and publishers that printing controversial religious material might carry very serious consequences.

In 1661 Grenoble's court condemned the work *The Anti-Monk, to Gentlemen of the Communion of Rome from the Town of Crest,* by Protestant minister Jean de La Faye, for its scandalous impieties and blasphemies. The court ordered La Faye sent to the galleys for life and fined him three hundred *livres.* The court also condemned the book's printer, Ezéchiel Benoît, for printing without a license; he was fined fifty livres. The book was publicly burned, and La Faye wisely fled to Switzerland. Foreshadowing Louis's edict banning all Huguenot publications three years hence, the *parlement* in 1682 condemned three Protestant works: *Interviews of a Father and his Son, Preservation against the Changing of Religion,* and *Treatise of Truth.* The first two the court deemed seditious and scandalous, and they were publicly burned. Booksellers in Grenoble who had sold these works were each ordered to pay fifty *livres* in fines to the king. Shortly thereafter, the *parlement* of Grenoble considered a fourth book, *Speech against the Rebels, Imprinted in the Desert,* which it condemned for "scandalous proposals, full of impostures and slanders against the Roman church."[71]

One needed not be a writer to find trouble with the French judiciary during this period; the court also took a strong stand against blasphemers who had spoken against Catholicism. In 1675 Grenoble's *parlement* issued a decree against Louis Rambaud, "who had caused much noise in the province," by profaning the mysteries of the Catholic faith. This outraged the Bishop of Valence and Die, who sought to prosecute him criminally. The matter was dropped when Rambaud agreed to remain Catholic. Apparently still restless ten years later, he drew the wrath of the authorities again when he chose to renounce his Catholicism. This action led Grenoble's *parlement* to renew the previous accusation of blasphemy, and Rambaud was condemned to beg forgiveness from God and king while on his knees holding a burning torch. Then his tongue was to be cut off, followed by hanging and strangling "until natural death ensues." His body was then to be burned. For good measure he was ordered to pay 1,600 *livres*.[72] Rambaud evaded authorities by slipping away to Geneva, but this case would have caused alarmed Huguenots across the province to take careful notice.

Giraud, his forbears, and his contemporary Protestant neighbors surely followed these cases closely and cringed at the trials, verdicts, and punishments. The outcomes no doubt prompted Protestant booksellers to exercise extreme caution when peddling their texts or vocalizing their religious beliefs. By the latter part of the century, under a weakened Edict of Nantes, Grenoble's court worked increasingly with church officials and took its cues from Versailles to suppress Protestant activities and belief. Giraud bravely peddled his Protestant works in the mountainous regions of the Hautes-Alpes and kept Alpine Protestants connected to the outside world, while supporting underground Huguenot social networks threatened by censorship and political centralization.

As part of his economic activities, Giraud provided a space—the buyer's home, the local market, or his own storehouse—where Alpine clients could meet with him and review the books and other goods available for sale. These economic encounters with his clients also served as occasions for cultural and political exchange. In meeting with clients, Giraud discussed his journeys and the latest news from Lyon, Grenoble, or Geneva. He reassured and supported those in need or seeking spiritual comfort, and provided Bibles, Psalms, and literature essential to their Protestant faith. Huguenot merchants like Giraud played a critical role in sustaining a religious movement that otherwise might have collapsed under increasing state pressure.

Giraud's subversion was well concealed under the guise of a successful merchant. His inventories of 1674 reveal goods valued at 10,480 *livres,* more than half the worth of a rich merchant of Lyon.[73] Giraud's account book discloses the nature of his capitalist ventures, which tended to center on providing merchandise and credit. In contrast to the urban bourgeoisie of the period, Alpine peddlers like Giraud rarely invested in land.[74] Giraud made his fortune principally from peddling and by furnishing loans to villagers within his social circle. Albeit doing so for profit, he provided opportunities for credit that were essential to the economic survival and well-being of many fellow villagers. Giraud's example was illustrative of an entrepreneurial spirit that prevailed among many of La Grave's Huguenots as they sought to transcend challenging circumstances.

As his religious life became more difficult and his business dealings more dangerous, Giraud reached the crossroads encountered by so many Huguenots in the Revocation era. In his livre de raison, Giraud does not explain his decision to leave. His anguish is very apparent in his escape narrative—perhaps deriving more from his distress in planning his secret escape than from the decision to depart France. Clearly this was a painful time for Giraud. He maintained the resources that allowed his family and himself to flee, but in doing so had to forfeit most of his possessions and property. Had he remained and continued peddling books—as others did—he would have had to confront the constant and baleful eye of state authorities, who outlawed the sale of most of his printed inventory. This surveillance and the potential repercussions of trafficking in Protestant works made his life impossible, as did the continuous pressure on him to abandon his faith and convert to Catholicism. His writing detailed priests collecting and burning Protestant works in local villages, suggesting that the book burning was uppermost in his mind, leaving an indelible imprint, urging him to depart.

By most modern standards, Giraud's world was harsh. People of the time suffered from repeated epidemics, poor harvests, and heavy taxation—not to mention religious persecution. A life of commerce brought new knowledge about the outside world and new social opportunities, but also new responsibilities. Villagers looked to Giraud, who was a pillar of their little community, to help solve problems and render aid in their plight. In the end, it was up to people like Giraud, a person of strong faith, to lead the way in securing a better future for himself but also for his religious community. Risking his life, he hid his books and began planning his escape.

TWO
緑%

Flight

GIRAUD'S NARRATIVE: THE LIVRE DE RAISON

When Jean Giraud returned home from a trip to Lyon in August 1685, he discovered his village under close guard by soldiers, many of whom had taken quarter in Protestant homes. His mother-in-law was among those under house arrest. Giraud's homecoming coincided with a French military offensive in the Hautes-Alpes that culminated a few months later in the Revocation of the Edict of Nantes, Louis XIV's official act banning Protestantism from France. From August 2, 1685, to July 29, 1686, Giraud chronicled in his livre de raison the terrifying events of those days as they unfolded in Dauphiné's mountain villages: dwellings plundered, residents fined and imprisoned, soldiers billeted in Protestant homes, forced abjurations. Numerous families, seeking to escape persecution, secretly abandoned their homesteads, leaving all their belongings behind. Those caught fleeing were imprisoned, sent to the galleys, or publicly executed. No one was spared, neither young nor old, neither rich nor poor.[1]

Giraud documented the toll of human suffering, and his notes reflect desperation, hostility, and disgust, especially with two town councilors, Félix Gay and Félix Paillas, whom Giraud referred to as "rascals."[2] Both men, who were Catholic, collaborated with and sought to assist in the *dragonnade*. His report recounted anguish, misery, and persecution, but also courage, faith, and perseverance. Documenting the persecution was dangerous, as Giraud frankly acknowledged: "Oh what misery and desolation these passages were to reap, if to fall between the hands of our enemies."[3] Giraud's livre de raison also shed light on how he interpreted his position in relation to other church members, many of whom were merchants. In some ways he emerged as the paterfamilias of his community, providing financial support to church members and maintaining correspondence with them in the hope La Grave's church might somehow be restored after the Revocation. Clearly, Giraud considered the events surrounding this cataclysm essential to record, and he used his account to preserve the deeds of the day and the history of his church for present and future generations.

Livres de raison were typically multigenerational, recording the extended financial history of family businesses and events such as marriages, births, and deaths. Rarely did one serve as a memoir, a "narrative recollection of a first-hand experience." This began to change in the seventeenth century, when some accounts, like Jean Giraud's, "began to take on the form of a story."[4] The narrative section of Giraud's *livre* recorded the events from September 1685, when what he calls the "storms" began, until July 1686, when he arrived with his wife and daughter in Geneva. He wrote contemporaneously, as events unfolded, hence the weekly, and sometimes daily, episodic nature of his composition.

What prompted Giraud to record these events? Historians have suggested that such a record might serve for the individual as a protest against the state's dominant narrative. This certainly was true for at least one Huguenot serving in Louis XIV's galleys, whose first-hand account challenged the power of royal absolutism.[5] Though memoirs became more common in the seventeenth century, few by Huguenots existed until the Revocation of the Edict of Nantes. There are notable reasons for this. Calvinism, unlike English Puritanism, discouraged personal reflection in writing: "Huguenots privileged threads in Calvin's writings that not only minimized the role of self-remembrance in sanctification but also actively disapproved of self-justifying personal narratives." By contrast, there were many Puritan examples of mem-

Pages from Giraud's livre de raison displaying list of church members,
their destination in exile, and date of death.
Courtesy of the Archives cantonales vaudoises, CH-ACV PP 713/1.

oirs and stories of self-reflection, representing the doctrinal emphasis
on "methodical self-discipline," and "high self-monitoring."[6] Despite
this doctrinal difference, Huguenot refugees of the Revocation were
driven to document their memories in order to demonstrate their
strong faith—that, despite all ordeals, they remained committed to
their God and church. Some abjurers, now ashamed, may have felt
compelled to pen memoirs to explain their apostasy. Once in their
new host community, they sought to make amends and repledged
their loyalty to the Protestant faith.[7]

Giraud's *livre* was a private document meant for his family, not the
public. And though it was replete with nonscriptural religious references, God was not central. It was, nonetheless, a personal testimony
to his faith. By recounting the circumstances in which his family and
neighbors abjured their faith under duress, he made clear that their conversions were coerced. Identifying the oppressed by name and telling

Members of the Chicot family from Giraud's livre de raison,
who settled and died in London. Other exiles journeyed from La Grave
to Cádiz and then to Amsterdam, to Bern, and to "Carroline."
Courtesy of the Archives cantonales vaudoises, CH-ACV PP 713/1.

their story, Giraud honored their memory. Like other Huguenot escape stories, Giraud's contributed to the formation of a larger community identity born from the experience of religious persecution and political domination. "Recounting their own past," writes David van der Linden, "gave Huguenots a new sense of purpose and belonging: it defined who they were."[8]

Perhaps more important than the narrative of events set forth in his *livre* was the individual tabulation of religious refugees that appeared near its end. Giraud identified by name, family, and village nearly 160 refugees who had been members of his church in La Grave. He also noted each church member's destination in exile, and year and place of death. Giraud mourned but sought to keep alive the memory of his dispersed community, many of whom were not only church members, but also neighbors, business associates, and relatives. As Ruth Whelan has shown in her examination of the writings of the Huguenot diarist

Élie Bouhéreau, Giraud's livre de raison served in the same fashion, "as an instrument whereby a broken community" could "be knitted back together." Distinctly early modern, Giraud's livre de raison represents both "collective as well as individual narrative space," linking family and community contemporaneously and through future generations in what Whelan terms "networks of filiation." In this respect, Giraud's *livre* memorialized his ordeal and also kept his religious community intact "through shared memories that simultaneously recall and recreate communal solidarity."[9]

Giraud's livre de raison lists members of the Monnet family who relocated to Vevey and Geneva. Giraud's sister Marie moved to Vevey but then settled in Erlangen. Giraud's sister Anne also moved to Vevey but eventually settled and died in Amsterdam. Other final destinations of La Grave's refugees included Kassel, Turin, Barcelona, and Aouste.
Courtesy of the Archives cantonales vaudoises, CH-ACV PP 713/1.

THE HUGUENOT STRUGGLE IN FRANCE

As a Protestant, Giraud belonged to a minority church that had survived the Wars of Religion, legal restrictions on their right to exist, and now, under Louis XIV, the end of those rights and a program of persecution. The historical struggles of these Huguenots were like those of other Protestant communities since the inception of the Reformation and the theological revolution of Martin Luther. Giraud's narrative documents the continuation of a long history of religious troubles and persecution of the Huguenot community that dated back to the previous century. French Protestantism, which first took root in the cities and towns in the sixteenth century, spread rapidly in France and led to religious conflict and civil war. The French Wars of Religion (1562–98) were bloody and chaotic and occurred at a time of extreme hardship, when the French population experienced harvest failures, epidemics, soaring prices, increasing levels of taxation, and a widening gap between rich and poor. The wars were not the cause of social and economic problems per se, but greatly exacerbated them. Huguenot nobles were the leaders of Protestant resistance in the sixteenth century, but ordinary Protestants also suffered. Noble Protestants who could fled the country, seeking refuge elsewhere in Europe. This was especially true following the St. Bartholomew Day Massacre. Non-noble Protestants left too but, with fewer overseas contacts and resources, had a more difficult time.

Sixteenth-century French Protestants faced challenges whether in exile or at home. Exiled Protestants did not always easily assimilate. If they stayed in their countries of refuge, they often had to navigate a new life facing unfamiliar surroundings, customs, and language. They also had to reestablish a livelihood at a time when economic hardship also plagued host communities. If they stayed in France, they had to endure the depredations of marauding soldiers, high taxes, and physical persecution, including massacre. Huguenot anguish and suffering were no secret in other parts of Europe. Elites and Protestant communities elsewhere had read descriptions in print and certainly heard by word of mouth from Huguenots who fled. It was in exile that the Huguenots began to formulate a new identity. They may have been dispersed, but as a reconstituted community they now believed their martyrdom distinguished them as a special people chosen by God. They were predestined to be saved. Whatever atrocities might befall them, they remained loyal to their faith, which, along with their sacrifice, was a sign of election.

Peace finally came to France, and civil war ended in 1598 with the promulgation of the Edict of Nantes. Although Henry IV had converted to Catholicism, he remained a defender of French Protestantism. The Edict guaranteed freedom of worship for French Protestants living in areas where Protestants had erected churches before 1597. It permitted Protestants to maintain garrisons and to hold offices. The *chambres mi-parties,* special courts that seated an equal number of Protestants and Catholics, were established in Protestant areas to guarantee them a fair hearing. But the assassination of Henry IV in 1610 saw a regime change that did not favor the preservation of Huguenot protections. Fighting renewed in 1628 when his son, Louis XIII, in seeking to enforce strictly the Edict of Nantes, went to war against the Huguenot south. The fall of the city of La Rochelle, a Huguenot stronghold, in 1628, effectively brought an end to their state within a state. With the Edict of Alès in 1629, the state no longer guaranteed Huguenot political or military rights. Protestants were permitted to worship but could no longer hold political assemblies or maintain fortifications.

Although their right to worship had been guaranteed, troubles continued for the French Protestants. They experienced a welcome respite from violence, but in the thirty years from the Peace of Alès up to the reign of Louis XIV, there was further diminution of their rights. With the end of the state within a state, the role and power of the Protestant aristocracy was seriously diminished, and the movement now underwent the ascent of the bourgeoisie to positions of leadership.[10] Catholic zealots who had never accepted the Edict of Nantes now sought to weaken the Huguenot church legally through its strict enforcement. "The most relentless adversaries of the Protestants were to be found among the clergy," writes Elisabeth Labrousse; "many of these . . . saw the re-establishment of religious unity in France as their prime task."[11]

The mid-seventeenth century was the zenith of the Catholic Reformation in France. Catholic religious orders engaged in serious campaigns to re-Catholicize Protestants, sending Capuchin missionaries into heavily Protestant rural areas, while Jesuits endeavored to secure Protestant converts in French cities. Civil authorities backed their efforts. All the while, the Protestants put their trust in King Louis XIII, the Just, hopeful that the king would sustain their remaining rights and privileges.

Put not your trust in princes. With the ascension of Louis XIV in 1661, the political situation worsened for the Huguenots again. Louis XIV steadily restricted religious freedoms in France by narrowly defining and more rigorously enforcing the Edict of Nantes. The result limited Protestant worship and religious activities.[12] Such measures increased the destruction of many Huguenot temples, including half of those in Dauphiné.[13] Some believed that the Edict of Nantes was never meant to be permanent. Louis XIV's stated goal in undoing the work of his grandfather was "one king, one faith, and one law," or as Labrousse explains, political unity through religious conformity.[14]

After 1680, the campaign against the Huguenots intensified. Louis's policies continued the razing of churches and offered financial incentives for conversion. The state also imposed new restrictions on Huguenot religious education and expanded the number of occupations prohibited them. Religious meetings were banned and procedures enacted for the Catholic indoctrination of Protestant children. Violence increased as the state sought more direct means of enforcement by quartering royal troops in Protestant homes. In what was called the first *dragonnade,* Louis unleashed his ill-disciplined dragoons on the Protestant population of Poitou during the winter months of 1681. Disorderly troops were lodged in the homes of Huguenots to compel them to convert, and Protestant residents were required to both house and feed these soldiers. While Louis XIV had imposed dragoons on other populations in the past to extract payment from and suppress disobedient subjects, the *dragonnade* of Poitou was the first time the crown used such drastic means to force religious assimilation.

The *dragonnade* of 1681 resulted in the forced conversion of around 38,000 and amplified Louis's resolve to extirpate Protestantism. The Truce of Ratisbon provided France temporary respite from its conflict with the Habsburgs and permitted the movement of an army previously stationed on the Spanish-French border inland to be lodged in Protestant homes; hence began a second, and more severe period of the *dragonnades*. In 1684 local functionaries, attendants, and royal troops worked together, and en masse abjurations resulted in Béarn, Languedoc, and Dauphiné. In just a matter of weeks, 30,000 had converted in Dauphiné, and 25,000 in Languedoc. Dragoons were also dispatched to other cities including Rouen and Bordeaux, the latter of which witnessed the conversion of around 60,000.[15]

These measures culminated in the Edict of Fontainebleau in 1685, which officially banned Protestantism in France, revoking all legal protections originally outlined in the Edict of Nantes of 1598. Historians disagree over the reason Louis decided on the Revocation at this time. Undoubtedly growing impatience with the pace of conversion was at its core, but a more favorable international situation may have contributed. The Treaty of Nijmegen of 1679, which concluded Louis's war with the Dutch, released the Sun King from his obligations to his Protestant allies, freeing Louis of their concerns over his treatment of the Huguenots. This new freedom allowed Louis to adopt more repressive measures.[16] Louis's war with the Dutch and their numerous allies had ended, but even with the respite from war, the Huguenots were a matter of concern; they remained a domestic group that might find common cause with foreign rivals seeking to thwart Louis's ambitions for empire.

In 1683 Louis married his second wife, Madame de Maintenon. A *dévot*, Maintenon represented the Catholic faction at court that opposed a moderate religious policy in favor of a more rigid and intolerant version of Catholicism. Under her influence Louis became more devout and, as the most Christian king, wished to make a grand

Catholic gesture. By this show of good Catholic faith he also hoped to ingratiate himself with the pope, who had been displeased by Louis's failure to render Emperor Leopold I military aid against the Turks when they threatened Habsburg possessions in the East.

Louis's position with respect to religious minorities was not unusual for monarchs of his era. Rulers of early modern states believed that their kingdoms were stronger and more stable if everyone adhered to one faith—the one, true Christian faith of the sovereign. Like France, other Catholic powers, such as Spain and Portugal, had a history of discrimination against non-Catholic populations. In the seventeenth century, Portugal banished its Jews, while actively suppressing Protestantism. Spain likewise expelled its Jews in 1492, and then the Moriscos—Muslims who had converted to Christianity after 1492—in the years 1609 to 1614. Except for the Dutch Republic, Protestant nations were generally no different when it came to their treatment of religious minorities. The monarchs of both Scotland and England, for example, enacted laws against Dissenters and Catholics alike, believing, like Louis XIV, that religious uniformity brought stability and national unity. For most nations during the seventeenth century, religious intolerance remained political reality.

Above all, Louis considered the existence of Protestants an affront to his power. For the divine monarch and head of the most powerful state in Europe, the toleration of a minority religion within France appeared to many as a sign of personal weakness. Louis's might rested on the effective use of state systems and the authority he derived from their coordinated efforts. Exercising command by overseeing both the French church and state, Louis could act decisively and with great force. The continued presence of the Huguenots threatened that autocratic supremacy and undermined his very notion of kingship.

GIRAUD'S FLIGHT

Before the Revocation, officials in Grenoble, the administrative capital of Dauphiné, had suspended the *chambre mi-partie* court and banned

Protestants from holding municipal offices. Civic officials expelled Protestant ministers from the city and in some cases executed them. Others were incarcerated, and their children held by the state.[17]

Writing at the time, contemporary and historian Elie Benoist depicted Louis XIV's crusade against the Protestants of Dauphiné in the years preceding the Revocation. Clearly partisan, Benoist's magnum opus, the *Histoire de l'Édit de Nantes,* accused the state, over the course of French history, of undermining Huguenot liberty through royal arrests and edicts that served to dismantle the Edict of Nantes.[18] Benoist included individual accounts of the persecution of Huguenot ministers and others across France. This presentation of the history of legal discrimination and its brutal effects played a crucial role in shaping the narrative of suffering and martyrdom that became central to Huguenot identity.[19]

In book five, which he published while in exile in the Netherlands, Benoist detailed the state's campaign against Dauphiné's rural Protestants. Louis XIV ordered the demolition of remaining Huguenot churches, and when religious gatherings continued in the countryside, it prompted an even more violent intervention.[20] In 1683, soldiers were sent to the wooded areas and mountains, where hundreds of Protestants were meeting in religious worship. Their devotion was met with violence, and many were arrested or murdered.

The Duke of Noailles attacked 210 men hiding near L'Herbasse, one hundred miles west of La Grave. Noailles's soldiers killed about 40 as the rest scattered through the woods. Nine who refused to convert to Catholicism were hanged from trees without trial. The same day troops went to Vernoux, where many others were hanged. In Chalançon the soldiers pillaged, burning what they could not carry. Women were raped in their homes, while others were murdered, including two men in their sixties. Both had refused to go to mass.[21] Truly execrable atrocities continued in the days to follow, totaling nearly forty incidents in the surrounding ten or twelve parishes. The bodies of the dead were either discarded in the river or left exposed on the road. Geraud Mercier, aged sixty, was hanged. Jacques Tinlaud, almost a hundred years old, died of a gunshot. Pierre Palix's arms were severed with a saber, and a pregnant Catherine Raventel was killed while giving birth. Soldiers then cut the face of one surviving child, aged eight, and the hand of another, aged five.[22]

Jean Giraud was keenly aware of the state's mounting campaign against his religious community. He recorded in September of 1685 that the dragoons in La Grave guarded homes by day, while Protestant neighbors fled by night, their homes looted after their departure. This was no voluntary exile. The Huguenot laity was forbidden to leave France; attempts to do so were punished in various ways, usually by incarceration and property forfeiture. Despite this, Giraud was willing to assist the escape of his sister Marie and brother-in-law Jean Monnet, together with his Chicot in-laws from the nearby village of Chazelet. The escalation of guards patrolling Giraud's house frustrated that effort. His sister Anne, her daughter and servant, and a nephew, however, did succeed in escaping to Geneva. Marie and Jean Monnet were less fortunate in a later attempt. Neighbors informed on them, and soldiers arrested them not far from their house. They were taken to jail in Grenoble, where they awaited appearance in court.[23]

An alarmed Giraud now undertook a plan to remove his wife, Magdelaine, and daughter, Suzon, to safety in Geneva. An opportunity presented when many villagers were permitted to attend a local fair and most dragoons were occupied keeping them under close watch. Giraud's home was left virtually unguarded. The chance came to naught, however, when the man available to assist the pregnant Magdelaine and her young daughter informed the family that he could only guide them to the top of the mountains; after that, they must fend for themselves. Magdelaine did not know the way, and her eight-month pregnancy certainly complicated matters. The plan to escape was thus rendered untenable and never realized. Rumors of the Girauds' intentions may have circulated, for shortly thereafter more dragoons were deployed to guard their home.[24] Meanwhile, the beleaguered merchant was beset with coercion from another source.

Kings always need more money, and Louis XIV stands as the

paradigm of the aphorism. The French nobility claimed exemptions from most taxation, leaving a heavy burden on the Third Estate—businessmen, merchants, professionals, shopkeepers, artisans, and rural laborers. As the number of Huguenots taking flight from La Grave and elsewhere steadily increased, so did the amount of debt they left behind in the nature of taxes, religious dues, and other fees. These delinquencies were demanded from economically successful Huguenots who still remained. Jean Giraud was one of the Protestant church leaders deemed responsible for these amounts despite the fact that he had always scrupulously paid his own personal taxes.

Officials sought information regarding the alarming number of departures of villagers and demanded payment for the debts they owed. Giraud consulted with other church leaders—Félix Giraud, Paul Jullien, and Daniel Grangent—to develop a proposal that would be considered a satisfactory compliance. After reviewing La Grave's consistory records, the men offered to pay whatever members of the consistory owed. This measure did not satisfy officials, and all were placed under house arrest. According to Giraud, the bishop demanded that La Grave's church pay not only what it owed but, in addition, all that was owed by thirty villagers who had previously fled La Grave. The men would pay the entire amount claimed or remain under house arrest and in due time be transferred to the prison in Grenoble.[25]

Whether Giraud paid the debts of those who fled is unknown, but Giraud was escorted to the prison in Grenoble along with Félix Giraud, Paul Jullien, and Daniel Grangent. The next evening all four men "signed" their abjurations. Abjuration required a formal renunciation of Protestantism and an official oath of loyalty to the Catholic Church. After the Revocation, state authorities sought to break Huguenot resistance by pressuring Protestants to abjure, and many complied to escape loss of property, imprisonment, or death. For the crown, abjuration symbolized the state's political and religious sovereignty. Abjuration for Protestants, traumatic and deeply personal, signified the loss of religious liberty and personal freedom. Many Huguenots who abjured, even if under duress, later expressed shame, believing they had betrayed their church and faith. Though the men had been freed, Giraud regretted the outcome terribly, writing that the intendant Berthon, "would offer neither rhyme nor reason, in such a cruel manner. The next day in the evening we signed unhappily after having cried during our imprisonment over our misery and pitiful state. This villain did not counter our proper sentiments and will. May God grace us by letting us weep for the rest of our days with great regret at having offended Him, and it pleases Him to regard us with great compassion."[26]

This was a momentous decision not only for one man's tortured conscience, but for the entire local community, Huguenot and Catholic alike. For his Catholic neighbors, it was important that Giraud's conversion be sincere. Giraud was a valued member of his community and his judgments had weight with church members, as well as with those with whom he conducted business. Catholic officials and neighbors knew this and undoubtedly sought greater assurance of the sincerity of Giraud's conversion than that of his Huguenot comrades.

His abjuration must have secured his release, for a few days later Giraud endeavored to free his sister and brother-in-law from prison. Giraud attempted to bribe and cajole, employing whatever connections were at his disposal, but to no avail. He finally admitted, "The ones who are loyal friends were the ones who hurt us the most." After the damaging testimony of several witnesses, presumably neighbors, and fearful of a negative judgment, Marie Giraud and Jean Monnet abjured their faith. The court released the pair after their abjurations and payment of court costs.[27]

The abjurations continued. Fellow villagers in Besse, Mizoën, Mont-de-Lans, La Faurie, and Clavans were pressured to swear allegiance to the Catholic faith, thus becoming new converts or *Nouveaux Catholiques*. Neighbors who had been in prison signed abjurations in order to be released. The role of the Catholic church was central; Giraud recounted four or five priests intervening and pressuring his neighbor Violente Grangent to convert. At the same time, Protestant neighbors and family members continued to flee France.[28] Departures were conducted secretly because of the ban on lay Protestants leaving France. The penalty for men was condemnation to the galleys; for women, loss of all material possessions. Of course, the very real possibility existed that, if apprehended and detained by extreme Catholics, any Huguenots refusing to abjure their faith on the spot faced summary execution.

Geneva attracted many émigrés due to its close proximity to France. According to Giraud, the Huguenot merchant Jean Bérard, his "cousin and friend," and Simon Vieux, Bérard's son-in-law, absconded to Geneva, with other Huguenot families following days later. Jean Bernard of Besse, along with his brothers Paul and Daniel, finally escaped, "arriving happily in Geneva" with thirty others and a caravan of eighteen pack animals bearing what property they could escape with. Giraud's mother-in-law and her daughter Manon, as well as her servant, were all pressured to sign their allegiance to the Catholic faith. Afterwards they successfully fled Chazelet for Geneva, where they were eventually reunited with other family members.[29]

Authorities grew especially suspicious of Giraud, undoubtedly for his role as a community leader and possible émigré accomplice. In La Grave, he remained under the dragoons' watchful eye. The bishop, who believed in conversion through persuasion rather than force, pledged to bring Giraud's community relief from the dragoons, but the situation only worsened. On December 15, 1685, a few weeks after the birth of Giraud's still-born son, the Marquis de la Trousse sent eight soldiers to La Grave, along with a *maréchal* to lodge specifically with Magdelaine, Giraud's wife. The *maréchal* arrived with orders to transfer her to the hospital in Grenoble, where it was believed she would be more inclined to convert. The threat succeeded; the following day Magdelaine abjured her Protestant faith.[30]

Giraud now drew additional suspicion after receiving an unsealed letter from a Savoy agent seeking wool for sale. The local curé, in conjunction with royal officials, questioned Giraud, who was adamant that he had no knowledge of the letter or its courier's intentions. Giraud was freed, but the letter's courier was sent to the galleys. The authorities no doubt suspected the man belonged to a group assisting Huguenots in their escape.

Meanwhile, an inventory of Giraud's father-in-law's property, which had been pillaged in his absence, was prepared. Presumably, Giraud's father-in-law was already in Geneva. In all likelihood, the inventory was executed in preparation for the family's departure, to cover the necessary costs and to escape with as much money as possible. According to Giraud, the court raised at least thirty *louis d'or* from the sale of his father-in-law's livestock. He noted as well that one "rascal," Paillas, appropriated fifteen sacks of grain from his father-in-law's granary in addition to blankets, tablecloths, napkins, taffeta, silver cups, and his sister-in-law's old clothes. The rogue "even took thirty *écus blancs* from the pocket of my mother-in-law," wrote Giraud, "all while in the presence of witnesses."[31]

Giraud soon found himself before a judge, interrogated about his mother-in-law, who had fled to Switzerland. Authorities probably conjectured that he was an accessory to her exodus, but they permitted Giraud to return home to his wife and daughter, where he began an inventory of his own possessions. Clearly, he had reached a decision to escape from France; now the Girauds waited for a propitious moment. With an eye to the future, Giraud disparaged the billeting troops, the harassment by local officials, and the confiscation of personal possessions: ". . . [I]t is a pitiable night that we are with persons of this sort. . . . They steal several possessions but they are only goods of this world."[32]

On a final trip to Lyon Giraud discovered that many Protestant shops, including that of his brother-in-law, Jacques Chicot, and other close friends, had closed. Following his return to La Grave, he was met with alarming news. Two groups of Protestants totaling 240 persons and twenty-eight mules had departed France for Switzerland. Learning of this, several priests took steps to apprehend the refugees, which authorities did at Saint-Jean-de-Maurienne. The captured men were transported to the prison in Grenoble and the women and young infants to the hospital. Paul Coing and Daniel Bouillet of La Grave and Ogier of Besse were condemned to the "galleys for life." Three others—Pierre-Bernard Camus, a young man named Masson, and Étienne Heustachy of Besse—were hanged, and their severed heads placed on poles. In early modern custom, Camus's head was placed at the entrance to the town to serve as a warning to all. Masson's grisly visage looked down on Giraud's garden. Giraud wrote:

> On the 26 June, day of Wednesday, the poor Étienne Heustachy, age twenty-three, was executed and his head exposed on a pole . . . and the other two led by archers to the grand prévôt of Mizoën, where the said Masson was executed and his head placed on a pole twenty paces from my garden at Besse, the said Masson was twenty-four. And Pierre-Bernard Camus, age of about thirty-eight, was executed in Besse, where his wife and family still were. His head was placed on a pole at the entrance of the village, and his body was dragged and discarded off the cliff.[33]

Clearly, not all attempts to flee succeeded, and the perceived leaders of those making the attempt were sure to pay a heavy price if apprehended.

An appalling and particularly gruesome event overtook Giraud when Thoinette Faure of Villar-d'Arêne, described as "rather bigoted with some of her kind," dug up his dead infant, removing it from its grave in order to have it baptized. Though Giraud had abjured his Protestant faith, he had failed to have his child baptized in the Roman Catholic church before its burial. Evidently having learned this, locals sought to secure the child's salvation by disinterring the body and having it baptized, over the parents' objections. The dead infant was returned to its sepulcher after baptism, and Giraud and his wife were horrified. "Can you believe to what state [we] were reduced," wrote Giraud, "treated in this way in our motherland." This incident exemplified, more than anything, the religious tensions within the community, at least among those who held extreme religious conviction.[34]

On June 15, the bishop of Grenoble visited La Grave and exhorted Giraud and his neighbors to fulfill their new obligations of confessing and attending mass. Giraud, in response, feigned ignorance—apologizing that he did not understand the new faith or know exactly what to do. That same day Jean-Étienne Bouchu, the new intendant of Dauphiné, stopped by Les Hières on the way to Briançon and lectured Giraud "brutally." Authorities were told to watch Giraud's actions carefully and, "if he escapes with his . . . effects, to write a report and send it to [Bouchu]." Bouchu's suspicions ran deep; he later placed a bounty of one hundred *louis d'or* on Giraud's head for anyone who caught him trying to flee.[35]

The persecution never seemed to cease. In July 1686, the intendant received complaints regarding delinquent debtors, who were thought to be hiding and considering flight. Among those under suspicion was Jean Monnet, Giraud's brother-in-law, who some thought had already secretly left for Geneva. Bouchu wrote to the councilor of La Grave that "he had learnt the said Monnet was not honoring his duty, and that he was actually hiding with the purpose of desertion." Bouchu confronted Giraud, informing him that Monnet must come forward or the community would risk serious repercussions. In response, Giraud proclaimed that his brother-in-law was in Provence attending the fair in Beaucaire, and produced a certificate from the Abbot of Grenoble, granting Monnet permission to travel outside the province. A week later the curé Planchet of Les Hières appeared on Giraud's doorstep demanding that Giraud confess and receive communion or suffer the outrage of dragoons in his home yet again. To satisfy the priest, Giraud agreed that he and his wife would attend confession the following week. The priest departed, wrote Giraud, "rubbing his hands with joy."[36]

At this point, Giraud decided to leave France. He had remained in his home nearly a year after the date of the Revocation. He had long contemplated his departure, but waited for the right moment. It pained him much to leave behind his home and current life, but a sense of urgency was now in the midsummer air. Giraud gathered those goods he needed for the trip and secretly arranged for guides to take him and his family across the Alps. On July 29, 1686, four days after the priest's visit, Giraud, with his wife and daughter, departed for Switzerland. At 10 o'clock that evening, an ally from Savoy stopped by to inform him that others, presumably guides and those willing to house them along the way, were ready and waiting. His two horses' hooves were wrapped in cloth to muffle their sound on the stones, so as not to alert neighbors. His wife carried Suzon, their six-year-old daughter, on her back. Giraud closed the door to the house for a final time, reverently putting himself "in God's hands."[37]

Giraud's sister Marie also fled at this time. All family members left with their guides, following different paths to avoid detection. It was pitch black and had rained the day before, producing more snow on the mountain tops. With no moon to light the way, Suzon and Magdelaine fell from their horse and wandered off the trail, the guides too preoccupied to notice. They were located, and despite the confusion in the darkness, the entire family and their guides reassembled. The weather was wet and cold; their clothes froze to their bodies and their boots froze up to mid-thigh. Magdelaine could not walk, and Suzon, from terror or stress or both, began to have stomach problems. Fearing for his daughter's life, Giraud wrapped Suzon with his coat and strapped her to the back of one of the guides. Bundled as she was, Giraud hoped she would stay warm. If not, Giraud wrote, "we would have to bury her at the Mountain Coin du Col that we were crossing."[38]

It was broad daylight by the time the group reached the mountain top. Each drank a half cup of fruit brandy. They descended the mountain, each taking a separate trail with his or her guide. They planned to follow different paths all the way to Geneva, and all agreed that, if one were discovered, he or she would feign ignorance of the others. All knew the rule: "for it is easier to free one than two or three." If questioned, they were to reply that they were heading to the baths in Aix-les-Bains. It was also decided that none would stay, eat, or sleep in the same house or inn at the same time. They all separated and began their trek once again, "under the grace of God."[39]

As they descended the mountain, "the sun started to appear on the top of the highest rocks," when, wrote Giraud, "we found some new courage." That evening Giraud dined in Saint-Jean-de-Maurienne, his wife a league behind, and his sister somewhat further away. At some point Giraud and his wife reunited, and both stopped for the night at La Chapelle near Montmélian. On the morning of Thursday, August 1, Giraud, Magdelaine, and Suzon entered Geneva. They were fortunate to be free; they were lucky to be alive. A new life beckoned.[40]

Marie was forced to contend with two perilous encounters in the final stages of her journey. First, when stopped by soldiers, Marie claimed to hail from Lucerne in Piedmont. They demanded money and her rings in exchange for her freedom. Then, about three and a half miles from Geneva, Marie was detained a second time and taken to a local judge, who made her pay a ransom of twelve *louis d'or* and her mule, which she gave up along with her remaining belongings. She was kept in the guardroom at Pont d'Arve all night until dawn, when she was finally released and permitted to cross the river into Geneva, arriving eight days after her brother and his family. Giraud recounted that she remained sick for nine weeks, and miscarried after only three months.[41]

The campaign against the Huguenots that caused Giraud and his family to flee actually represented a transitional point in the larger evolution of the power of the state and its institutions. Both popular and institutional violence had long been associated with religious controversy in France. In the previous century, ordinary citizens took matters into their hands, resorting to popular violence to compel religious conformity, while the state inflicted torture and held brutal public executions to illustrate its sovereignty.[42] The tossing of Camus's torso off the cliff harkened to the days of the Wars of Religion, when French subjects joined in the barbarous rounding up and massacre of Protestants. As in days past, bloody public executions, both popular and institutional, symbolized the violent eradication of heresy, the continued existence of which was perceived to threaten the general well-being and salvation of the Catholic community. Public mutilation

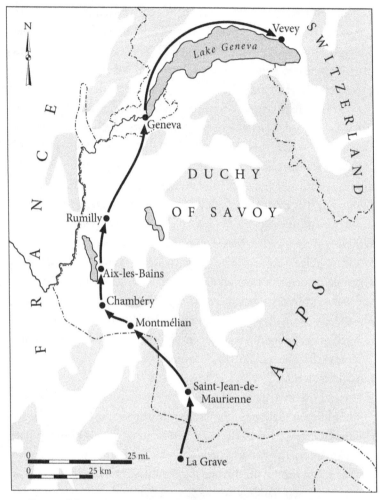

Route of Giraud's Flight from La Grave to Vevey, per his livre de raison

of Camus's corpse constituted an additional level of humiliation and punishment, reserved for those who were believed to represent the greatest public threat.

By Giraud's time, mass coercion by means of the billeting of troops in Protestant homes and organized campaigns against Huguenot communities can be seen as exercises in governmental power more familiar to modern states, as was Louis's detention of thousands of Huguenots attempting to flee his kingdom. When Heutachy, Masson, and Camus refused to abjure and make the sign of the cross, they were executed and their bodies posthumously mutilated. But such dreadful fates were the exceptions. Most who resisted conversion or caught fleeing were incarcerated either in Grenoble's prison or hospital. Imprisonment as punishment suggested a new discipline and re-education with respect to one's proper role and duty as a member of the Christian community, and even more important as a subject of the crown.[43]

Giraud's account shows that Louis XIV succeeded in synthesizing informal and formal networks into hegemonic structures. The monarch achieved control by gaining the consent of regional and local actors who may or may not have directly benefited in real terms from an expansion of royal power, but who willingly gave their approval to a traditional set of cultural values that served to buttress royal power and its patron-client relationships. Plunder, confiscation of personal possessions, imprisonment, quartering of troops, forced abjurations, banishment to the king's galleys, and public execution—all speak to an operation of force on a scale so ferocious it was only possible with the commitment and support of multiple regional and local actors. As Giraud's narrative attests, the Revocation in Dauphiné involved the expert manipulation of military figures and agencies, functionaries of the courts, officials of the church from the highest echelons to the lowest village priest, and many private citizens, all working in concert.

So, how centralized were Louis XIV's institutions of state? One opinion is that Louis's standing army—symbol of royal strength and a tool readily deployed to suppress popular uprisings and rebellion—was an instrument of coercion only effective if directed in conjunction with "a variety of other institutions and forces that were organized along military lines but that existed outside the traditional military hierarchy." Historian Roy McCullough has noted that "the coercive power within the French state remained decentralized to a surprising degree."[44] For this reason and others, the state did not succeed in converting or eliminating the Huguenot minority of France. As many as 20,000 Huguenots escaped Dauphiné; as many as 200,000 fled France. Many who remained, despite abjurations and outward conversion, continued Protestant worship in secrecy, in the caves, forests, and rural meadows.[45]

Huguenot ministers returning to France from exile sustained an underground movement of Protestant assemblies despite the state's best efforts to suppress it. Known as *l'Église du Désert* (the Church of the Wilderness), this southern rural movement began as early as 1683, when ministers in Languedoc began preaching from the ruins of razed churches. These groups were bold. In 1702, Protestants from the Cévennes revolted against the crown, launching a bloody civil war known as the Camisard Uprising. This insurrection persisted until 1704, with intermittent clashes until the demise of the Camisard leader, Abraham Mazel, in 1710.[46] Such prolonged agitation and conflict attested to Huguenot resilience and the manifest limitations of royal power.

Upon departing France, Giraud undoubtedly found himself in reduced circumstances, as he had left behind his home, his land, livestock, and almost all of his personal belongings. He took with him only what he could carry. He likely took gold and liquid assets he could sell, small, portable valuables like spoons, jewelry, and precious stones. He pondered how he would live once relocated and how he would support his family. As a lender, he could have tried to recover amounts owed him, though collection would have been difficult as many of his debtors were still living in France or had relocated elsewhere. Many of those indebted to him were no doubt now destitute. Alternatively, he could pursue financial support from his host city or seek loans from other Huguenot immigrants with available resources. Giraud now contended with a new, unfamiliar environment, separated from his community, which had scattered in the wake of the Revocation. During this unsettled time, he contemplated how a new community would greet him and how he would reestablish the business ties and network of clients that were essential for his livelihood.

The trauma Giraud experienced weighed heavily. He chose not to explain why he kept an account of his escape and the dissolution of his community; more important, he does not explain what it meant to him. How did Giraud make sense of the multitudinous atrocities and persecutions he and his community experienced? His blow-by-blow account detailed the wicked misdeeds that provoked his angst and desperation. And Giraud's escape narrative betokened his fortitude. He knew God was testing him and his people, and apprehended that he could not waiver. In addition, as paterfamilias, it was his responsibility to document the events for posterity. In exile, there is no record that Giraud confessed his conversion, a common practice the persecuted undertook to make amends and be reaccepted into the community of the faithful. Perhaps any shame he felt for his abjuration was expunged by his written account, in which he had recorded his true commitment and loyalty to his faith. Although Giraud's personal narrative drew no biblical parallels and lacked scriptural references, his descriptions, like those of other contemporaries, indeed constituted an act of personal piety, his recorded suffering a sign of election, and his resettlement a representation of God's favor.

Giraud with his wife and daughter arrived in Vevey, their final destination, in January 1687. The family were among seven hundred other Huguenot refugees who came to live in this little town on the eastern shore of Lake Geneva. In recording their suffering and the ordeals they endured, Giraud's narrative was a testament to Huguenot sacrifice. Stories of oppression and loss transformed victims into martyrs. The Huguenots of La Grave may have abjured, but they also displayed courage and strength, forced to conceal the faith that carried them through their tragic ordeal.

The Huguenots in Giraud's story lived up to their calling. Giraud's Church in La Grave was destroyed—no physical church remained—but its people, Giraud's community, lived on in the hearts and minds of those who endured. Giraud and his community would endeavor to sustain long-standing ties, forging new meaning and direction from the remnants left behind. As a cultural intermediary, Giraud played an important role in framing and communicating refugee experiences. In more specific terms, his record helped to make sense of the Revocation and the near annihilation of the Huguenot community, not among an urban elite but among common Alpine people both before and after their diasporic experiences.

THREE

✖✖

Giraud's Community of Exiles

Jean Giraud, his wife, Magdelaine, and six-year-old daughter, Suzon, arrived in Vevey, Switzerland, on January 26, 1687. The previous summer, the family had evaded the dragoons patrolling their native village, La Grave, and its neighboring French hamlets, cautiously slipping away to safety in Geneva. As they crossed the Alps from France into Switzerland, Huguenot immigrants like the Girauds embraced a new identity. They were no longer rebels, or Louis XIV's *prétendue réformée*, but now *réfugiés*. This designation was in general use in late seventeenth-century Vaud and can be found in many cantonal and municipal archival sources.[1] *Réfugié* was a specification like *habitant* or *bourgeois*, and particularly denoted a Calvinist who had fled France to escape religious persecution, one who likely required special attention and support.[2] With around seven hundred others, Giraud settled in Vevey, a town of a few thousand situated on the eastern shore of Lake Geneva in Vaud, one of the Swiss cantons that gave sanctuary to Huguenot refugees.[3]

The French refugees who found their way to Vevey faced numerous challenges. If they did not have a contact to provide shelter, they had to make arrangements for a place to dwell. Municipal authorities helped by subsidizing lodging. If they had the resources to purchase food and medicine, they did so; otherwise they were, again, dependent

Seventeenth-Century Scene of Vevey, print by Matthäus Merian, 1650.
Copyright © *Historical Museum of Vevey,* Copyright © *Municipal Archives of Vevey.*

on municipal charity for temporary relief. Finding employment also
posed obstacles. Some pursued their previous trades even though locals, resenting the competition, fervently opposed them. Others lived
off their savings and investments. Most important, refugees had to
adapt to a new civic authority and new culture. The people of Vevey
spoke French, greatly facilitating the refugees' transition to a new life,
but other challenges awaited. As with refugees throughout Europe,
the newcomers' presence in Vevey resulted in tension and hostility
with the native population. Refugees sought social acceptance through
abiding by the civic rules of their host city and tried to establish new
personal ties, vital for economic and social survival. And within their
small group, the fugitives from France, through traditional strategies of
marriage and godparenthood, maintained social relationships essential
for reconstituting their lost community.

The exodus of refugees arriving in Vevey bore witness to a pattern of European religious persecution that began in the fifteenth
century. Since that time, various states had mounted campaigns to
expel minorities from their borders for religious reasons. During these
years, Europe saw mass waves of religious refugees, including Jews and
Muslims, Anabaptists, and other Christians forced into exile. Eccle-

siastical and state officials, borrowing from the medical terminology of the Middle Ages, dubbed religious minorities a "contagion" that needed "purging" from the community. By excising the contagion, through either forced conversion or expulsion, the state restored the community to social unity and purity.[4] Such thinking continued into the seventeenth century, when states, more centralized than before, applied power against religious minorities at unparalleled levels. Notorious examples included the expulsion of 300,000 Moriscos from Spain between 1609 and 1614, and, as we have seen, the flight of Huguenots from France in 1685.

HUGUENOT DIASPORA

Historians estimate that between 150,000 and 200,000 Huguenots fled France following the Revocation of the Edict of Nantes in October of 1685. Many settled in Protestant states: England, the Dutch Republic, the German Protestant lands, and Switzerland. Of the 40,000 that fled to Switzerland, about 6,000 came to the Pays de Vaud, many of them arriving from the provinces of Languedoc or Dauphiné.[5] The final destinations of the families who were members of Giraud's church were widely dispersed geographically with much overlap in routes of migration. Many from La Grave, including Jean Giraud, came first to Geneva, and continued from there along one of the emigration routes to Yverdon-les-Bains, Morges, or Vevey. Giraud's records of fellow church members reveal that, from those points, some families proceeded to the northern cities of Kassel, Winterthur, Erlangen, and Amsterdam. Others continued as far north as London, and then westward to Dublin or across the Atlantic to "Carroline."[6]

Giraud did not discuss the lives of these families during their years in exile, but he did provide an extant list by prénom and family surname of all attendees of his church in La Grave, giving each individual's final destination in exile and his or her year of death. This list essentially documented the diaspora of Giraud's church and attested to Giraud's strong desire to keep his religious community in some sense intact by this record. Of equal importance, it showed that Giraud in exile maintained an elaborate communication network, possibly founded by means of his various commercial contacts, that enabled him to stay connected with relatives and fellow church members. Such networks suggest that a well-developed system of social support was established, spanning great distances. Familial and church-related networks undoubtedly enabled refugees to pool resources and possibly provided a web of contacts with access to capital for investment. Most important, refugee networks of this kind demonstrated the transnational features of the Huguenot community which, following the Revocation, found itself dispersed among various national and cultural settings. Huguenot refugees like Giraud were undoubtedly adaptable. Many were experienced in international commerce, while others exercised craft skills that were desirable and transferable.

Although many European nations were sympathetic to their plight, Huguenot refugees in the seventeenth century were not always well received. Countries vacillated in policy (or simply lacked a national policy) with respect to them. Geneva offers an interesting study. Thousands of refugees fleeing France crossed through Geneva en route to other countries. Between 1680 and 1689, Geneva rendered aid to around 28,000 refugees, and about 3,300 stayed, comprising one-fifth of the city's population.[7] In addition to bringing traditional trades and crafts, Huguenot refugees arriving in Geneva opened workshops for making silk thread, stockings, ribbons, taffetas, and other fabrics. They greatly aided in the industry of print calicoes and contributed to the growth of watchmaking trades by apprenticing themselves to established Swiss watchmakers. Some engaged in the illicit trade in cloth and "other wares" they smuggled into Geneva through their connections in France.[8] Over time tensions between refugees and the native population mounted, especially during the last decade of the century when the city experienced housing and food shortages. Native Genevans grew less tolerant of foreigners, who competed for jobs and charitable support. A slump in the standard of living and rising prices drove the city's merchants to demand that authorities

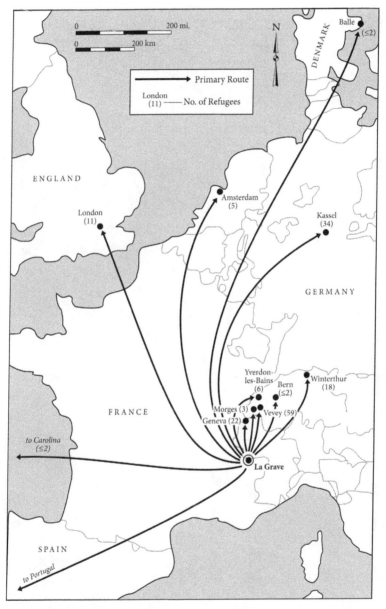

Primary Routes of La Grave's Exiles, per Giraud's livre de raison.
The great majority of La Grave's refugees fled to Vevey, Kassel, and Geneva,
followed by Winterthur and London.

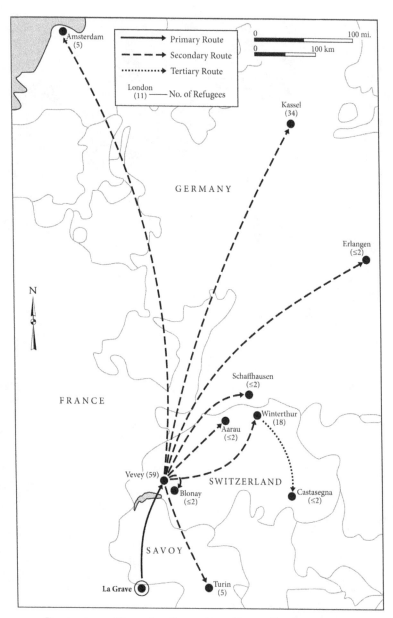

Destinations of Secondary Routes from Vevey of La Grave's Exiles,
per Giraud's livre de raison.

restrict the refugees' commercial activities.[9] As early as 1685, Geneva had taken steps to expel Huguenot refugees from the city. The most economically successful were permitted to stay, and, though they denied them full status as citizens, Geneva's municipal authorities did finally permit 1,235 to remain in the city as "inhabitants."[10]

Refugees faced varied receptions and challenges in other host nations. England saw nearly 50,000 Huguenot refugees settle in its lands, with around 30,000 taking up residence in or around London by the start of the eighteenth century.[11] London drew Huguenot refugees for a number of reasons. The administrative capital of England, it was a major center of manufacturing and a hub of international commerce. Also, London already possessed a prominent community of Huguenot immigrants who had made the city their home generations earlier. Huguenots brought with them craft skills the English greatly valued, and they augmented England's cloth trades. The French refugees also contributed to jewelry and watchmaking, silversmithing, papermaking, and the manufacture of felt hats and mirrors.[12]

For the most part, the English sympathized with the Huguenot immigrants and gave generously to their aid. As early as 1689, the king warmly welcomed the refugees, offering them protection and petitioning for their citizenship, which Parliament initially rejected but finally granted in 1709. Still, the high number of refugees pouring into London at times generated tensions between the native population and immigrants. London's silk weavers, for example, objected to the presence of Huguenot artisans, alleging that they did not satisfy the full terms of apprenticeship and took jobs from native residents.[13] Feelings in London ran especially high in the last decades of the seventeenth century when popular inflammatory, antipopery rhetoric directed against Louis XIV and the French reached its peak.[14] Despite their refugee status, Huguenot immigrants could be the targets of anti-French animus and hatred.[15]

While many Huguenot refugees fled to London and Geneva, large numbers headed for Holland. Some 35,000 left France for the Dutch Republic following the Revocation. It was attractive for a number of

reasons. The Dutch had a strong economy, and authorities there offered incentives to encourage settlement. Also, there already existed a
network of Walloon churches that welcomed refugees. The economic
incentives offered Huguenot refugees with skills and means were well
known: charitable loans, free acceptance into guilds, tax exemption,
and, in some cases, citizenship. In some situations, Dutch authorities
permitted Huguenot entrepreneurs to employ cheap labor from or-
phanages. Sailors, skilled artisans, and merchants were willing and able
to take advantage of the numerous incentives Dutch officials made
available. Along with them came French bookmakers and printers
who, after settling in the Dutch Republic, published a wide range of
French books, newspapers, and journals for the international market.
So many contributed, no doubt lured by policies of limited censorship,
that historians have credited Huguenot immigrants with initiating
the early Enlightenment in the Netherlands.[16]

Despite their overall positive reception in the Dutch Republic,
French refugees struggled there, too, and found themselves in fierce
competition with native Dutch industries long since established. Many
Huguenot entrepreneurial enterprises did not survive, including print
shops and bookstores. By the close of the century, the Dutch Republic,
falling into a state of economic depression, "became saturated with
refugees," precipitating "antagonism and heightened economic rivalry."
Subsequently, many Dutch municipalities after 1690 ended privileges
originally purposed for the assistance of Huguenot refugees.[17]

VEVEY'S HUGUENOT REFUGEES

As elsewhere in Europe, Swiss authorities were predisposed to do what
they could for uprooted refugees, offering aid in the most urgent of
circumstances. In time, however, authorities both in Bern and Vevey
became less inclined to furnish relief for a number of reasons. Economic conditions began to worsen for the population as a whole, and
the cost of relief exceeded Vevey's capacity to provide it. Native-born
artisans, mainly members of the bourgeoisie, protested the continued

presence of refugees who competed for work and jobs. And the presence of French Protestants stressed the alliance system fundamental to keeping peace between the Swiss cantons. Swiss authorities, both in Bern and Vevey, appreciated those refugees possessed with their own resources who could contribute to the economic improvement of Switzerland through manufacturing and shops that brought commerce and employment. Nonetheless, by the close of the century, officials took steps to expel many by establishing strict terms of residency. The fluctuating policy between accommodation and removal that came to characterize immigrant policy in the years following the Revocation reflected the competing interests between rival camps in power—those who either sympathized with the refugees and recognized their contributions, and those who saw the refugees, at least the poor ones, as a detriment and drain on economic resources.

Shortly after the Revocation, Bern, the municipal authority over the Pays de Vaud, took immediate action and provided emergency assistance to the 6,000 refugees swelling the canton. During this mass influx, cantonal authorities dispensed free public housing and in some cases covered the refugees' transportation costs. The Pays de Vaud's network of hospitals also assisted fleeing refugees by granting temporary housing, food, medical care, and assistance in securing further passage. In 1683, Bern had created a Chamber of Refugees for the specific purpose of addressing refugee-related concerns. The Chamber played a pivotal role in raising and managing charitable donations, which were augmented when the Reformed Conference established an additional fund in the amount of 30,000 florins, which all states were expected to endow. This measure was followed by the founding of a Chamber of Commerce, which subsidized refugee businesses and manufactures. As with cantonal authorities, Vevey granted charity to individual refugees and families and dispensed relief through the city hospital.

Municipal records indicate that civic authorities additionally supported refugees by providing them temporary residency and, in some cases, permission to work. Others were allowed to open boutiques.

In one case, for example, municipal authorities granted permission to the Huguenot woman Magdeleine Masset "to earn a living as a refugee."[18] Such strategies for relief paralleled programs elsewhere in Europe such as the Netherlands and Geneva where state authorities sheltered and met the immediate material needs of Huguenot refugees.

While many refugees continued on to other destinations, the names of those who remained in Vevey occasionally surface in the town's municipal records. On November 23, 1685, for example, Félix Giraud, "merchant of La Grave" and "resident of Lyon" (an obvious relative of Jean Giraud), appeared before municipal authorities requesting permission to remain in Vevey.[19] His early arrival, over a year before Jean Giraud and his family, may partly explain why other family members chose to relocate there. Members of Jean Giraud's church in La Grave also appear in Vevey's municipal records. Jacques Faucher, a merchant from La Grave, requested permission to stay on August 19, 1686. Three weeks later Jean Bertet, another refugee, did the same.[20] The following January, Vevey granted charity to the refugee widow Galor, also a former member of the church. That spring another Giraud relative, Jacques Gravier, appeared before municipal authorities seeking the right to sell his merchandise.[21]

Although refugees settling in Vevey represented all walks of life, nobles, rentiers, and merchants accounted for the vast majority who immigrated. Between 1680 and 1705, the city granted work permits to 203 French refugees, many of whom were engaged in the professional and commercial domains. Others were employed in agriculture, or the textile and clothing, leather, watchmaking, and bakery trades.[22] The city could be less hospitable to artisans seen as competitors. Artisans to whom the city granted permission to work usually had to comply with certain restrictions as municipal authorities imposed limitations to protect native industries. Bakers, for instance, could use only flour obtained from the town granary. Other artisans paid fees or agreed to work limited hours. For example, city officials permitted one refugee to open a spice shop as long as he paid their tax.[23] Two others paid a habitation fee and agreed to contribute to the relief of the poor.[24]

Then there was the case of two refugees whom city officials agreed to tolerate for an interval of six months, as long as the local bourgeoisie lodged no opposition.[25] Also accepted was a refugee surgeon who had served in the army of William of Orange, on condition that he did not open his own surgery shop. In a similar case, a refugee with a résumé of various skills and some extended experience in Geneva was allowed to make wigs but not to act as a surgeon.[26] A carpenter from Mizoën was permitted temporary work but was encouraged to seek employment elsewhere after the winter.[27] The same held true for a baker from Languedoc; municipal authorities permitted him to exercise his craft only through the winter, after which he agreed to retire.[28] Such restrictions and directives no doubt made the economic transition to life in Vevey more difficult for artisans than for elite refugee families.

Although the Swiss offered assistance through the 1690s, Vevey's refugees experienced mounting local resentment reflected in reduced emergency relief and fewer economic opportunities. By 1694 the terms for residency and the right to exercise one's profession had tightened. Economic conditions had steadily worsened for the overall population, with wheat shortages in 1693 and 1698 making bread unaffordable for many families. The city's refugees competed with Vevey's native poor for access to resources and employment. In March 1699 the municipal authorities declared, at the request of a hospital administrator, that only the Swiss with the greatest need should receive bread "to the exclusion of the Savoyards and their neighbors."[29] Municipal minutes indicate that Vevey observed close contact with Bern throughout the troubled decade, heeding requests and directives with respect to the refugees. In at least one communique to Bern in July 1701, city officials, undoubtedly seeking additional financial help from authorities there, emphasized the challenges of supporting twenty-two refugees each month in such dire times.[30]

Local authorities proposed diverse projects beyond emergency relief to address the widespread poverty and indigence that beset their city. In 1693 they propounded a scheme to send refugees to Ireland.[31]

Later, in 1704, an anonymous letter was entered into the city's minutes that proposed a rather elaborate program for eliminating poverty in Vevey. Its author presumed that the origin of poverty was not economic, but rather a matter of personal morality, what he referred to as laziness or idleness:

> My thoughts regarding the project I envisaged for manufacture in the town of Vevey were not to propose profits . . . as so many people have done in different places (for some time) but uniquely to abolish the laziness of so many beggars and church dependents that we have to maintain by fault of their presence here, where I was assured that in a couple few months, I do not wish to say a few years, all the dependents that we feed in their idleness today and they and their descendants shall be relieved of public expense . . . so that we shall never have to see this type of person begging in the streets and at doors.[32]

Accordingly, the writer felt, Vevey should eliminate poverty by establishing a workhouse where the idle would be kept and made to work, and freed only when they had demonstrated their industry. "Those imprisoned who desire their liberty and wish to leave should work incessantly to become worthy and shall not be allowed out apart from under the condition that if they are idle and become a beggar they shall be more strictly incarcerated, to study in the work that they will have been taught. Those others who have not yet been apprehended in order to be incarcerated should make efforts to not go there, to work at something and to neither beg nor even to ask for any part of any subsidy."[33] The letter's author did admit some hesitation at pursuing such a drastic solution. He noted that in the past those "wanting to establish silk manufactories and other woolen stuffs, in order to make excuse for those foreigners of whom we assist," ultimately encountered "diverse difficulties . . . which are the reason for which they failed." Any doubts notwithstanding, he went on to describe his plan for a workhouse, a rather sophisticated complex for housing the poor. The building was to be erected near running water and provide an area for all livestock needed for the household. The proposed structure included cooking and dining facilities, where all would take meals at specified hours (men and women separately). Two large rooms were reserved as sleep areas, where men and women bunked in segregated adjacent units. This separation of husbands and wives was surely proposed as a disincentive for residents to linger. The work to be performed remained unspecified, but one may infer carding, spinning, and knitting, as the production of woolen stockings was the explicitly stated objective. Everyone in the workhouse who learned to knit would be "obliged to work for their bread in this trade." They would be provided wool and were expected to produce a finished product of appropriate weight.[34]

While a workhouse resident, one would learn a trade and follow social discipline. All would be required to hear the workhouse minister's Sunday and Thursday morning sermons, expected to observe their Sunday afternoon catechism, and pray morning and evening at the designated hour, usually at the beginning and end of mealtimes. Those who disregarded these regulations were answerable to an "absolute Superior," armed with the authority to withhold food and to use corporeal punishment if necessary.[35]

Authorities in the seventeenth century, like the writer of this proposal, typically considered poverty a personal moral failing—or at least distinguished between those who were deserving of relief and those who were not. States enacted poor laws allowing for the provision of outdoor relief in food, clothing, and other basic necessities to those deemed deserving. The deserving poor usually consisted of those who found themselves destitute for reasons beyond their control. Their numbers included widows, orphans, the disabled, the elderly, and those left penniless from natural disaster. The Huguenot refugees who received relief in the immediate aftermath of the Revocation were initially included within this definition. Along with outdoor relief, poor laws also supported workhouses such as the one described. Workhouses housed and fed the able-bodied indigent in exchange for their labor. Their harsh and demanding work regimens, which were more a punishment than relief, served to deter dependency.

Whether or not the city ever actually instituted such a plan is unknown, but municipal records indicate that Vevey's authorities supported Huguenot artisans and manufacturers who employed the poor.[36] Surviving contracts dated from 1684 to 1704 also show that municipal authorities proffered free lodging to refugee entrepreneurs, supported workshops and stores for up to two years, and rented tools and equipment to them, such as spinning wheels, forges, and cauldrons, for the life of their enterprise.[37] City officials acknowledged that they had "attracted workers with diverse incentives such as lodgings, looms, and other things . . . [and had] constructed fulleries, employed a shearer and a dyer, . . . [which] are working still at the present day and making full progress."[38] A public woolen factory was established in November 1704 and equipped with spinning wheels and looms to employ the poor. Of great concern to city officials was the fear that their investments would sour, consigning many refugees to the "deepest poverty."[39] To prevent this, they occasionally advanced refugee entrepreneurs capital, in one instance an impressive 2,000 *écus blancs*. In another case, the city extended free lodging and an interest-free loan to a Huguenot refugee from Romans, Pierre Soyez, who opened a woolen factory that employed three apprentices from Vevey's poor.[40] In October 1703, Gédéon Tapernon, a refugee from Montelimar who had previously lived in Geneva, offered to establish a factory for the manufacture of small fabrics. Municipal authorities agreed to furnish him with housing, spinning wheels, and tools if he would hire the indigent.[41]

Notwithstanding these measures, many within the ranks of the local bourgeoisie sought to block the residency of refugees and any official approval allowing them to pursue their profession in the city. Municipal records document the concerns of those who felt that far too many refugee merchants were seeking bourgeois status.[42] Vevey's bourgeoisie further complained that refugees had not been contributing sufficiently to the relief of their compatriots, and in January 1695 all refugee merchants and artisans were required to pay the habitation fee.[43] The next month the city's gunsmiths lodged a complaint against a refugee gunsmith, who had apparently settled in Vevey without the city's permission.[44] Likewise, Vevey's master bourgeois shoemakers objected to a refugee shoemaker by the name of Ogier, who sought to open a shop "to their detriment."[45] Refugee surgeon Jean de Gardonange's request to exercise his craft was met by opposition from his local fellow surgeons, as were the requests of refugee tanners, which were outright rejected "being that there is already a great number of tanners" in town.[46]

Surgeons immigrated to the Pays de Vaud in especially high numbers. The total number of surgeons, including both native and émigré, increased from 71 in the years prior to the Refuge (1675–80) to 117 by 1705, a rise attributed to the influx of Huguenot refugees.[47] Vevey's authorities approved work permits for a dozen of them, but some already established surgeon refugees sought to block the residency and employment of those who arrived after them. One was Cyprien Levade, a master-surgeon who immigrated in 1681 and quickly ascended to the bourgeoisie, securing a seat on Vevey's Council of One Hundred and Twenty in 1689. He then sought to prevent the residency of new refugee surgeons, registered complaints against them, and successfully won cases in 1687, 1689, and 1697.[48] He obviously believed the competition of newer surgeons threatened his business, and consequently exercised his power and influence to restrict their practices.

The need to keep the peace among the Swiss cantons dictated Bern's immigration policy as much as did economic considerations. Vaud was one of thirteen cantons, along with a number of cities, communities, and lordships, that comprised the Swiss Confederation. The thirteen cantons and other entities were united by a complex web of alliances that had evolved since the Middle Ages into a more formally integrated nation-state by the early modern era. By 1648, the Swiss Confederation had become a sovereign republic, and though each canton exercised self-governance, the cantons worked cooperatively in setting foreign policy. The influx of Huguenot refugees into Vaud and other Protestant areas in the late seventeenth century exacerbated religious tensions between Catholic and Protestant cantons, thereby threatening to dissolve the delicate alliance system that was the foundation of peace and cooperation among them. Bern, which had previously resisted Catholic political pressure on the issue of immigration, eventually capitulated, and agreed to take stronger measures facilitating the transfer of Huguenot refugees to other lands.[49]

Bern's refugee policy continued to pivot into the 1690s. In 1694 all refugees were ordered to leave Vaud, inaugurating a six-year initiative of resettlement, with some even returning to their native France.[50] Despite this policy, Vevey continued to receive refugees. As late as September 1703, twenty-one refugees from the southern French town of Orange arrived via Geneva.[51] Vevey provided them lodging and financial assistance and granted some residency and permission to work. For example, one week after his arrival, city officials granted Étienne Meure the right to remain with his family in Vevey and exercise his profession of surgery, albeit only according to his rank.[52] City officials altered the terms of his stay the following June, allowing him to remain as "non-bourgeois," on condition that he pay a hundred francs and register with authorities.[53] The same conditional residency was extended to David Besson and Susanne Plumette, also refugees from Orange, but all others were ordered to depart for Germany by the following week.[54]

What had changed that resulted essentially in this expulsion of refugees? In 1699 the situation of the French refugees in Vevey had dramatically altered. That year, Bern reissued its original mandate calling for the withdrawal from the Pays de Vaud of all remaining refugees not members of the bourgeoisie. This demand, well organized and well executed, resulted in the emigration of one-half of Vaud's refugees; those who stayed received permanent residency.[55] The 1699 mandate required that municipal officials compile two lists: those who would be permitted to stay and those who had to leave. Most refugees were assumed to be foreigners and granted residency only after they had successfully petitioned city officials, and many retained the label "refugee" despite having received permanent residency. It was not uncommon for those accepted into the bourgeoisie and naturalized to be still identified as refugees in official documents. The refugee status of parents or grandparents—even if they had also been naturalized—might continue to be noted in the official documents of their offspring who were among the native born.

Vevey's municipal authorities also adopted an official system of classification that divided refugees into five categories according to wealth and occupation.[56] The first class included all those admitted to the *grande bourgeoisie* (the precise requirements for inclusion are unknown due to the torn and absent section of the relevant municipal minutes). The second class consisted of members of the professions and successful merchants, including the La Grave refugee and relative of Jean Giraud, Paul Chicot.[57] These *petite bourgeoisie* held the same privileges as members of the first class except for the right to vote for council members.[58] Occupations identified in the third class encompassed refugee drapers and a spice merchant for whom they could not find a place elsewhere. The fourth class consisted of numerous artisanal trades and manual laborers without property.[59] The fifth and final class subsumed the poor and infirm.

Naturalization was predicated on successful application and reception into the Vevey bourgeoisie.[60] Successful candidates had commonly achieved the top rank in their area of work. Artisans, for example, had usually ascended to the rank of master. In addition, it was not uncommon for candidates to pay an initiation fee; authorities were known to broker deals permitting candidates to pay in installments or in kind. Those applying might also have donated to charity as a show of their support for the community and to please community leaders. Bourgeois status was inheritable, and natural sons could succeed their fathers. The Huguenot refugees who remained in Vevey following Bern's mandate of 1699 had presumably attained the rank of bourgeois—either *grand* or *petit*—and were, de facto, naturalized citizens, enjoying the right to both reside and practice their profession within the city.

Though the total number who applied for entrance to Vevey's bourgeoisie is unknown, nineteen refugee petitioners were admitted into the *grande bourgeosie* between 1680 and 1700, and seventy-six were received into the *petite bourgeoisie* between 1700 and 1720. A third category of ninety *habitants perpétuels* was accepted after 1700. These were refugees who had not ascended to the bourgeoisie but sought legal residency. *Habitants perpétuels* had the right to remain in the city for an unlimited period as long as they observed social norms and abided by municipal regulations.[61] In all likelihood, Giraud qualified for this final category. What is clear is that city officials privileged the higher social echelons and the more successful artisans in their determinations to extend permanent residency. Economic success, social status, and sometimes financial influence approaching bribery afforded these elite refugees security not extended en masse.

MARRIAGE STRATEGIES

During the early modern period, families formed alliances through marriage, and refugee families in Vevey pursued marriage strategies to forge the right relationships for social and economic survival. Marriages strengthened existing ties between families, and fostered new outside relationships. These connections, financial and emotional, were a longstanding European custom, and were even more vital to survival for a refugee community. Marriage brought together not only two individuals, but two families.[62] This union typically involved exchanges of property and dowries, especially for those involved in commercial enterprises, and expanded kin networks and the pool of potential partners and clients.[63] Such was certainly the case for the peddlers of the French Alps, and later for the Huguenot refugees of Vevey. Giraud's own marital strategies back in France are unknown, but in all likelihood followed one of three different patterns discerned among Vevey's refugee population. Some married fellow refugees from their hometowns; some married refugees from other French towns; and some married outside the refugee community altogether.

Though customary in La Grave, it was less common for refugee families in Vevey to marry someone from the village of their birth, simply because the number of available partners from one's hometown was greatly reduced in exile. Research confirms the endogamous nature of Giraud's French Alpine merchant community, an actuality supported by reconstructing the family and church networks Giraud detailed in his livre de raison.[64] Many members of Giraud's church in La Grave were related through marriage, and some continued to marry into families from La Grave once in Vevey. This included the marriage between Paul Monnet, Jean Giraud's nephew, and Magdelaine Mallein, the daughter of Louis Mallein, a relation through marriage of Jean Giraud's sister Anne.[65]

Marriage among Huguenot refugees from different regions of France was more common. For instance, Marie Mallein, whose father Jacques was a La Grave merchant, married Claude Balcut, Doctor of Medicine from Pragela (in Dauphiné), in 1687.[66] Likewise, Blaize Bouchardon, a dyer from Lyon, married Judith Froncillion of Grenoble in 1688.[67] This pattern continued with the marriage of Marguerite Robert of Privas (in Vivarais) to Jacques Bandin of Auvergne in 1703.[68]

Vevey's Huguenot refugees also married outside their community, and from 1685 to 1722 did so 43 percent of the time. After 1699 refugee marriages plummeted. There are no refugee/nonrefugee marriages recorded between 1700 and 1704, and they resume only in modest numbers after 1705.[69] Why the decline in these unions between refugees and natives, marriages that certainly established a crucial link with the Swiss community? One likely explanation for the upswing and then abrupt drop in refugee marriages in general is the increasingly strained relations with the community. By the late 1690s, many families were experiencing increasing pressure to leave Vevey and many were compelled to do so after the decree of 1699. All marriages dropped precipitously. This included marriages between refugees and fellow refugees (or their offspring) and those of refugees and native inhabitants. So, from 1695 to 1699 marriages in which both parties were refugees or descendants thereof peaked at an average of six per year. After 1699,

Marriage Patterns among Refugee Families of Vevey

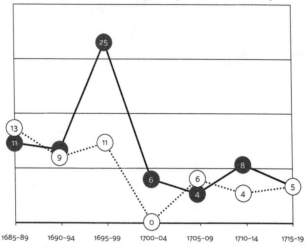

— Number of marriages where both spouses are refugees or the children of refugees
⋯⋯ Number of marriages between refugees and native inhabitants

Huguenot refugees married at the remarkably low rate of only one union per year. Although the reason for the hike in refugee marriages in the late 1690s, which represents the highest level during the Refuge, is unclear, the noticeable decline afterwards certainly occurred because of the sudden and massive departure of refugees.

STRATEGIES OF GODPARENTHOOD

Godparenthood, like marriage, provided an important path for early modern families to extend their power and influence beyond the traditional kin group. Godparenthood emerged in the Middle Ages as a guarantee to parents that their children would be cared for in the event of their parents' deaths. Godparents also assured that a child, once baptized and removed from the taint of original sin, received new spiritual guidance to welcome him or her into the community.[70] The practice of godparenthood endured into the early modern era, when Jean Calvin and other reformers rejected the Catholic position that baptism was a ritual act of cleansing or served to remove the taint of original sin. For Calvin, the sacrament of baptism symbolized a person's admittance to Christian society.[71]

Godparenthood continued in importance to Huguenot families in the sixteenth century as their leaders endeavored to revise the practice.[72] For Catholics, the Council of Trent called for the reduction in the number of godparents to one godfather and one godmother, a practice Catholic countries were slow to adopt. Far more extreme was Calvin's initial desire to eliminate godparenthood altogether, as he was convinced there was no scriptural basis for it. He soon observed that godparenthood was as popular among Protestants as it was in the lands of his Catholic adversaries, and he compromised by limiting the number of godparents to one, the godfather. This restriction never took hold, as most members of the Reformed faith continued the custom of multiple godparents, attesting to the social importance and continued relevance of traditional godparenthood to ordinary people and their communities.[73] While the practice of having only one godfather and one godmother eventually became standard, Vevey's parish registers for the late seventeenth century demonstrate an enduring preference for multiple godparents beyond two. By these means, as we shall see, the Giraud, Chicot, and Monnet families established strong and lasting ties that offered a support network in a new and highly uncertain life.

One way to recognize the relationship between the baptized child and his or her godparents was by bestowing on the child the first name of a spiritual parent. The refugees of Vevey followed this practice. Boys took the first name of their godfather, and girls their godmother. In cases with two godfathers, boys took the first names of both. Jean Giraud's son, Jean Claude, for example, was named after both godfathers, Jean Berard and Claude Barcet.[74] The same occurred with Félix Giraud's son, Simon Paul, who bore the name of both his godfathers, Simon DeLor and Paul Chicot.[75] This practice, widespread not only among Huguenot refugees but also the general Vevey population, spoke to the importance of godparenthood as early modern families sought to establish strong ties of affinity between blood and spiritual kinship.

Godparenthood often brought unrelated families together through vertical relationships that were less common in marriage.[76] Historians have noted how families in the early modern era used the custom to build patron-client relationships. Such arrangements brought protection and economic support, and were readily pursued by families concerned with securing their social position and financial future. Historian James Farr contends that nobles in Dijon frequently served as godparents to the infants of artisans, not out of friendship, but to legitimize their power. During an era in which social hierarchies were affirmed through acts of deference, the custom of godparenthood was a way for families to demonstrate fidelity to social superiors, thereby affirming the social order. "Ritual kinship," says Farr, not only forged the bonds of social support, but also created "vertical ties of trust," serving as a "mechanism of social control."[77] In a vertical relationship, a godchild was paired with a godmother or godfather whose status was socially superior to that of the child's blood parents.

In the case of Huguenot refugees, parish registers for the years 1685 through 1721 provide examples of vertical relationships forged through godparenthood. A prime example was that of Paul Tallemant, Sieur de Lussac, a Huguenot refugee from a prominent banking family with ties to the aristocracy of La Rochelle. Tallemant served as godfather to a number of refugee children, including the daughter of previously mentioned Félix Giraud.[78] Similarly, Étienne-Laurent Matte, a refugee connected to a banking family in Geneva, served as godfather to one of Félix Giraud's sons, Étienne Laurence.[79]

Some refugees opted for godparents who were from less prominent families from different regions of France or who were native inhabitants of Vaud. Between 1685 and 1706, 328 refugee children in Vevey were baptized—all with at least one godparent—attesting to the popularity of the practice. A slight upswing in baptisms occurred after 1695, followed by a steep drop in 1699. This pattern, as with refugee marriages, reflected the demographic changes of the city, including the departure of around one-half the refugee population. Also, in the 1690s fewer refugees were identified as godparents. In the first seven years

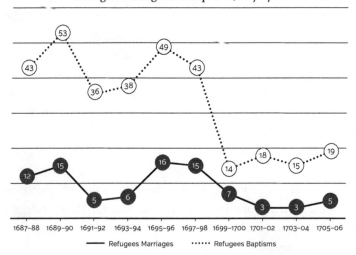

Refugee Marriages and Baptisms, 1687–1706

Refugees Marriages ······ Refugees Baptisms

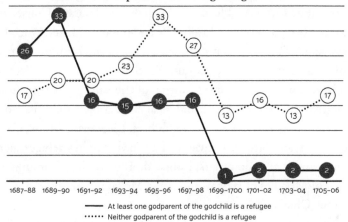

Patterns of Godparenthood among Refugee Children

—— At least one godparent of the godchild is a refugee
······ Neither godparent of the godchild is a refugee

of the Refuge, almost 70 percent of refugee children had at least one refugee godparent. This number could be higher in actuality since some nonnative godparents possibly remained unidentified in the baptismal registry. Families during the early years of the Refuge clearly preferred fellow refugees to serve as godparents to their children regardless of the godparents' regional origin. From 1695 to 1706, this number dropped to around 24 percent, indicating that an increasing number were native godparents. This data suggests that from the mid to late 1690s, refugee parents sought to solidify social ties with the native community through the practice of godparenthood.

Vevey's parish records reveal three important patterns with respect to the selection of godparents. First, a chosen godparent could be a French refugee from a region different from that of the birth parents. Second, close family members, such as brothers and sisters or grandparents, might be selected as godparents, a practice that became more common in later centuries. And third, families might seek godparents who were locally prominent native inhabitants, a clear strategy of vertical integration with a cohort both outside their kinship group and separate from the refugee community.

The Pez family chose this final strategy for their son, Randolph Paul, for whom they selected four godparents: two godfathers, Paul Tallemant de Lussac and Jean Randolph du Tavel, Grand Conseil of Bern, and two godmothers, Tavel's wife and Susanne Herald, wife of a Vevey banker.[80] The carefully considered naming and baptism of Anne Louise Faucher, daughter of Jacques Faucher and Susanne Chicot of La Grave, combined all three strategies of choosing godparents from among family, fellow refugee, and local elite. Anne Louise Faucher also had four godparents—two godfathers, Lieutenant Morel, likely a local elite, and Jacques Gravier of La Grave, a fellow refugee merchant—and two godmothers, Louise de Blonay, of the prominent family of Morelles of Blonay, and Anne Mellain, a family relation of Susanne Chicot.[81]

Strong family ties among the Giraud, Chicot, and Monnet families are reflected in the baptisms of Paul Chicot and Anne Mallein's sons, Jean-Jacques and Paul.[82] Jean Giraud and Jacques Monnet, along with their wives, served as godfathers for Jean-Jacques, while Paul Monnet and Marie Chicot served as godparents to Paul. Of the families mentioned, the Chicots appeared most adept at securing locally prominent godparents for their offspring. Jacques David Chicot, son of Paul

Chicot and Anne Mellain, claimed David Bonn, Bourgeois of Bern, as one godfather.[83] Likewise, François Falconet, a local judiciary official, served as a godparent to Paul Chicot and Anne Mellain's daughter, Marie-Anne, while Monsieur De La Cour, a municipal councilor, and Monsieur David Commandeur, both local notables, served as godparents, in conjunction with their wives, for Paul François, son of Paul Chicot and Anne Mallein.[84]

ROLE OF THE CONSISTORY

As Huguenot refugees forged important relationships through the bonds of matrimony and godparenthood, they also took care to demonstrate loyalty to their new environs by conforming to the local laws and rules of social discipline that regulated Vevey society. Civic authority was predicated on the belief that God justified the social hierarchy and public order, with the family as its fundamental social unit. Consequently, religious ideology found expression in both public life and at home. Observing the Sabbath through regular attendance at church and supervising one's children's religious education were salient markers of religious devotion, and also evinced a firm commitment to the community. Religious ideology penetrated every level of society, establishing fundamental principles and laws by which all lived; it defined relationships, daily interactions, habits of work and leisure, and dress and material life.

As the dominant class, members of the bourgeoisie were expected to model Christian virtues, not only in governance, but in social daily interactions and manners. A prayer recorded in the city's council captured the religious sentiment combined with a notion of civic duty that defined them as God's magistrates on earth and their governance of Vevey as God's work:

> King of kings and lord of the lords, we present ourselves before
> your throne to confess our sins to pray that you freely pardon us
> for the love of Jesus Christ our lord, and especially as it is better

to lead the people by the order of the superior and subordinate powers you have made us, it is an honor to commit ourselves to the magistracy and care of the administration of things. . . . First of all, we beg you to share with us the Graces of your Holy Spirit and . . . as rested with Moses and the seventy men of Israel, who were his deputy for the conduct of this people, give us a wise heart . . . so that we can properly carry out the exercise of a significant charge, and then singularly we are called to the direction of both property belonging to the public and those affecting the poor . . . [We] have the grace to proceed in purity of conscience, our hearts are disposed to renounce entirely to our particular interests, to attach ourselves only to the good and to the advantage of the public, banished from the midst of us this abominable sin. . . . Keeping among us a good union and holy harmony, which forms in our minds the desire of employing ourselves in the same way to procure the advantage of this public, flex the hearts of those who are subject to our conduct, that they obey our good regulations and all the rest of us are redundant to your honor and glory, and we may the rest of our days live a quiet and peaceful life, this is what we ask you in the name of your son Jesus Christ.[85]

God had granted them the power to enforce His laws, and above all else, their duty was to ensure community peace and harmony and public compliance with civil authority. This was based, of course, on Reformed belief and principles.

In 1537 Bern introduced in Vevey the *consistory*, a new mechanism for promoting social discipline.[86] In Reformed Swiss communities, the chief purpose of this regulatory body was to instill the principles of the Reformed faith and uproot Catholicism. By the late seventeenth century, the elders of the consistory of Vevey also endeavored to eradicate popular practices and beliefs, resolve family and community disputes, thwart aberrant Protestant movements (i.e., Pietism), punish illicit sexual activity, and ensure strict adherence to religious practices, such as attending church regularly and abstaining from work on Sunday. Above all, the consistory during Giraud's day maintained and promoted a cohesive community of godliness. Men and women, rich and poor, refugees and natives—all were obliged to adhere and conform to its disciplinary efforts.

Vevey's consistory was composed of both ecclesiastical and lay leaders (usually two or three of each) who heard cases weekly concerning improper behavior or misconduct. Those accused presented their cases before the consistory of elders, who listened, interrogated, and rendered punishment, usually in the form of censures, fines, and/or imprisonment.

The Swiss Protestant reformer Ulrich Zwingli had earlier sought to clarify the relationship between church and state in the Protestant world. He believed communities should charge city magistrates with the responsibility of social discipline. According to historian Bruce Gordon, Zwingli held the belief that only a select minority truly embodied Christian faith. Although discerning between the elect and the damned proved impossible, Zwingli posited that an overall societal transformation was attainable, with governing magistrates serving as the catalyst for change. For Zwingli, scripturally based laws applied uniformly to all. He believed that "Human righteousness . . . [should] be tempered by obedience to scripture and the ordinances of worldly magistrates," while divine righteousness, or faith, was "beyond the apprehension of the other humans." In short, "Christian magistrates" must concern themselves "with human righteousness in the hope of facilitating divine righteousness" even though the final reckoning was between the individual and his maker.[87]

For this reason, authorities in Bern had the final say with respect to all matters of church doctrine and practice, and, though those who served in the consistory heard cases and administered punishments, they did so on behalf of the city, not the Swiss Reformed Church. Although Switzerland was known as a republic, no system of courts or a provincial parliament existed to check the power of executive authority. Nor did the Reformed Church exercise an independent voice as was the practice in other Protestant countries. To the contrary, by the seventeenth and eighteenth centuries, the Reformed leadership of ministers had come under the direct and absolute authority of Bern. As historian Vivienne Larminie has noted, the ministers' "disciplinary and pastoral activities were conducted under the watchful eye of the local Bernese bailiff," and "all appointments . . . were finally decided by the Council of Bern; all ministers were bound by oaths of loyalty to orthodoxy and to their political masters."[88]

Reflecting the ascendancy of Bern's authority over Vevey's ministry, including refugee ministers, were mandates issued by Vevey's municipal officials just a few months following the arrival of the first refugees. The town councilors publicly proclaimed the regulations governing the functions of new ministers, and left no doubt that their activities came under Vevey's administrative authority.[89] Its prerogative was again exercised in the spring of 1704, when city officials complained that the ministry had altered the times for public preaching and catechism without first obtaining the city's consent. On this occasion the ministers successfully appealed, and city officials finally agreed that the ministers could hold catechism on Friday in order to instruct the city's youth, rather than preach the usual Friday sermon.[90]

At a later date, city officials called two ministers to answer to charges that they had neglected their duties by not properly instructing the poor in their catechism. The pastors were quick to concur with city officials and agreed to mend their ways, fully aware that if they failed to do so, both would appear before the consistory for further punishment.[91] The Regent for the Poor also received a reprimand for his deficiency "with respect to instructing the poor in the catechism," and was told that his job would be forfeited if he did not show improvement in his duties. City officials also warned fathers that they were responsible for teaching their children the catechism or would face a call before the consistory for any neglect thereof.[92]

Refugees were as likely to commit infractions as were native churchgoers. Consistory records from 1688 to 1710 for the town of Vevey suggest that refugees regularly violated community norms and mandates, especially when it came to activities involving leisure, popular culture, or the sins of the flesh.[93] During this period, the consistory heard cases involving drunkenness, lewdness, blasphemy, public insults, fighting, and assault. In 1689, Johan Morin, "poor laborer and idiot," of Saint-Julien-en-Quint of Dauphiné appeared before the consistory to respond to the charge of blasphemy. While inebriated, Morin had raised his glass of wine before numerous witnesses and exclaimed, "I drink to the health and glory of my God, his apostles according to St. Paul, and the faithful of Jesus Christ."[94] Admitting to blasphemy, Morin languished in prison until the end of the month.

In Vevey, as elsewhere in Europe, tensions appeared within refugee families, among unrelated refugees, and between native dwellers and refugees. Verbal exchanges and physical confrontations recorded in consistory records reflected this strain. Antagonism between native dwellers and refugees indicates that there was some level of xenophobia. In one example, the consistory heard a case against Jean Dumont, whom they condemned for blasphemy and "unwisely professing against the refugees."[95] A complaint was registered by Barretier, the daughter-in-law of a refugee, who accused one Johan Oberson, bourgeois, of defiling her cheese in the market and calling her a whore, along with other insults.[96] Disputes sometimes turned physical. The consistory reprimanded the sons of two local townsmen, a merchant and a refugee, for physically quarreling on Sunday.[97]

Other behaviors not tolerated included gambling and dancing on Sunday, lapsing in religious practices, and violating sumptuary laws. The consistory condemned refugee baker Johan Chernaux for gambling and compelled him to forfeit his winnings from a game of billiards.[98] Likewise, the consistory urged the sons of the refugee Monsieur Combe to refrain from gambling with cards at late hours in the cabaret.[99] A young refugee daughter was cited for having wed while in possession of a rosary.[100] Another was called to task for wearing strips of silver silk braid, an obvious violation of the sumptuary laws.[101] The consistory regularly censured both native townspeople and refugees for dancing on Sunday, apparently a common practice. Jean Giraud's brother-in-law and business partner Jean Monnet was condemned and fined for holding a dance party at his house that included a refugee minister and numerous others.[102]

But the most common cases the consistory heard involved illicit sexual activity, termed *compagnie charnelle* (carnal companionship) and *copulation charnelle* (carnal copulation). These cases usually concerned pregnant young women called before the consistory to name the putative fathers of their soon-to-be children. It was not uncommon for young couples to engage in sexual intimacy prior to marriage, and neighbors, family members, coworkers, and employers were usually accepting as long as the couple was of suitable age and rank. In such situations, family and community members assumed that the couple were bound for marriage.[103] Problems arose after pregnancy when the prospective groom refused to marry the young woman by either denying paternity or by professing he had made no promise to marry.

Unwed pregnant women appearing before the consistory in Vaud often claimed that the men responsible had sealed their proposals with a gift, a practice common at this time. Gifts accompanying marital promises in Vaud included a gold ring, a pair of gloves, buttons and a silver stamp, and an *écu blanc* and *eau de toilette*. Testimony usually entailed naming the young men and providing detailed accounts regarding where, when, and the number of times sexual intercourse had occurred. Witnesses often corroborated such testimony. Pernette Passez, for example, admitted to *copulation charnelle* with Joseph, son of Jure Claude Ormond, three different times, while Jeane Grande Jan disclosed a carnal relationship with David Michod, *potier d'étain*, four times in the town of Lausanne.[104] Once this took place in a room with a stove, another time in the boutique.[105] Lucresse Merlin confessed to *copulation charnelle* with David Jant Chatillions twice inside Monsieur Berdoz's barn, and Louise Guyond informed that she had lain with the valet of a butcher of Morges on two occasions in the afternoon while traveling along on the great road between Cully and Sephorines.[106] She regretted not recalling the young man's name.[107] In another case, the consistory compelled a blind girl to name the father of her child, whom she confessed was the refugee weaver Antoine Vernet.[108]

The men accused, who the consistory usually called to answer for their conduct, might acknowledge the deed, but often denied that they had made any promise of marriage or that they were responsible for the pregnancy. Frederick Clerk, for example, admitted he had engaged in sexual activity, but since the timing did not coincide correctly with the child's birth, he posited someone else must have fathered the child.[109] David Michod also recalled his sexual encounter with Jeane Grand Jan, but as defense claimed that "nothing" of him "was left inside her body."[110] The refugee Benjamin Mercier considered economic hardship a reason for evading the responsibility of fatherhood, though he agreed to marry the young lady in question even if working in the fields as a refugee paid only one-half what he had earned in France.[111]

Pregnant refugee women often leveled charges of broken promises of marriage. Such misunderstandings may have originated from separate perceptions of culturally based marriage practices. In one case, the consistory decreed that both parties would "fulfill their obligations of the sovereign law."[112] The townsman Johan Noé de La Vaux protested his status as husband even though several refugees attested to his public oath. La Vaux's refugee wife, Danielle Minard, presented as evidence of the marriage two *louis d'or*, which she claimed La Vaux had given her as part of his promise. A rather different situation existed in the case of the daughter of a refugee, Modeste Marguerite Vasserot, who at first denied she was married but later, appearing with her father before the consistory, finally confessed that she had indeed signed, "with the proper hand," the matrimonial promise. Though it is not clear if she was seeking a divorce, she did admit that while she had a great friendship with her husband in the past, she was not fond of him anymore.[113] At other times, persecution and flight led to confusion regarding marital status. In one such case, the consistory sought to settle a matrimonial matter regarding a refugee couple who had married in France during the "persecutions." Though the couple produced a marriage certificate, they had not been properly wed in the Holy Reformed Church. The consistory, as in all difficult cases, referred this matter to authorities in Bern.[114]

For the Vevey consistory, a major reason for their interest in contested relationships, engagements, and marriage was to reduce the number of illegitimate births. Its records indicate people engaged in illicit sexual conduct with seeming impunity. Certainly this was true for male heads of household, whose impregnation of their female servants appeared to have been a rather common occurrence. The consistory condemned refugees who impregnated their servants and refugee wives who gave birth shortly after marriage.[115] These women were undoubtedly vulnerable to the sexual advances of their masters, but still were called before the consistory to answer questions regarding their supposed indiscretions. Blame was often misplaced as women, considered morally weaker than men, were thought to be naturally licentious and prone to sexual misbehavior.

Though community leaders frowned on illegitimate births, the church continued to baptize children born out of wedlock, including the illegitimate infants of refugee parents. The likely reason was that the community celebrated childbirth, even of those infants who were illegitimate. The community also praised couples' fertility. The recorder of births for Vevey noted, for example, that despite the economic hardship of providing for numerous children, Nicolas Gerard had fathered in total thirty-six children by three separate legitimate wives, unquestionably a notable accomplishment for a lantern maker living in the late seventeenth century.[116]

Still, church leaders discouraged illegitimate unions. Community leaders believed that illegitimate births begot poverty, which resulted in further debauchery. Early in the eighteenth century, the magistrates of Vevey outlined for authorities in Bern what they believed were the chief causes of poverty in their land, together with possible remedies. The document submitted spoke with specific relevance not to French refugees but to outsiders from Corsier, who arrived daily in Vevey and were such a burden that its citizens considered themselves overwhelmed by "the Poor." Parishioners contributed little to their upkeep, compelling city magistrates "to beg of the directors of the parish aid to keep their poor to themselves." The author went on to condemn "debauchery" in its many forms: spending money in inns, on foreign lotteries, and on clothing and furnishings, tobacco and coffee usage, and gambling. As remedies, the author recommended requiring fathers to teach their children a profession enabling them to provide for themselves, creating additional employment opportunities for those who found themselves occupied in the vineyards for only five or six months of the year, and discouraging couples from marrying until able to sustain themselves as a family unit.

Specifically, for city magistrates, "premature marriage," connoted a couple proceeding to wed without sufficient means to provide for themselves and their offspring, and was an obvious cause of poverty in Vevey. They submitted: "The large number of premature marriages that take place amongst many young, domestic people, and others who have neither house nor profession, and who do not save money to pay for the cost of the wedding, and are prepared to work the land with no provision, are obliged to borrow and if they are struck by illness or the harvest is mediocre they are thus reduced to penury. . . ." They noted that experience showed people should not marry "until they are old enough or have the means to support themselves and a family," and proclaimed tellingly, "This land is so over populated that as soon as there is a year with little grain . . . that most are obliged . . . [to] incur considerable debts in order to buy cereals in order to live, which puts them into penury." [117]

Officials in Bern blamed the high number of illegitimate births on the influence of foreigners. Indeed the concerns of Bern, as well as those living in Vevey, arose in response to the local economic pressures and general economic crisis of the last decade of the seventeenth century. The Supreme Council noted that "whores" in our land "accuse unknown foreigners in order to hide others," and "they give themselves over to foreigners . . . to become pregnant." They argued that illegitimacy made worse the economic crisis of the area, that the country "is filled with illegitimate children who overwhelm the communities and snatch the bread from the mouths of the legitimate children of the land." Given the continuing high number of these cases—pursued by the consistory more than any other indiscretion—it would appear that efforts to control this behavior were ineffective. In December 1698, Bern's Supreme Consistory sternly directed city magistrates to eradicate illegitimacy, stating: "... we have found it necessary to put out relevant orders to stop this evil, and to this effect, we have made it known and ordered by those present that in the future those whores who accuse foreigners as being the fathers of their illegitimate children, before or after they have given birth, should .... be obliged to leave our lands and country...."[118]

For some, "foreign" Huguenot refugees were convenient scapegoats for the social ills that amplified Vevey's economic challenges. In truth, they were no different from native inhabitants when it came to vice. Both refugees and native dwellers gambled, danced, fought, drank to excess, and engaged in illicit sexual activity. The civic powers of the Swiss consistory meant that Reform doctrine infused Vevey society. In order to mold a model Christian community, Vevey's officials policed both the public and the most intimate details of private life. French refugees like Jean Giraud clearly learned to comply with city ordinances and Bern's mandates of social discipline. In all, the records exhibit very little resistance to Vevey's consistory.

After a treacherous journey across the French Alps, Huguenot refugees settling in Vevey found themselves in a new and, for many of them, unfamiliar foreign land. Their faith carried them, and now they sought solace in the generosity of the Christian brethren who sympathized with their situation. Huguenot refugees established trades, businesses, and livelihoods, but not without great struggle. As time passed, native residents began to oppose their presence, as did officials in Bern, who considered the refugees a burden in hard times. While Vevey provided charity and permitted many refugees to exercise their craft, policies regulating poor relief and residency fluctuated, and their situation grew more precarious during years of dearth.

Refugee families sought to reconstitute their community by relying on traditional strategies of marriage and godparenthood. Members of the community married refugees from different regions of France and sometimes prominent locals, who also served as godparents to their infant children. Such strategies highlight the measures taken to secure social alliances essential for survival. These networks, now more than ever, constituted essential safety nets in the perilous world of refugees.

As foreigners living in a new place, refugees were prone to the same temptations and weaknesses that led many of the Swiss citizens astray. Their trials and tribulations as a persecuted minority and as religious refugees made them no less susceptible to drinking, swearing, gambling, or carnal pursuits than the rest of the species. This meant that consistory records included details of the many refugee infractions of the high moral code associated with Calvinist communities. Like everyone else in Vevey, some Huguenots observed municipal ordinances and civic norms, and some did not.

Despite the Huguenots' best efforts at assimilation, nearly half left after 1699, and their shrinking community underwent a concomitant sharp drop in refugee marriages and baptisms. Only those with financial assets and desirable skills remained and achieved legal residency. Jean Giraud was one such fortunate individual who adapted and made a place for himself and his family by establishing the right social connections and engaging in those entrepreneurial pursuits his host community clearly valued.

FOUR

Émigré Livelihoods

Finally settled in Vevey, Jean Giraud's family invested in four kinds of business: watchmaking, peddling, moneylending, and book sales. Giraud's activities as an exiled merchant and businessman spoke to his resourcefulness, and were a response to larger economic trends. Since the early Middle Ages, the Swiss Alpine region served as an important crossroads for traffic from the Holy Roman Empire to France, Spain, and Italy, but was not a region of remarkable economic significance. The land was heavily wooded and sparsely populated. Vaud's municipal workshops of artisans, including those in more urban Lausanne, met the commercial needs of these localities, but the surrounding lands barely produced enough to sustain the canton's population. Economic development improved slowly in the sixteenth and seventeenth centuries, and French refugees played an important role in promoting capitalist expansion in Switzerland.

Historians have long remarked on the economic benefits of Huguenot migration to Britain, Prussia, the Netherlands, and the Swiss cantons, but the economic impact of the Huguenot exodus on France has been less well studied. Those Huguenots who left France following the Revocation tended to be the more prosperous merchants and artisans, whose assets and skills were easily transferable. These refugees invested in new ventures and brought with them new skills and technologies. Their departure deprived France of capital, commercial wealth, and craft talent. Louis XIV's Comptroller-General of Finance,

Jean-Baptiste Colbert, for one, understood the economic importance of the Huguenots to France.[1] However, some historians have since argued that the economic impact of the Revocation on France was negligible, and that France's economic challenges of the late seventeenth century were due more to Louis XIV's expensive, disastrous wars and fiscal policies than to the departure of the Huguenots.

The initial impact of the migration was salutary for the economy of the region. Huguenot refugees arriving in Vevey after 1685 introduced better methods of viticulture and the cultivation of mulberry trees for breeding silkworms. They encouraged the planting of vegetable gardens and fruit trees and established cloth factories and other manufacturers.[2] They founded tanneries, print houses, and a dye store, and opened some of the region's first retail shops.[3] These displaced Huguenots encouraged cultural diversification through their commercial ventures and material consumption. Unknown to Jean Giraud and his fellow refugees at the time, they were performing a small part in a larger scheme of economic change that not only characterized the seventeenth century but was foundational for the one to follow.

Many Huguenots who reestablished their livelihoods in Vevey were entrepreneurs who promoted capitalist enterprises. In medieval society, feudal elites and landowners with seigneurial rights were economically predominant. In the sixteenth century, early European entrepreneurs made money by deploying their capital in small-scale manufacture, which typically occurred in people's homes. These early entrepreneurs did not necessarily possess craft expertise, nor were they necessarily directly involved in manufacturing itself. Rather, they provided the capital essential for funding the production process. Along with investment in manufacture, early entrepreneurs and capitalists participated in credit and finance schemes, and in regional and international trade—systems of economic organization that were the necessary preconditions for the rise of industrial capitalism in later centuries. Equally significant, villagers and townspeople working from their homes in the seventeenth century began producing goods for the market, rather than only for the home. Their desire to possess new products encouraged their pursuit of increased income through new forms of employment and money-making; this, in turn, led to greater monetization (rather than barter), a growth in commerce, and increased levels of consumption.

Important to the development of early modern capitalism was the "putting-out system" or cottage industry. In the putting-out system entrepreneurs with capital employed cheap, surplus labor, usually in the countryside because it was outside the jurisdiction of the medieval guilds with their rules and restrictions. Capitalists provided raw materials like wool to the rural worker, who spun or wove for a piece rate, the amount paid when he claimed his yarn or semifinished cloth. Thread and cloth produced in this manner were cheaper than that made in the guild's workshops because peasants working for the capitalist were not bound by the guilds' exacting quality controls and price regulations. Cash-poor peasants residing in the countryside acknowledged the opportunity to earn extra money and, for this basic reason, welcomed entrepreneurs. In the early modern era, most peasants were in some way involved in the putting-out system, which employed many women who considered spinning an essential skill.

Besides employing rural workers in the countryside to work from their homes, capitalists also hired workshops of artisans, especially in the field of textiles, the leading industry of the seventeenth century. In this arrangement, merchants provided master artisans and their workers with raw wool, which the latter then carded, spun, fulled, dyed, or wove, turning the raw material into semi-finished or finished products. Merchants would then collect and sell, sometimes exporting this cloth. The guild master, and the artisan journeymen and apprentices beneath him, worked for a wage. As with the rural cottage industry, the merchant-capitalist investor often knew very little regarding the actual manufacturing process, but proved very adept at coordinating the various supply chains entailed in the process to get his product to market.

Swiss authorities permitted entrepreneurs to employ rural workers who labored for wages at home or sought temporary employment in neighboring towns in one of the local trades. According to Hermann

Kellenbenz, most Swiss peasants of the early modern era engaged in spinning to supplement their meagre incomes: "Especially in areas mainly given over to cattle breeding, where labor was less in demand than it was in agricultural areas—in England, Belgium, and Switzerland, for instance, we know that every member of the peasant families, from the children to the grandparents, earned money from spinning, and some from weaving."[4] Usually part-time, this seasonal work, whether carried out at home or in a workshop, afforded a crucial increase in the income of the working poor and peasants, especially when harvests were bleak and resources scarce.

A similar process evolved in the burgeoning watchmaking industry. Entire families of poor mountain villagers were employed as skilled or semiskilled workers in an elaborate putting-out supply chain that, in time, became the foundation of Swiss watchmaking production. Genevan horology comprised high-end fabrication, "but the heart of Swiss mass-production," writes David S. Landes, "lay in the mountains and valleys of the Jura, in Neuchatel and the Vaud, where a poor agricultural and pastoral population had learned to make the most of long periods of snowy idle time between harvest and sowing—to the point of giving up farming altogether, renting their land to outsiders from Bern and elsewhere, and devoting themselves full-time to the manufacture of watch parts."[5]

Termed *établissage,* this form of putting-out involved the distribution of watch manufacture among various rural workers, mainly peasants and rural artisans living in poorer districts. They assembled watches in small workman's shops and in private homes year round, especially during winter months when agricultural work was unavailable. *Établisseurs* furnished the tools and watch pieces needed to construct the semifinished products. They performed as early modern entrepreneurs who took advantage of cheap labor in the countryside and coordinated the production and distribution of watch products as they were prepared for final sale.[6]

Both Jean Giraud's nephews, Paul and Jacques Monnet, played roles in establishing the watch industry in Vevey, having been watch-

Oignon pocket watch by Paul Monnet of Vevey, ca. 1700, front view.
Photograph courtesy of Grigory Talalay.

makers there from the early years of the Refuge.[7] Paul arrived in Vevey
from La Grave shortly after the Revocation and became apprenticed
to an established refugee *horloger*.[8] Over time, Paul developed his
expertise, specializing in *oignon* pocket watches.[9] As a master watchmaker, he likely managed the manufacture of watch parts as well.
Vevey became a major center for their production, where workers
manufactured pieces for Genevan watchmakers who had difficulty
obtaining the semifinished products in their own city. Most of these
components were dials made "almost exclusively in Vevey."[10] The
town's watch industry continued to grow through the mid-eighteenth
century, featuring as many as 29 *horlogers* and 400 other laborers,
mostly dial makers.[11]

A lengthy list of watchmaker's tools that appears in Giraud's livre
de raison could either be Giraud's, as he is the owner of the livre de
raison, or may have belonged to one of Giraud's nephews.[12] Jean
Giraud's brother-in-law and former business partner, Jean Monnet,

Oignon pocket watch by Paul Monnet of Vevey, ca. 1700, side view.
Photograph courtesy of Grigory Talalay.

Oignon pocket watch by Paul Monnet of Vevey,
ca. 1700, close-up of face.
Photograph courtesy of Grigory Talalay.

Oignon pocket watch by Paul Monnet of Vevey, ca. 1700, back view.
Photograph courtesy of Grigory Talalay.

came into possession of Giraud's livre de raison sometime in the early eighteenth century, following Giraud's death.[13] More than likely, the list of tools appearing in the account book belonged to one or both of Jean Monnet's sons.[14] Whether Giraud or one of his nephews was the owner of the watchmaker tools may never be known, and why the Monnet family, who came into possession of the account book, took it upon themselves to hold and preserve the *livre* also remains unclear. What is certain is that the Monnet and Giraud families remained closely connected following their flight from La Grave and probably engaged in business undertakings together once in Vevey as they had in the past.

Giraud was not a watchmaker but may have sponsored his nephews' undertakings. A 1696 census showed that Jean Giraud lived off his investments, supporting himself mostly through moneylending and commerce.[15] As the *livre* was transferred to the Monnets, Giraud's role may have become that of financier, capitalizing the manufacture of watch components used for building *ébauches*, the main body of the pocket watch, while his nephews managed the workforce, supervising production. When the *ébauches*, dials, and other semi-finished parts were ready, Giraud, acting as *établisseur*, had them finished locally, or sent to a master watchmaker in Geneva. Given his former commercial activities in France, it made sense that Giraud and his nephews were part of a new preindustrial enterprise evolving in western Switzerland.

Jean Giraud's oversight of the assemblage and sale of watches coincided with his peddling of lace products. In fact, *établissage* and the lace industry served as the protoindustrialized backbone of western Switzerland's transitioning economy during the seventeenth and early eighteenth centuries. Budding capitalists contracted, mostly to rural women, for the production of semi-finished lace products. As with spun wool, these country folk manufactured lace accessories easily sold to tailors and seamstresses working in urban areas for use in completing their dresses, menswear, or household products.

Giraud fit this entrepreneurial profile, probably funding the production of watch parts while also peddling women's dress embellishments, which included a great deal of lace, to city women and residents in the surrounding countryside. As past is prologue, the "inventory of linens and other things for young women," appearing in Giraud's account book preceding the inventory of watchmaker's tools, suggested a female clientele of young mothers and unmarried women wishing to augment their trousseaus.[16] A silver mirror, dressing gowns, shirts, petticoats, aprons (some with lace), hankies, towels, tablecloths, a dress coat, *engageantes* (attachable sleeves, some with lace), undergarments, a needle case, sewing cushions, baby clothes, bonnets (some with lace), trinkets, head caps, and mousseline embroidery for the toilette—all appear in Giraud's inventory for young females. Many textiles were made of taffeta and lace or with lace trim. Other items were made of flannel, cotton, mousseline, and grisette, an inexpensive woolen material typically worn by poorer women.[17] Giraud may also have commissioned lace production for his peddling business, though this was not indicated in the inventory.[18]

Moneylending was a natural collateral offshoot for Huguenot entrepreneurs in the Protestant community. The practice turned a profit for the capitalist and helped sustain members of the Huguenot population in need of money. The example of the widow Marie Giraud, a La Grave refugee and likely cousin of Jean, is instructive. She supported herself through lacemaking, and an examination of her 1698 death inventory suggests a godly woman, who lived humbly.[19] Marie left behind some kitchen items and a few home furnishings. A copy of the New Testament, two copies of the Psalms (one in large letters and the other with music), and two religious titles, *Le baume de Galaad* and *Le voyage de Bethel*, attest to Marie Giraud's piety.[20]

Other articles in her inventory provide insight into her livelihood. Marie owned an indeterminate number of spindles, along with seven handkerchiefs, seventeen shirts, thirty-four bonnets, and twenty-two caps, some with lace. The quantity of these items intimates that Marie sewed at home and sold her output to itinerant peddlers and shopkeepers in town. At her death, she owed Jean Giraud a considerable debt of more than sixty-four *livres,* an indicator that Giraud, as a financier, likely sponsored Marie's piece work at home, enabling her to provide for herself. Whether Jean Giraud expected full repayment of the entire amount owed him is not known. Her death inventory reveals that Giraud bought the New Testament, carpet, tablecloth, iron pot, and copper cauldron.[21] He also purchased her twenty-two caps along with thirty-four bonnets.[22] Most likely Giraud intended these purchases for resale, or he may have obtained them in exchange for the waiver of some of her debt. Marie's death inventory undeniably showed the survival and continued importance of economic ties between members of Giraud's former church following their exile. Refugees like the widow Marie relied on Giraud's financial backing and altruism and perhaps on the support of other members of her original church to relocate and reconstruct her life in Vevey.

Alternate forms of home production are also revealed in Vevey's probate inventories. During the early modern era, in Europe, the family household was the basic social and economic unit. Husbands and wives, children, and perhaps extended kin such as grandparents, cousins, aunts and uncles lived under the same roof. Households strove to preserve self-sufficiency, outfitting their own clothes, producing their food and fuel, and maintaining their dwellings—in essence meeting all the economic needs of the family. At this time many families began looking beyond the household for certain provisions. Peasant families interacted with itinerant peddlers or merchants involved in cottage industries, offering their labor in exchange for wages to purchase household goods. Some sold their homemade consumables, like butter, cheese, eggs, or vegetables from their gardens, and items of home manufacture, such as lace or yarn, either in the market or to middlemen in exchange for coin or credit. Household scarcity, exacerbated by the inability of home production to satisfy the economic needs of the family, encouraged the emergence of capitalist enterprises.

As demand for homemade products and services grew, so did the volume of manufacture; as a result, various successful home manufacturers converted their homesteads into workshops. In other cases, homesteads became retail shops. These small enterprises were located somewhere near one's home, typically in a shop or workshops positioned adjacent to the household or on the ground floor of a multi-floor dwelling, with the family's private quarters above. The ubiquity of common tools for home production, especially spinning wheels, distaffs, winding reels, and lacemaking tools, along with volumes of cloth of different varieties in household inventories, verifies the reality that Vevey's businesses and shops were an extension of household manufacture.[23]

Death inventories describing the many tools and materials employed in household manufacture are revealing records of the stages of capitalist production. They also illuminate the roles women played in early modern capitalism as both wage earners and entrepreneurs.

The death inventory of Gomorée Sara Challain, together with the *assignal* of Anne Deboulaz, both Vevey residents, are instructive. While it is unclear if these women were refugees (neither was identified as such in her death inventory or assignal), it is important to note that refugee women likely engaged in comparable home production for the market once they received municipal approval. Vevey's census for 1698 identified refugee women who supported themselves through lace-making and sewing, probably done in the home as piece work. Other refugee women were engaged in domestic work or owned and operated shops.[24] Vevey's municipal records reveal that the city considered the petitions of at least three single refugee women who sought town approval to open boutiques. Vevey approved the applications of the widow of Monsieur Girandet and Demoiselle Marie Poutrelles, but dismissed a third—that of a Demoiselle Macaise.[25] City magistrates did not legally object to women owning and operating boutiques because petty retailing was an occupation generally reserved for women.[26]

When she died, Madame Gomorée Sara Challain, a minister's wife, owned a spinning wheel and a wide variety of sewing parapher-nalia, exemplifying the overlap in production for the home and for the market. Her textiles and accoutrements included lace and silk collars and sleeve ends, bits of taffeta and cotton thread, ribbons, blue upholstery and small bands of tapestry, pieces of embroidered cloth, buttons, cloth of many colors, gold and silk sewing thread, and pins.[27] Madame Challain traditionally spun or sewed for the family and supplemented household needs by spinning and sewing at a piece rate for a local merchant or tailor. Such piece work was acceptable socially as an extension of home labor. According to Evelyn Welch, "a consci-entious housewife had the capacity to make up conserves, sweets, and medicines or turn linen into embroidered coifs, elegant chemises, and cushions."[28] With sufficient earned capital, a housewife in time might expand her activities by transforming the home into a sewing shop or fabric store, offering fashionable garments and other supplies, and in the process shifting her status from wage-earner to entrepreneur.

Anne Deboulaz's *assignal* inventory for 1696 consisted of a wide variety of fabrics, pieces of satin and silk, London serge, lace, taffeta, embroidery, Dutch cloth, Indian handkerchiefs, Chinese cotton stockings, combs, thousands of pins (many English), ribbons, soap, writing paper, writing desks, spices, bouquets, spinning wheel cords, and 20,050 curtain buckles.[29] In early modern Vaud, an *assignal* was a legal document by which a husband pledged his property to his wife as collateral to assure his wife's right to her dowry in the event that he died or the couple separated. Many master artisans and members of the bourgeoisie in Vaud pledged their shops with all their merchandise to their wives. This was the case with Anne Deboulaz, whose husband guaranteed the entire contents of his shop to her. She did not technically own this shop or its merchandise, but exercised the right "to enjoy it until her dowry claim was paid in full."[30] Like many other wives of shopkeepers and master artisans, Deboulaz likely played an important role in operating her husband's shop.

Based on the store's contents, Deboulaz might have made clothes for men and women, sewed for home furnishings—curtains and upholstery—and made and repaired hats, as twenty hat cords were also listed. Like Gomorée Challain, Deboulaz likely began by selling her labors to a local middleman, who purchased her yarn, thread, sewn or repaired clothes for distribution to a merchant or tailor. At the same time, with sufficient capital and a clientele, Deboulaz moved from sewing for merchants to serving customers directly by operating a shop that offered popular fabric and fashions. Dominated by local markets and peddlers up to the seventeenth century, commerce in Vevey changed radically with the establishment of the retail shop. Huguenot immigrants were some of the first to open these small ventures, including the Chicot family who operated a boutique in Vevey in the 1690s.[31] By 1763, around twenty-eight merchants, many of them shop owners, resided in Vevey. Almost all of these shops were owned by Protestant refugees or their descendants.[32] In Vevey, the permanent shop emerged as an important fixture, and allowed for regular access to market goods, helping villagers to fulfil their needs with dispatch rather than waiting for market day or the appearance of the peddler.

In contrast to Anne Deboulaz and Gommorée Challain, Jacob Lemonon's death inventory hints at a possible example of mechanized spinning. Discovered among Lemonon's possessions was *une grande machine ou moulin à filer*, or "a great machine or spinning mill." This device appeared in his inventory in 1696, six decades before Hargreaves's spinning jenny debuted in England. It would seem that Lemonon owned and operated some kind of atypical spinning machine. Lemonon's *moulin à filer* was identified in conjunction with an assemblage of other textile-related tools and products (a spinning wheel, spools, packets of string, and balls of thread). Though it is not known exactly how Lemonon's *moulin à filer* worked or in what ways it differed from conventional spinning wheels and other spinning apparatus of the time, this example illustrates a transitional moment when one Vevey entrepreneur shifted from producing strictly for the home to manufacturing en masse for the market.[33] Probate records did not describe the productive capacities of Lemonon's *moulin à filer*. They do, however, suggest the existence of a greater and more complex capitalist enterprise.

One Vevey refugee named Servière operated a silk factory of considerable size. The Bernese encouraged Huguenot émigrés to establish silk-producing facilities, which were subsidized by state-supported cultivation of the mulberry trees that nourished the worms needed for silk production.[34] With this assistance, silk manufacturers obtained, at a reduced price, the raw material used in production. Servière's death inventory reveals a silk factory, a *grand moulin à soye*, equipped with 167 silk bobbins, 28 naked bobbins, 47 bobbins *de filoselle* (of floss silk thread), 141 bobbins *garnis de filoselle* (trimmed of floss silk thread), 20 other bobbins *garni de soye* (trimmed of silk), 37 iron spindles, 4 quarts of silk, balls from which to make silk, an auger, a weaver's shuttle, an ordinary silk reel/spindle, several button molds, and a loom. What role this Huguenot refugee played in introducing silk technology to Vevey is unknown, but the number of bobbins and other silk-related items that appeared in his factory imply a highly developed enterprise. Servière no doubt manufactured silk for local clients and possibly for more distant markets, depending on the volume of production.[35] By the time of his death in 1699, his business had fallen into disarray because the mulberry orchards had been abandoned and silkworms were no longer procured locally. For reasons unclear, silkworms in 1696 began dying all over the countryside, leading to the unemployment of silk workers throughout the region.[36]

If typical, Servière's business operated as a workshop, employing a number of workers under the same roof. In the early modern era, these enterprises could be quite large, occupying dozens of workers in one place. More often than not, they arose in the countryside, where merchants and other entrepreneurs employed families and teams of workers, providing them the raw material to spin, weave, full, or dye cloth for a wage. In time, workers concentrated in one place under the same roof, the forerunner to the modern factory. Unlike work in the home, factories utilized supervisors who managed the hours and pace of production, and greatly minimized the control of employees over their work environment.

When Giraud arrived in Vevey, he found himself at the center of a rather cosmopolitan community. Like other places Huguenot refugees settled, Vevey was clearly affected by international commerce and rising consumerism. Under Bern's ascendancy, commerce in Vevey flourished. Taxes and levies were low, and tolls not excessive.[37] Meanwhile, the town underwent the arrival of hundreds of Huguenot immigrants from different regions of France, along with visitors from Germany, England, and other parts of Switzerland. Immigrants like Giraud brought with them their skills and also their cultural values—their appreciation for certain kinds of reading, politics, forms of etiquette and cuisine, styles of dress, and home decor. Vevey was home to an eclectic body of tastes and customs. Of course, as we may gather from his La Grave possessions, Giraud likely entertained international contacts long before the Revocation. Even so, his residence in Switzerland marked a moment in his life when he lived with a new mix of people arriving from diverse locations in France and other parts of Europe. With the notable exception of his book inventory, Giraud's lists of possessions in Vevey did not reveal an accounting of his personal effects as was the case in La Grave. Nonetheless, study of the books he had available for sale, and the inventories of the possessions of other refugees similarly situated, provides insight into the commercial world he inhabited.

In Vevey, Giraud became an important purveyor of books in a vibrant trade with ties to publication houses in Geneva and Lausanne and as far away as Amsterdam and London. Although little is known of the book trade in Vaud in the seventeenth century, prominent publishers in Geneva such as Chouet and Tournes, well established since the Reformation, likely supplied Vaud's regional book sellers. Print shops in nearby Yverdon and Lausanne, although of less renown, may have also been a source for Vevey's regional book trade. Before he left France, Giraud was already connected to international trade circuits, and the resettling of family members in two important publishing centers, London and Amsterdam, no doubt widened that trade network. Large publishing houses in the Netherlands also had agents operating in many cities across Europe.[38] Giraud's records give little indication of his travels once in Vevey, although he may have visited international book fairs or corresponded with publishing agents in other cities.

Giraud's inventory of books from 1702 suggested he was connected to the book trade in Amsterdam. Following the Revocation, that city became an important center for the translation and production of English titles into French;[39] many featured in Giraud's book possessions of 1702. For this reason, Giraud's inventory epitomized the new international trade in French titles that grew after 1685. Many Huguenot printers and booksellers continued their work abroad in Dutch publication centers, and published for their refugee brothers and sisters, residing in émigré communities throughout Europe. These French translations, whose authors were from England, the Dutch Republic, and elsewhere, hastened the trend of French supplanting Latin as the new *lingua franca,* or international language.[40]

The volume of books available in Vevey's shops indicated an increasing readership as rates of literacy rose gradually everywhere in Europe in the early modern era. Literacy spread among the general populace in part due to the production and dissemination of cheap newsletters, leaflets, and other ephemeral literature that more people could afford. Material in the vernacular reached larger popular audiences that did not comprehend Latin but could read their printed native tongue. Protestants, with their emphasis on the individual reading of scripture, were more literate than Catholics, men more than women, and nobles and wealthy merchants more so than common people.[41] By the late seventeenth century, people were learning to read for work, worship, and personal enjoyment.

The inventory of books included in Giraud's livre de raison, recorded in his hand in 1702, sixteen years after his flight to Vevey and close to the time of his death, provides a window into his intellectual world and the people with whom he socialized and did business. Examination of the book inventory for Vevey suggests a trade with an international clientele both well traveled and well educated, especially in topics of contemporary politics and history. His Dutch travel guide provides an interesting case in point. Published in the early eighteenth century, it presented a highly detailed step-by-step guide that included street names, international flags, and other identity markers to assist in commercial navigation about Amsterdam.[42] A city of vital commercial importance, Amsterdam's robust and international economy made the city a primary economic hub in Europe at this time. Likewise, an account book on tariffs and tonnage, listed in the inventory, was also meant for the foreign traveler or merchant seeking instruction in calculating tariffs set by varying international standards. Clearly, Giraud dealt with a client base that was mobile, commercial, and experienced in international travel and exchange.

Books on history and politics indicated a readership that was interested in matters of state. A few texts Giraud listed as books of "controversy," suggesting his awareness that the possession and circulation of certain books was illegal and dangerous, at least in France. The largest number of the books listed in Giraud's literary inventory carried religious themes, indicating the continuing relevance of faith to his customers and the critical importance of the book trade to the French Protestant community in the years following 1685.[43] The majority are devotional pieces—many sermons, editions of the New Testament, the Psalms, and the Anglican liturgy; there were also works on prophesy, Reformed Church Discipline, Christian faith and virtue, and religious conscience. In terms of age of publication, Giraud's books spanned over 150 years, with the earliest printing date being 1543, the latest 1705. The date, publisher, and city of origin for most of the works are not listed, although Geneva, Amsterdam, London, Louvain, Saumur, and Charenton are all inscribed as the source of others. Of those texts so identified, most were published in the latter decades of the seventeenth century. All the books except one had French titles, and most were related to French history, politics, or the Reformed faith.[44]

Nowhere in his livre de raison did Giraud elucidate his personal political beliefs. The books that appear in his inventory of 1702 nonetheless provide some indication of his own political leanings and certainly that of his clientele. Giraud's books revealed a manifested interest in antimonarchical authors. In addition to a "work of controversy" by author of the *Vindiciae Contra Tyrannos,* Philippe DuPlessis Mornay, are included the anti-Catholic *Metamorphoses de la Religion Romaine* written by the notorious double agent Huguenot spy, Jean Aymon, and Gatien de Courtilz de Sandras's *L'Alcoran de Louis XIV* (*The Koran of Louis XIV*), a polemical dialogue against the Sun King. Works of this kind signaled an important turning point in Huguenot politics: gone were the Huguenot apologists of the past, who supported the Bourbon monarch as their protector.[45] Louis XIV, now the focus of Huguenot animus, was considered as much a threat to Protestantism and Christian civilization as the pope.

Equally provocative works listed were those on political prophecy and writings by English Whig authors. Reminiscent of earlier English radicalism, the apocalyptic works of Pierre du Moulin, Pierre Jurieu, and Huguenot physician Jacques Massard attested to the appeal of

Huguenot millennialism.[46] Works by English Whigs, including two sermons in French translation by William of Orange's personal chaplain, Gilbert Burnet, *Give Thanks to God for the Deliverance from the Conspiracy Made against King William,* and, most important, *A Sermon Preached at the Coronation of William III and Mary II, King and Queen of England* also figured among Giraud's books, as did the *Cabinet of Jesuits* by Titus Oates, the Popish Plot conspirator whose infamous allegations fueled London's anti-Catholicism in the years leading up to the Glorious Revolution. Why Giraud kept such titles remains a mystery; perhaps his clientele included English exiles who had also sought refuge in Vevey after the Stuart Restoration.[47] The presence of Whig and Huguenot polemicists adds credibility to the claim that the Revocation served as a rallying cry for the Whig cause. As historian Geoffrey Adams puts it, "Jurieu" (the Anglican priest cum French heretic) "was convinced that the survival of European Protestantism was linked to the destiny of William of Orange."[48]

Bernese officials feared the spread of heretical literature and sought to control what works were published and read. Some scholars contend that press control in Europe in the seventeenth century was highly sporadic and had minimal economic impact on the book trade.[49] Although the overall effectiveness of Bern's policing efforts in the Pays de Vaud is difficult to gauge, the freedom to publish was limited. At the beginning of the century, with the exception of Lausanne, where the academy supervised the press, all works in Vaud had to be approved by censors in Bern and, later, by bailiffs or local councils vested with policing authority. In the Pays de Vaud, Bern possessed the sole right to print schoolbooks and academic theses, while bailiffs and local councils surveilled printers and book shops. Works on religion and philosophy generated the most controversy. In 1683, for example, Bern issued a sovereign mandate to the bailiffs of the Pays de Vaud banning the treatises of Spinoza. Six years later, Lausanne's booksellers were made to swear an oath not to sell the works of Catholics, Lutherans, Quakers, and other heretical authors.[50]

Bern's policies of censorship were part of a larger program compelling subject populations to conform in both thought and practice to the state's conception of a model Christian community.[51] Vevey's consistory records make no mention of concerns over religious prophecy or political propaganda of the kind Giraud kept in his inventory, though Pietism, a new spiritual renewal movement of German origin, did worry authorities. German Pietism originated in the seventeenth century and spread across the Holy Roman Empire, Switzerland, Scandinavia, and the Baltic countries, emerging in different forms. Difficult to define as a movement, the idea of personal connection to God was a fundamental component, with roots in German mysticism.[52] Pietists were close adherents of biblical doctrine that stressed personal devotion and stalwart Christian living. Their assemblies were called *conventicles*. These were small gatherings, usually in someone's home, in which those present conducted Bible readings and held discussions. The Pietist movement challenged the Swiss and German Reformed churches, both of which endeavored to exercise authority over the interpretation of scripture and ensure doctrinal compliance through regular church attendance. The Pietists challenged the Reformed authorities by offering a different path for spiritual awakening and union with God, nourishing the religious needs of some who found the formal church lacking.

A number of Pietists were brought before Vevey's consistory from 1701 to 1704. Most were single women (a few were married to prominent men) who had failed to appear in church for the weekly Sunday sermon, choosing instead to worship together privately in their homes.[53] At least three, including two sisters, were French refugees.[54] In 1704, the consistory reviewed the case of a Pietist, the widow Campamar, for failing to attend sermons or partake in the holy sacrament. Campamar told the consistory she was not disposed to do so.[55] Upon similar inquiry, Mademoiselle Le Loy told the consistory she could not attend the sermons or participate in the holy sacrament as a matter of personal conscience.[56]

Women were predominant in the movement. Those who lacked education comprised the more radical elements and engaged in prophecy.[57] Aside from François Magny, an influential Pietist leader who had the support of local Vevey nobles, the most notable Pietist appearing before Vevey's consistory was a German blind girl of unknown age.[58] Unnamed, she sang spiritual songs in German and was suspected of prophesying and speaking against Reformed tenets. She denied these charges, and among others, claimed that at gatherings she only spoke of pious things.[59] Consistory elders were probably alarmed by this disabled child, whose religiosity invoked the enduring popularity of the idea that God communicated through the weak and less fortunate. More important, she represented a challenge to patriarchy, as women were permitted to hold Bible study in their homes only under the authority of a male head of household.

In fact, Bern's concern with Pietism stemmed in part from the liberating effect the movement had on women, and its potential for upending the social order. Officials believed Pietist "maids" were "using the excuse of serving God to avoid their earthly masters." Authorities were further alarmed "by the hubris of maids who decide without consulting their masters which church to attend." Pietist wives in Bern who were attending religious gatherings late at night "unsupervised" and "uncontrolled," and "without consulting their husbands" were funding "religious causes." In 1699 the Great Council convened in Bern to address the rising problem of Pietism. Among its reasons for suppressing the movement were the needs to "keep a unified church with a clear dogma" and "to stop women from neglecting their families and housework."[60] To quell the movement, Bern banned Pietist texts and assemblies, and sent many adherents of the "New Birth" into exile.[61] Quickly falling in line, Vevey's consistory denounced the Pietists, proclaiming their religious activities tantamount to insubordination and heresy. David Vassoroz, Giraud's friend and fellow book peddler, owned a work on Pietism, a book Giraud assessed at the time of Vassoroz's death. While not a Pietist himself, Giraud was at least familiar with the movement through this connection.

Giraud's possession of works on Huguenot religious prophecy would certainly have discomfited Vevey's authorities although there is no evidence of this in the historical record. Like Anglican authorities and conservative Huguenot elites who found works on Huguenot prophecy unsettling, authorities in Bern held similar reservations, as they were fundamentally restrictive with regard to religious practices and beliefs outside the official tenets of the Reformed Swiss faith. Bernese authorities took a strong stand against Pietism and Cartesianism, and expelled three French prophets in 1711.[62] Still, Giraud, living in a town of a few thousand, managed to trade in controversial works without drawing the attention of city officials. He surely exercised prudence and discretion, skills acquired while trading in Louis XIV's France. He also may have received protection from influential Huguenot benefactors. Perhaps officials in Bern were less concerned with Huguenot prophecy, and regarded Pietism the more serious threat.

Of course, municipal officials would have approved of Giraud's works of political propaganda that were anti-Catholic and pro-Whig. In the late seventeenth century, Bern, like other Protestant cities, was caught up in the confessional struggles of the era. Despite an official position of neutrality and confederation with the Swiss Catholic cantons, Bern appreciated William III as a bulwark against the mighty Catholic state of Louis XIV perched on its western border.[63] The Bernese held common cause with the anti-Catholic, pro-Whig volumes that stocked Giraud's shelves and, possibly for that reason, had no desire to censure or punish him.

Another book owner, David Vassoroz, owned a boutique in Vevey, but likely pedaled his wares in Vevey's city proper and the surrounding countryside. Vassoroz sold books along with other small, everyday items that could be easily transported like ribbons, gloves, English pins, lace, soap, and German thread.[64] At his death Vassoroz possessed twenty-three volumes. Included were commonly held texts: a copy of the Psalms, a Genevan Bible, a catechism, and works on devotion and personal piety. Less conventional were *The Arithmeticians' Alarm Clock, the Height of Arithmetic* (1626), *Metaphysics* (n.d.), and the *Response of Blaise Pascal to Father Noël* (1647).[65] The first title was a five-hundred page book on arithmetic, and the second a work on metaphysics, author unknown. The third publication was the mathematician Blaise Pascal's reply to the Jesuit Étienne Noël, a refutation of the assertion that a vacuum was not possible in nature. In this response, Pascal employed an empirical approach using the scientific method. Other religious works were included, notably those by Huguenot authors Pierre du Moulin, Jean Claude, Pierre Jurieu, and Charles Drelincourt. More unorthodox was the controversial French Pietist Jean de Labadie's *Déclaration de Jean de Labadie* (1650).[66] Conceivably, Vasseroz and Giraud operated in the same trade circuits. They shared a keen interest in religious works, including works on Huguenot prophecy.[67] As book merchants, the two helped develop and kept alive the informal networks essential for serving the various intellectual and religious persuasions of Vevey residents during these tumultuous times.

Vassoroz's example also illustrates how iterant peddling and shops spread new consumer goods, including printed materials, into the countryside. The practice of selling small household articles in combination with printed materials has drawn comment as being characteristic of seventeenth-century English and Dutch peddlers operating between the town and country.[68] The presence of "peasant handkerchiefs" within Vassoroz's inventory attests to his commercial connection to the countryside, while other items, notably silver rings (fifty), children's ties and stockings, and swaddling bands (over forty), demonstrates that young women and mothers were an important clientele.[69] Above all, merchants such as Giraud and Vassoroz were part of what Jan de Vries calls a "retailing revolution" that led to shops and peddlers gradually supplanting "markets, fairs, and direct guild-controlled, artisanal sales."[70] This change provided a greater variety and quantity of consumer goods, making merchants like Vassoroz and Giraud integral partners in the consumer revolution.[71]

Most households in Vevey typically owned either a single Bible, a catechism, or a book of Psalms; those with larger private libraries possessed works that reflected wider intellectual and cultural interests. Jean Eneau, for example, owned a copy of Nicolas Bonnefons's *Le jardinier françois*, a sort of companion volume to his cookbook which, according to historian Donna Bohanan, was a major turning point in the history of French cuisine.[72] Bohanan contends that Bonnefons's work led to a new kind of cooking, in which cooks employed seasonings to enhance the natural flavors of dishes. This style of cooking "resulted in a simple cuisine" in which "the best seasonal products the farm and countryside could produce became a new luxury."[73] Jean DeSoches, surgeon-bourgeois of Vevey, André Save, doctor of medicine, and Philippe Aiguisier, principal of Vevey's college, comprised an erudite readership with collections of works in both Latin and Greek. In addition to a Bible and works on hunting and falconry, DeSoches owned a book on treating musket wounds and another on iatrochemistry, a kind of early biochemistry.[74] At the time of his death in 1689, André Save owned several works by physicians, including Paracelsus.[75] The works he owned were in Latin except for a French translation of Plutarch's *Lives*.

Philippe Aiguisier (or Eguizier), of Marseilles, possessed numerous books by classical and Renaissance authors. He had been a priest in France before converting and fleeing to Switzerland, where he assumed the position of College Principal of Vevey in 1689.[76] While in Vevey, where almost all college teachers were Huguenot refugees, Aiguisier imparted humanist learning and education. Younger students at the college learned the catechism and Latin, following Comenus's and Erasmus's grammars. Older students studied logic, rhetoric, and religion. They learned to write, read Pufendorf, and memorized Virgil. They also staged Racine's *Thébaïde* and performed La Fontaine's Fables and epigrams as declamation exercises. While at the college, Aiguisier also wrote and directed plays that were publicly performed. The plays he directed had allegorical themes that resonated with Huguenot audiences. *Joseph*, or the *Exaltation of the Just Persecuted*, was a drama that alluded to contemporary events: the starved Egyptians were the desperate Huguenots; and Pharoah's debauchery was Louis XIV's depraved court.[77] *Joseph* was meant to inspire Huguenot audiences by demonstrating that hardship could be overcome through faith and trust in God.

Grammars, dictionaries, and Bibles appeared in Aiguisier's book inventory, as did the works of classical Roman poets Publius Papinius Statius, Marcus Annaeus Lucanus, and the Roman African playwright Publius Terentius Afer. Humanist authors included Alsatian Renaissance encyclopedist Conrad Lycothenes, Latin dramatist and pamphleteer of the German Reformation Thomas Naogeorgus, and the Dutch philosopher Desiderius Erasmus. Aiguisier also possessed the works of Italian Renaissance historian Oarzio Torsellino, Czech philosopher and pedagogue, John Amos Comenius, and the Huguenot polemicist and theologian Charles Drelincourt. Aiguisier's faith did not preclude the presence of works by Catholic contemporaries. Most notable were the works of Italian cardinal and devotional author Giovanni Bona, and Jesuit cleric and poet François Antoine Pomey.[78]

In contrast to the book inventories of Aiguisier and other social elites, shopkeepers' stocks generally addressed the reading preferences of common households. Anne Deboulaz, for example, offered multiple volumes of catechisms, spiritual song books, grammars, alphabet books, copies of the Psalms, prayer books, and other devotional texts.[79] Marguerite Moret sold books with comparable titles.[80] Their inventories highlight the role women shopkeepers played in fostering a culture of private devotion. In Vevey many of these offerings were read in homes where families regularly engaged in private worship, a practice as important to Reformed communities as church attendance.

The ABC books, catechisms, and Bibles Deboulaz and Moret sold were fundamental to Protestant education and literacy.[81] These commercial activities extended a commitment to the moral instruction of the family from the home into the public sphere, as the shopkeepers assisted mothers and fathers in the religious education of their children. In the Protestant home both parents taught their children how to read. Fathers instructed in matters of faith and led the family in worship; mothers instilled in their children the importance of prayer. Some Protestant households became schools, with the mother serving as mentor and teacher. In 1679, authorities in Lyon noted three Huguenot women operating primary schools in their homes. These women taught children using familiar and standard materials: alphabet books, the Bible, and catechisms.[82]

The high number of catechisms—132 stocked between both shops—deserves comment regarding their significance to the Reformed community. Not unknown in the Middle Ages, the catechism became standardized during the sixteenth century as Protestants used the printing press to spread their religious message and doctrine. A popular early example was Martin Luther's *Small Catechism* (1529), which consisted of a dozen pages of questions on the Ten Commandments, Apostles' Creed, Lord's Prayer, and the Sacraments. Replete with illustrations, Luther's catechism was specifically purposed for children and the illiterate rural population.[83] Jean Calvin's *Formulaire d'instruire les enfants en la Chrétienté* (1541) and Charles Drelincourt's popular *Catéchisme ou instruction familière sur les principaux points de la religion chrétienne* (1642) followed.[84] Drelincourt's contribution, first developed for his own family, included a concise version for small children, which was still in use after the Revocation.[85]

The catechism, short or more extensive, typically consisted of a summary of religious principles in the form of questions. They presented complex theological positions in a clear and accessible manner to readers who were poorly educated. Parishioners read and memorized the catechism, and through their recitations internalized religious belief and dogma. In this way, the catechism served as a tool of Protestant indoctrination and as an instrument for promoting social solidarity at a time when religious allegiance was of cardinal importance. In Vevey, the destination for many people from different regions of Europe, the catechism and other Reformed practices instilled within parishioners a sense of common religious identity. Though many early Reformed catechisms were intended for the home (fathers were expected to instruct their wives, children, and servants), both clergy and the laity composed and used catechisms in schools, church services, and the military.[86]

The numerous catechisms kept in shops indicated a preference for rote learning. Yet Deboulaz also sold the Colloquies of Desiderius

Erasmus, unspecified works of John Amos Comenius, and Aesop's Fables, an indication that though Protestant parents considered the study of scripture and the catechism as foremost in a child's moral education, humanist studies and moralistic theories of learning were also important.[87] Alphabets and educational texts taken together with material articles, such as children's beds, chairs, cradles, toys, and clothes (also found in Vevey's inventories), support the claim that the early modern era witnessed a "substantial investment" in objects meant for children, at least among the upper and middle classes.[88]

The variety of books in Vevey's private households presents a picture of a community with diverse interests. While residents continued to purchase books of piety, prayer books, Bibles, and other religious texts, their reading was enriched by works on cooking, commerce, mathematics, politics, history, and literature. Lettered professionals owned books on philosophy, philology, and medicine, while local shops stocked simpler fare, indicating a community devoted to literacy and religious education. The humanities, math, science, medicine, cooking, and the art of hunting—all appealed to the educated in Vevey. Clearly, Jean Giraud belonged to an eclectic community of individuals whose intellectual interests encompassed more than religious works alone.

Far removed from the world of books, flourished fashion. Retailers in Vevey sold a wide range of vibrant textiles that originated from across Europe.[89] A concept that became an economic as well as cultural force in seventeenth-century France, fashion set the style in furniture, home furnishings, tableware, gardens, household textiles, clothes, jewelry, and in hair styles and personal accessories like umbrellas, parasols, canes, handkerchiefs, and adornments for the head such as wigs, ribbons, and hats. Her *assignal* inventory indicates that Anne Deboulaz stocked 119 doll faces, or *visages de poupée*.[90] Some of these may have delighted young girls as children's dolls, but the majority were miniature advertisements for current fashions or what literary scholar Rori Bloom refers to as "objets d'art."[91] Starting in the seventeenth century, dress fashions were displayed through France and other regions of Europe in miniature form and worn by dolls, or *poupées de mode,* which were distributed to shops and fashion houses across Europe. Fashionable styles were certainly advertised through print, but the tangible *poupées de mode* sported popular styles in storefronts.[92] Deboulaz promoted her fabrics and other articles, educating Vevey's citizens regarding fashionable attire through the dolls displayed in the family store. Local tailors also imitated French fashions, sometimes to the disapprobation of the authorities. In 1705, Vevey's consistory chastised the city's tailors for failing to comply with regulations that forbade commerce "in the new foreign fashion sold in France called *falbalas.*" The ban included any skirts or other kinds of ornamentation considered "useless" or "very expensive."[93]

The inventories of four well-stocked Vevey hat shops illustrate the importance of men's hats as markers of social class and occupational identity. Foreign and regional styles inspired men's dress locally. Hats were highly desirable and commercially profitable, if the high volume of hats that stocked Vevey's shops at this time is an indicator. Notaries identified 820 hats in the inventories of three merchants from 1688, and 263 from a sole inventory in 1700.[94] At his death, the Vevey hat merchant Philippe Gauches possessed 42 hats of the *façon codebeck* French design. Little is known of the *chapeau de codebeck* other than it was a French hat. The notary identified another 22 as *codebeck de Rouan,* likely a style that originated in the northern French commercial center of Rouen. The *chapeau de bourg,* or hat of the town, was either a local city or village hat, or a hat possibly worn by the bourgeoisie. The *chapeau de brignolet* presumably originated in the southern French town Brignoles and was conceivably created in the shape of a briolette, a particular diamond cut popular in the seventeenth century. Wigs were also fashion statements, though no inventories of wigmakers or wig shops have survived to shed light on men's wig choices.

These inventories reveal patterns of consumption that coincided with the expansion of international commerce. In the later seventeenth and early eighteenth centuries, people from all walks of life owned more goods—clothes, utensils, and household articles. Some items were obtained from great distances, demonstrating the influence of international commerce on local consumption. In addition to French fashions and the international book trade, examples of other global articles that found their way into Vevey homes include Sinhalese cloth, Moroccan slippers and saber holsters, Chinese cotton, and Turkish and Persian carpets. As a consequence of rising prosperity, Vevey residents appreciated other new creature comforts, such as *fauteuils*, a kind of early armchair, bed warmers, foot warmers, cushions and pillows, nightstands, mirrors for enhancing lighting, felt slippers, umbrellas, and parasols. Although the modern bedroom had not yet emerged, the seventeenth century witnessed a shift towards styles of architecture and home furnishings that promoted privacy. Paramount were screens that served as dividers within rooms.

Equipment for the kitchen also became more elaborate. Inventories show, in addition to the standard medieval dripping pans and cauldrons, special pans for frying fish (*poêles à poisson*) and pans for cooking chestnuts. Some listed even more specialized equipment such as a gingerbread mold, a toupin (a type of jug with a stick-like handle), tart pans, pie pans, and funnels, including one specifically designated for making beignets.[95]

The death inventories of distinguished Huguenot refugees illustrate even more robust patterns of consumption. Paul Tallemant, Sieur de Lussac, arrived in Vevey in 1685 and was admitted to the bourgeoisie shortly thereafter. He was the descendant of Huguenot nobility from La Rochelle. His father was Pierre Tallement, banker of Bordeaux and Paris, and his sister Marie was the wife of Henri de Massue, Marquis du Ruvigny. His uncle François was an abbot and chaplain to the king of France and member of the distinguished *Académie française*. These family members figured among Louis XIV's *nouveaux convertis*, but Tallemant, along with one nephew and niece, refused to abjure their Protestant faith. French authorities imprisoned and then later expelled his nephew, and his niece slipped away to England. Tallement landed in Vevey, and took a great interest in fellow refugees who were less fortunate. He played a pivotal role in their care and well-being, receiving and holding charitable contributions on their behalf. The total amount Tallemant bequeathed to the poorer Huguenots of Vevey was extraordinarily generous, a large portion of his total estate that was valued at a little more than 10,000 *livres*.[96] His generosity extended to serving as godfather to numerous refugee children, including one child who was a relation of Jean Giraud. Tallemant's social circle was certainly more elevated than that of Giraud and his family, but the two men were no doubt acquainted through their church.

The belongings described in Tallemant's death inventory reflect a material world and lifestyle consistent with a man of his social standing and class background. Though a generous man with tremendous compassion for his fellow refugees, his was not a life of self-denial; his death inventory also proved he lived well. Among items listed were a gold ring with a large sapphire and diamonds, denominations of money, a goblet of silver and gold, two great silver candelabras with silver candle extinguishers, a silver bowl, silver salt cellars, a knife with silver handle, and silver forks and spoons.[97] Like many of his day, Tallemant appreciated the virtues of coffee and owned a particularly elaborate set up for preparing and serving it: a wooden box to hold his coffee, with a special sack inside to hold brown sugar, and three Levant coffeemakers made of tin. To serve, there were six small coffee spoons, twelve earthen coffee cups, and eighteen other coffee cups. His most dear possessions were likely his pocket watch, paintings of idyllic landscapes, two small *épées* (dueling swords)—one with a silver handle and sheath, the other with a handle of silver and gold—and a saber with a damask blade and silk cord to carry it. Items for setting a fashionable table included Venetian tablecloths and napkins, along with seven vases. Objects that provided insight into his personal grooming habits included tweezers, a mirror *de toilette*, several wigs and wig powder, an English knife with agate handle, a brush for his head, an ivory comb for his wigs, and small rods for ironing his clothes. Tallemant also owned a special chest for storing his chamber pot,[98] and a number of screens for personal privacy, the finest of which had walnut feet and was made of fabric that matched his bedding.[99]

He also owned other luxuries that were typical of the era's more prosperous households. His home was decorated with Indian and Persian carpets. A wardrobe held his ample assortment of clothes and personal effects: handkerchiefs, shirts, ties, silk vests, Dutch sleeves, breeches, stockings and leggings made of English cloth. He accessorized with several sets of eyeglasses (with steel, black horn, and silver frames), parasols, and steel shoe buckles. As was customary of notary inventories, his bed was elaborately described as a highly valued possession. It was canopied and outfitted in pink silk and double yellow taffeta, including eight curtains. With the bed were two wool mattresses, along with Indian and Tunisian blankets. The remainder of the room's furnishings included numerous chairs.

As was customary in elite households, Tallemant received visitors in his bedchamber. Rooms were still multipurposed to a considerable extent, and the social nature of the bedchamber explains the value attached to a beautiful, canopied bed. The furniture in the chamber included four armchairs upholstered in fabrics to match the bed, two armchairs of Chinese satin, and four armchairs with red background and black stripes. Four additional walnut chairs, lined with straw and upholstered to match the bed and carpet were also present, allowing Tallemant to receive a larger gathering of friends in a well-decorated environment.[100]

Another refugee acquaintance of Jean Giraud was the gentleman Étienne-Laurent Matte. With his two brothers, Étienne-Laurent owned a large banking house in Livourne, Italy, which his father had founded. Originally from Montpellier, the Matte brothers became internationally renowned bankers, whose commercial activities spanned Asia, the Indies, the Middle East, and the Americas, and whose expertise in international matters was sought by the most prestigious courts in Europe: Louis XIV consulted Étienne-Laurent concerning the French Royal Navy during its tour of the Mediterranean. With the Revocation, Étienne -Laurent left France for Vevey and rejoined his brother Pierre, who had already settled there. He brought to Vevey his banking expertise and international connections, and became an important patron for the Huguenot refugees, assisting orphans and serving as godfather to a number of Huguenot children, including the son of Félix Giraud. After a grave illness, he died in Vevey in 1697.[101]

Like Tallemant, Étienne-Laurent Matte maintained a home furnished in a style comparable to that of other European elites. As customary, the inventory of his possessions began with the chamber in which he slept. Outfitted abundantly in crimson textiles, it bore testimony to the power of fashion and period tastes. There was a crimson *chaise roulante*, or armchair with wheels, nine crimson taffeta curtains with silk cords for his canopied bed, and crimson damask curtains garnished with green tapestry and brocatelle (a kind of patterned broadcloth) for his bedroom windows. There were additional valences for his bed, including one of satin and another of red London serge, the latter complemented by five Indian covers.[102] Matte's appreciation for comfort and luxury was further revealed by a clock, a number of silk and Turkish carpets, mattresses, silver and brass candelabras and lamps, bed warmer, and mirrors—the last likely employed to enhance interior lighting. The twelve screens listed in Matte's inventory attested to his appreciation for privacy, and five family portraits emphasized the importance he placed on his lineage. Both privacy and sentimental objects became key signifiers of status and wealth in the next century.[103]

Matte's kitchen and personal possessions were equally impressive, implying wealth and high social station. The quantity of fine linens associated with his kitchen is staggering—some forty-seven Venetian napkins with matching tablecloths and hand towels. The mass of linens for the kitchen was necessary for Matte to host dinner parties and gatherings on a regular basis. His table was outfitted with a predictable array of soup plates, dinner plates, and serving dishes.[104] Among his more private possessions were a diamond, a desk, a silver stamp (or seal), medals, two hunting rifles, a pair of pistols, a marble checkerboard, denominations of money, and three small cases, one for traveling (*étui pour voyage*).[105] Notably missing from this long list of possessions was an enslaved Turkish subject he brought with him when he immigrated to Vevey.[106]

The extensive personal inventories of Paul Tallemant and Étienne-Laurent Matte demonstrated that both men appreciated comfort and luxuries. Different coin denominations, among both men's possessions, spoke to the international nature of their work, especially in banking. Only the very wealthy in Vevey could afford articles procured from distant places. The possession of such items as clocks, Turkish carpets, comfortable furniture with elaborate upholstery, and expensive kitchen items like coffeemakers, candlesticks, and silver flatware communicated wealth and high social status. Both Tallemant and Matte were pillars of their community, who entertained regularly. They were also arbiters of taste. The French aristocracy strove to establish its preeminence through upscale material culture, as a way of distinguishing itself from Europe's commoners. Vevey's bourgeois refugees aped Europe's elite, simultaneously projecting an aura of cultivation and sophistication that served to justify their power and social standing in Vevey.

In contrast, the 1724 death inventory of Magdelaine Chicot, Jean Giraud's widow, indicated that she lived modestly. Chicot possessed a wardrobe and several chests and baskets for storing her linens, which included curtains for her windows. She owned ladies' shirts, coats and skirts, caps, cutlery, a mirror, tablecloths, napkins, and forks and spoons. These items showed an appreciation for table manners, privacy, and household respectability; her bed, mattress, and reclining armchair denoted an affinity for comfort. Likewise a mirror and iron for straightening linens showed a regard for appearances.

Married to an entrepreneur and merchant, she was accustomed to accumulating property for safekeeping. It was an era when middling families exercised ingenuity and forethought to maintain a decent lifestyle in hard times. Her *louis d'or,* diamond, rings, forks and spoons were assets that could be easily stored, transported, and, when necessary, liquidated. No Bible or other reading materials were recorded among her effects.[107]

Her personal belongings were sold at public auction, the proceeds going to her three nephews, Marq Henri, Jacques, and Michel

Chicot.[108] These three brothers, whom her husband Jean had taken charge of when they were left parentless in London in 1694, were now grown, possibly with families of their own. Though it is open to question, Magdelaine Chicot's nephews were likely still living in London when she died, demonstrating the close connection refugee families maintained over distances, generations after the Revocation.

Chicot outlived her husband by sixteen years, and it is unclear how she supported herself following his death. There is no indication that she remarried, and she left behind no account books. Two promissory notes due her, one for 900 *livres* and another for 1,600, are evidence of the possibility she lent money to others as her husband had. At the time of her death, her few personal possessions of worth were likely what remained of her original dowry and what her late husband left her.[109]

Giraud left no will and few account records while in Vevey, so as with his wife, Magdelaine, it is difficult to gauge the extent of his holdings or property at the time of death. What is clear is that before arriving in Vevey, Giraud was a merchant-peddler of some means. His success as a businessman before his flight is supported by his merchant mark, which graces the cover of his account book.[110] Some historians contend that merchant marks evolved from architectural talismans or runic letters, which medieval merchants later adapted by adding crosses and other geometric forms that symbolized a ship's mast or yard.[111] Giraud's merchant mark, found only on the front cover of his *livre,* took the form of a heart with a number four ascending from it, the four being the traditional insignia of the merchant.[112] Jean Giraud's initials appeared inside the heart along with a small star or hexagram with a dot in its center. The star, an emblem identified in earlier merchant marks, likely represented Christ, or more specifically the traveling Magi, who relied on the star of Bethlehem to guide them in their journey.[113]

Merchant marks became more widespread when the Hanseatic League, along with other merchants and professional and craft groups, used them to designate ownership of goods and occupational identity.[114] In both the Middle Ages and early modern era, merchant

Jean Giraud's Merchant Mark.
Courtesy of the Archives cantonales vaudoises,
CH-ACV PP 713/1.

marks could be found imprinted on the outside of barrels or materials designated for transport and on books, letters, rings, paintings, and architecture.[115] Giraud's merchant mark was clearly used as a form of identity and supports the contention, borne out by a close reading of his accounts, that he was a merchant engaged in widespread international commerce. Though a pious man, Giraud was also a proud businessman and likely relied on the image of merchant to carry out his trade in religious works during the persecution in France and during his relocation in Vevey. Giraud's merchant mark is further evidence of the fundamental importance of commercial networks in sustaining the Huguenot community.

Though it is less clear how Giraud's business fared in Vevey, Huguenot merchants like Giraud, though resented by some of the native population, helped usher in an entirely new economy and society in this region of western Switzerland. Giraud and other family members arrived in the Pays de Vaud in the late seventeenth century, a time of

developing capitalism. The death inventories of contemporary Huguenot refugees show that international trade coincided with new patterns
of consumption. Books, clothes, and household furnishings delineate
a cosmopolitan community that experienced increased levels of prosperity despite economic fluctuations and downturns. More people
were producing for the market and purchasing more things, including
articles from distant places. Although the connection between the
Huguenot diaspora and the spread of French fashions is unclear, shop
inventories and other records indicate that French fashions flourished
in Vevey. Also, refugee enterprises like Giraud's infused more money
into the economy, enabling ordinary people to make monetized decisions about their leisure.

People could now afford books and games and enjoyed pastimes
such as drinking in cabarets and shopping. In short, the residents of
Vevey communicated their religious and civic pride in the clothes
they wore, the books they shared, the manner in which they decorated
their homes, and in their daily interactions, especially the commercial
exchanges and conversations they had in shops, homes, and church.
The consistory militated against excess, but so did one's inner nature.
Through their consumption, Huguenot refugees and native residents
alike endeavored to achieve an aura of respectability, while projecting
social status and rank as esteemed and godly members of Vevey's
religious community.

FIVE

℀℀

A Peddler's Cosmos

I n chronicling significant events in his livre de raison, Jean Giraud often noted, in addition to the day of the month, the hour of the day. Neither clock nor watch was listed among his personal possessions in his *livre,* but the frequency with which he noted the time of day, and the remote position from which he recorded events, high in the mountain villages of the Alps, indicates that he owned a personal timepiece. As a peddler, Giraud's business dealings required him to travel from La Grave to nearby cities that included clockmakers' guilds established in the previous century.[1] Neighboring towns and cities possessed public clocks as aids in regulating urban life.[2] These encounters undoubtedly familiarized Giraud with a modern time-keeping culture. Still one might ask what use a peddler like Giraud, who spent much of his time in the rural mountain areas of the French Alps, would have for a watch in the 1680s.[3]

During the sixteenth century, few people had access to personal timepieces; their ownership was generally restricted to the wealthiest members of society.[4] By the seventeenth century, this group expanded to include the commercial classes and those with a special interest in the technology of timekeeping.[5] Despite this, pocket watches remained expensive objects, appreciated more for their aesthetics than their practicality. Giraud's timepiece, carried as a piece of jewelry, was probably an *oignon,* a seventeenth-century pocket watch, fat and round, shaped like the vegetable for which it was named.[6] As a luxury item, the watch served as an indicator of Giraud's rising social status and mark of acceptance among others who shared his habits and sensibilities. As a man who kept meticulous records of fellow church members, and who dealt with detailed issues of accounting such as calculating interest owed, Giraud undoubtedly valued the watch's capacity for time measurement. In this respect, his watch evidenced his own technical aptitude and sophistication, qualities increasingly attractive to those who appreciated the era's technological achievements.[7]

Giraud's personal narrative of the Revocation of the Edict of Nantes began with a description of soldiers descending on La Grave and neighboring villages in the fall of 1685:

On the 2nd of August 1685, I, Giraud, departed from La Grave for Lyon to see the conclusions since the thunderstorms were gradually strengthening little by little, and arrived in Bries on the way back to La Grave. On the 25th of August, the Day of St. Louis, one half hour before dawn, Sieur Monnet, my brother-in-law, and I saw a meteor in the sky like a rocket that was coming around Grenoble and that was going in the direction of Briançon and passing through La Grave. The rocket was seen for approximately an hour before sunrise, where it passed as far as Pragela, more than 20 leagues away.[8]

Tellingly, Giraud associated the Revocation with a Catholic feast day but also recorded the clock time, "one half hour before dawn. . . ." and "one hour before sunrise." By connecting the start of the "thunderstorms" with a Catholic feast day, Giraud practiced a conventional method of dating events by connecting them to a religious or holy day.[9] Even so, Giraud's notes showed that he appreciated documenting events according to the more modern clock time. In fact, "one half hour before dawn" and "one hour before sunrise," may be interpreted as a hybrid of clock time and sun time.

Giraud established chronology in his livre de raison by marking the occurrence of events by the day and hour, and sometimes the half hour. On occasion, he determined the time of events by estimating the number of hours remaining before sunrise or nightfall. Giraud wrote: "The Marquis de la Trousse sent eight dragoons and a field marshal to lodge with my wife. The marshal arrived three hours from night at Les Hières . . . to take my wife to the hospital in Grenoble in order to change her religion." Often, Giraud preferred noting the time on the hour, like "two in the afternoon," "ten in the evening," or "at midnight." Giraud wrote, for example: "Having crossed everywhere separately, we went to sleep in Aix, each in his/her own lodgings; and the next evening in St. Julien, each stayed in his/her own lodgings. . . . And on Thursday, August 1st, we made our entrance into Geneva at eight o'clock in the morning by the grace of the Lord." On one occasion, Giraud mentioned minutes. Giraud wrote that his daughter was baptized on Tuesday, April 13 at 8 o'clock in the evening on "the 11th day of the crescent moon." He continued that the 23rd of March being the new moon, on "the 2nd of April at 2 o'clock and 34 m in the morning. . . . God gave me a daughter in Vevey in Switzerland in the Canton of Bern." More often, Giraud designated time in approximate intervals, for example, "around" the hour. He wrote that "On the 29th of April there departed from Mizoën, Besse, and Clavans around midnight two bands of 240 persons with 28 mules. . . ."[10] In each case, Giraud demonstrated an appreciation for clock time, mostly in approximate terms, suggesting he had internalized timekeeping in broader half hour and hourly intervals. Telling time by the minute was, at least in the 1680s, still relatively new.[11]

Those who kept clock time in the seventeenth century often associated it with astronomical cycles, like the monthly phases of the moon or the rising and setting of the sun, calculations familiar since classical times. Giraud's notes indicate that the moon was still an important reference point. In one instance, when his sister Marie and brother-in-law Jean Monnet were apprehended, Giraud mentioned the approximate time, moon phase, and weather: "And my brother-in-law Monnet and my sister Marie, his wife, were taken and arrested about 500 paces from their house at the place called Aux Veires at about ten o'clock in the evening. The moon was full and the weather was very serene." The family entries in his *livre* also established his use of the phases of the moon for charting the births of at least five children. His earliest entry is for 1680: "On October 3, 1680, God gave us a daughter, the day of Sunday . . . at five o'clock in the evening, the twelve day of the moon." Again, in 1683, Giraud wrote, "My wife is pregnant with a boy. Fat Thursday counts as the 26th of February, the last day of the moon on which he expired following his birth." In a later entry, Giraud noted that on November 27, 1689, at "10 o'clock in the evening and the 26th [day] of the moon, God gave us a boy."[12] People living during the early modern era believed that the moon affected the weather and daily events, and duly planned activities and tasks such as bloodlettings and commercial transactions around its phases. People also believed that the position of the moon on the day of one's birth determined health and fate.[13] Giraud's notations connecting lunar cycles to the weather and his children's births suggests he possibly shared these popular superstitions.

The moon also served a more practical purpose. During his flight across the Alps, Giraud noted the difficulties presented by the night's darkness, a consequence of the failing moonlight, "*la lune étant défaillant.*"[14] Giraud's comment illustrates the challenges darkness posed for traveling at night. Remarkably, some seventeenth-century watches and clocks disclosed the phases of the moon so that their owners would know when moonlight was strongest for night travel.[15] Whether Giraud's timepiece included this uncommon feature is unknown. Certainly, Giraud's entry of "failing moonlight" in his livre de raison demonstrates the moon's importance to early modern merchants and other night travelers.

In the seventeenth century, the French led the way in European watchmaking.[16] Louis XIV subsidized the developing industry. Scientists receiving support included the Huguenot Christiaan Huygens, who made several advances in timekeeping. Soon the English and Swiss rivaled the French in the science of clock and watch manufacture, in part due to the departure from France of skilled workers.[17]

Jean Calvin had, in the previous century, banned jewelry making and encouraged many Protestant lapidaries to convert to watchmaking. At the same time, Huguenot refugee horlogers fled to London and Geneva in increasing numbers, an exodus that culminated after the Revocation in 1685.[18] As a result, Switzerland and England overtook France in innovation and production, as the former leader lagged far behind technologically.[19] By the late seventeenth century, Geneva and London served as preeminent hubs of the watchmaking trade.[20]

Within Giraud's livre de raison is a section entitled "Inventory of Tools of Our Deceased Father" which lists a range of tools associated with watchmaking, including a "horloger's compass" and a "watch to place in the front of the boutique . . ." for public notice.[21] The livre's notes are rudimentary and provide only a glimpse into the processes workers followed for assembling ébauches, the central, unfinished round component of pocket watches. Giraud does not explain why he or his nephews entered the watchmaking trade. Presumably, they became aware of the demand for semifinished watches while traveling through Geneva on their way to Vevey. Needing to reestablish themselves after their family's Swiss relocation, either one or all three chose the watch trade as a potentially profitable enterprise.

On a personal level, Giraud came to understand the practical importance of personal timepieces and their popular fascination, especially among Huguenot merchants and technology enthusiasts. The family's decision may also have stemmed from his Huguenot world view, heavily influenced by the idea of predestination and a mechanical perspective. For Huguenots trying to make sense of difficult personal circumstances, the watch may have symbolized God's universe in microcosm. For those seeking support and guidance, possession of a pocket watch demonstrated confidence in the divine order—past, present, and future. In much the same way that possession of a Bible represented confidence in God's laws and word, so too the pocket watch, God's machine in miniature, symbolized confidence in the stability and perpetuity of God's rational cosmos.[22]

Usage of timepieces occurred concurrently with new developments in scientific instruments and tools of measurement that astronomers, physicists, naturalists, craftsmen, and mariners eagerly adopted. The seventeenth century beheld the development of the telescope, microscope, barometer, micrometer, adding machine, thermometer, and pendulum clock.[23] These inventions were the products of a scientific age, when natural philosophers, astronomers, and mathematicians honed instruments to improve their accuracy. These refinements enabled scientists to obtain more precise data from their experiments. Scientific innovation coincided with a parallel trend among artisans, who began to view the world as definable and measurable. Ultimately, Giraud's interest in accurate documentation corresponded to a general awareness among artisans and scientists in the Huguenot community of the benefits of these advances.

Huguenot religious texts reflected the importance of instrument technology to the Huguenot reader. In their devotional works, ministers sometimes demonstrated a popular appreciation for technology by creating religious metaphors using comparisons with navigational or scientific instruments. In one instance, Huguenot minister Denis de Bouteroue, in his work *The Response of the Good Angels to the Angelic Voices of the Bad,* compared the Bible to a compass.[24] Ministers read and kept abreast of the latest scientific advances, many believing that scientific investigation was a worthy endeavor that ultimately celebrated God's universe. Some perhaps deliberately tailored their sermons to reach audiences embracing the new science. The application of scientific and technological metaphors in Calvinist sermons would have held special appeal among merchants and tradespeople, professionals, and others whose livelihood depended on a working knowledge of new technologies, especially in the areas of navigation, cartography, optics, printing, and medicine. Most impressive, Huguenot sermons revealed that the movement's religious leaders were relying on the authority of mathematicians, astronomers, physicians, and natural philosophers, old and new, to promote the Calvinist faith.

The minister Pierre du Moulin, whose works Giraud hid from Catholic authorities and which later appeared among Giraud's Vevey book inventory, was a case in point. Moulin was the leading Huguenot polemicist of the first half of the seventeenth century.[25] His sermons and other works, which were widely read among the Huguenots, were published in several editions, and included his *Accomplissement des prophéties: où est montré que les prophéties St. Paul et de l'apocalypse et de Daniel touchant les combats de l'église sont accomplies,* which predicted the destruction of the papacy in 1689.[26] Moulin was well aware of new scientific developments, and did not always agree with them.[27] Moulin, for example, rejected the theories of Copernicus. He wrote:

> The entire globe of the earth is motionless. But some parts of the earth may be moved by earthquakes: For the opinion of Copernicus which maintains that the earth revolves around the Sun is not admissible: For if the earth revolves in circles, making each day some ten thousand French leagues by turning on itself, a stone thrown into the air would fall some or two hundred leagues far from the place from which it was thrown. Simple bodies, like the elements, have only one natural motion in a straight line: But by this doctrine, the earth by this circular motion would have two natural motions. One in a circle, the other in a straight line . . . Holy Scripture says the earth never moves.[28]

Moulin nevertheless recognized the advantages new instruments brought his audiences, both craftsmen who labored to earn a living and scientists who studied nature. In one sermon, Moulin spoke of the contemporary study of Pythagoras: "The Pythagoreans find themselves veritable in some way, asserting that the heavens by the rapidity of their movement render a melodious sound, and a sweet harmony."[29] On another occasion, Moulin referred to a planetary phenomenon that enthusiasts of astronomy likely appreciated: "It is this happy day, in which the Sun of justice, after a forty-hour eclipse, has resumed its clarity, to shine forever and never go to bed."[30] Elsewhere, Moulin wrote: "Mathematicians bend their brains to look for perpetual motion, and never come to grips with it. This is what God has done with the rivers, from whose source they rise from the earth, against the inclination of the water which is always to descend.... Astronomers who have measured the growth of celestial bodies find that the Sun is at least one hundred and sixty-two times larger than the whole earth."[31] Moulin maintained the superiority of sciences to the crafts, a common way of categorizing knowledge in the early modern era: "One science is subordinate and beneath the other, if it borrows its principles, and when the conclusions in the higher are the principles in the inferior: as Optics is below Geometry, and Music below Arithmetic ... one science depends ... [on] another, as the art of making bridles depends on the art of cavalry...."[32] The rhetorical application of scientific and mathematical metaphors to communicate religious points begged the question of whether Huguenot ministers were seeking to communicate the intellectual compatibility of science and religion or to cultivate audiences influenced by scientific culture. Either way, this rhetoric shows that early modern science had taken its place as a new authority within Huguenot dogma.

One area of special interest to Moulin was lens optics, a field distinguished by landmark advances during the seventeenth century.[33] Moulin liked to employ the term *lunettes* (spectacles) in his religious works, drawing parallels between the guiding accuracy of the Bible and the corrective visual effects of optical lenses. "The word of God is as a set of *lunettes*," wrote Moulin. "It helps us see things human sapience cannot teach."[34] Moulin acknowledged the practical importance of eyeglasses for ordinary people. "We see elderly people learning a foreign language," he remarked, "and with *lunettes* reading an alphabet." Finally, in a nod to the importance of scientific discovery, he commented that "*lunettes* [assist] for reading more clearly the book of Nature."[35] Moulin compared the jealousy of the envious, who attempted to identify negligible faults in others, to the way a telescope "*lunettes Hollandoises* [sic]" exposed sunspots.[36] The sun is so illustrious, that its spots are trifling, in the same way the praiseworthy are the objects of gossip by those who seek to "attach imperfections to others" while bypassing their "virtues." He wrote:

Envy is generally bad, a plague which infects the human race, a vice that corrodes the heart, which dries the bones, which punishes justly those who are tainted. It is a vice which is tacitly opposed to God : because he [who is envious] poorly shares what God has done. . . . Come the gossips who attach imperfections to others, and overlook the virtues: in much the same way flies that lay on galls and on ulcers. The luster of praise of others offends the sight of the envious. It twists and turns badly the best actions, which carry a sinister interpretation. In the same way *lunettes Hollandoises* [*sic*] find spots on the sun.[37]

Moulin employed the same metaphor in comparing the envious to those who readily mislead. As a set of lenses locates spots on the sun, the envious easily distort, "twist," the virtuous actions of others. Although he applied the term spectacles in this example, he clearly meant a telescope: "Envy . . . does not stop there. Just as mirrors represent always the left everything that is to the right, so gossips twist the better actions by a sinister interpretation, and find trouble where there is none. Their eyes resemble spectacles that find spots on the body of the Sun."[38]

Moulin enjoyed the clock metaphor and employed it frequently in his sermons and devotional texts. Familiar with hourly timekeeping, he noted it more than once in his printed texts. This metaphor communicated various religious points, and achieved almost universal currency among Huguenot audiences. There were many variations on the theme. Though valued for accurate time measurement, public clocks sometimes malfunctioned. Moulin acknowledged this fact and used it in his *Sermons sur quelques textes de l'Écriture Sainte,* where he compared lying to a clock striking at the wrong time and to boxes of drugs that were incorrectly marked: "But the most common vice of language and the most natural, and to which we have the greatest inclination is lying, by which man disguises his thoughts, is forged in a hundred ways, like clocks that show the time but strike at another, or boxes of drugs, which have deceptive labels, rhubarb outside, but inside arsenic."[39] The use of such metaphors indicates the practical importance of clocks during the seventeenth century as people became more accustomed to hourly timekeeping. In another example, Moulin acknowledged the time-measuring capacity of the clock, a phenomenon he must have presumed was quite familiar to his audience: "We preach the word of God as a clock, the arc of our attention only holds beyond the hour: but the hands dictate the time. We would like to teach by the measure, but treat without measure placing all limits on instruction, but not on greed."[40]

Though he once owned a shop in Lyon, and was likely accustomed to life with public clocks, Giraud undoubtedly had to adjust, as did other refugees, to Vevey's disciplined religious life regulated by the chiming of church bells. Usually located on the town square, public clocks in the seventeenth century rang at regular intervals to remind parishioners of their obligation to appear for religious services. Placed high in the church, itself typically centrally located, clocks held special religious and civic significance. The town of Vevey sought to erect its first public clocks in 1397, and in 1451 installed a clock in St. Martin, its oldest church.[41] Whereas Lyon had public clocks set to chime to designate Catholic religious services, Vevey's public clocks rang regularly for Protestant assemblies. In the late seventeenth century, Protestant tolling regulated the religious life of Vevey's citizens, ringing at quarter and half-hour intervals for sermons, prayers, catechism, and for feast days at Easter and Pentecost. The city council minutes detail the chime regulations for the city:

> On Sundays, between the Spring Equinox and the Autumn one, the bells shall be rung for the morning sermon with the first strike at six o'clock of the great bell, the second strike at half past six of the second bell and the third at a quarter to seven of all the bells and this for a quarter of an hour. After the Autumn Equinox at seven, half past seven and at a quarter to eight. For the catechism at eleven o'clock precisely, the third bell shall be rung continuously for a quarter of an hour. For the evening sermon the first strike at one o'clock, the second one at half past one and the third at a quarter

to two, as each morning throughout the year. For the four feast days, at Easter and Pentecost they [the bells] shall be rung with the first strike of the great bell at four o'clock, the second at half past four of the second bell and the third at quarter to five of all the bells. . . . The third bell shall otherwise be rung for prayers on the four Saturdays before each of the first Sundays of communion as ordained and on the four other eves of communion they shall be rung for the preparatory sermons, two strikes at the noted hours, the last with all bells during a quarter of an hour. . . .[42]

Vevey's municipal rules regarding time and the ringing of public bells attested to the degree to which city authorities sought to regulate the religious lives of town residents. The timing of worship with the chiming of bells at regular intervals also engendered a sense of community since all were presumably participating in the same religious services.

In addition to regulating religious life, public clocks abstractly symbolized God as prime-mover and creator of the rational world system. Many Huguenots appreciated the Renaissance position that posited a universe guided by spiritual forces (laws) that God had set in motion at the time of its inception. Such thinkers, many of them natural philosophers and theologians, envisioned the universe as operating according to rational, universal laws that were largely immutable. Traceable to the scholastic debates of the Middle Ages, this concept was not new, but it gained momentum during the seventeenth century. Natural philosophers and mathematicians, like René Descartes, espoused a universe governed by mathematical principles, and popularized the mechanical perspective. Jean Giraud in some sense embodied this new view and represented it in microcosm. His watch operated according to precise, predictable measurements, as did Vevey's public clock, as did the universe. In the same way God's creation was stable, consistent, measurable, and predictable, the watch in Giraud's pocket existed as a miniature replica of God's divine plan, also predictable, reliable, stable, and precise—a beautiful example of the perfect Cartesian order God had created.

Though a peddler, Giraud understood the concept of historical periods and perhaps saw certain eras as cosmologically significant. The books he sold represented a wide range of topics and provided unique insight into Giraud's mental universe and that of his clientele. Giraud's books and artifacts indicated that he was intrigued by other worlds. His ostrich eggs, pictures of the *Seven Wonders of the World,* and history books, in particular, portray a man curious about other places and times. With his knowledge of history, Giraud was aware that events and eras occurred at distinct moments, had a chronology, and varied in terms of historical importance. Time was not merely in the moment; it had a past and a future, with distinct epochs, some more critical than others. Above all, his possessions evinced that his was an expanded cosmos containing other places and histories long past, or, in the case of apocalyptic works, expected to come—all understood in relation to his own lived experience. It is impossible to know for certain how Giraud epistemologically interpreted the texts he read and the artifacts he owned, and he did not record any personal reflections regarding his belongings, other than his need to preserve his books. Nevertheless, one can speculate that Giraud selected texts that he and his contemporaries thought were helpful for understanding and framing their life experiences. In his work, *The Cheese and the Worms,* Carlo Ginzburg shows how the simple Italian Renaissance miller Menocchio interpreted works by relating them to his peasant world view and his personal concrete experiences. Similarly, historians may speculate on how Giraud made sense of life before and after the Revocation in light of his recorded experiences, material life, and understanding of time.

Despite studies arguing that seventeenth-century Calvinists viewed any given events in life as no more holy or sacred than others, Giraud's inventory of texts seems to suggest otherwise—that he believed that he and his clientele were living in a unique and religiously significant time that warranted recording.[43] Giraud's selection of certain history books—such as the *History of the Reformed Faith,* which remained hidden in the course of the "storms," and his *Abridged Account of the*

Most Remarkable Events that Happened in the Return of the Walden-sians to Piedmont, from August 16, 1689, to July 15, 1690—indicate that he sought to better understand his own people through their unique history and those of others who had suffered from similar acts of religious persecution.[44] *The Count Tékély,* a work of historical fiction, told of a Hungarian prince who, while working with the Ottomans, led a Protestant revolt against the Austrian emperor. Little wonder that Giraud, who guarded his Huguenot beliefs so fiercely, found such a story inspiring. Giraud's possession of histories of the cities of Geneva and Lyon contributed to shaping his historical consciousness and, at least in the case of Geneva, his sense of Huguenot identity.

The prophetic works of Pierre Jurieu, Pierre du Moulin, Jacques Massard, and Michel Nostradamus were also present in Giraud's 1702 Vevey book inventory, and they provide additional clues regarding Giraud's understanding of religious and/or historical identity. The first three were books of Huguenot prophecy and markedly political, while the last work by Nostradamus was that of a prominent and respected Catholic physician known for his published predictions.[45] Taken together, these apocalyptic works, histories, and Huguenot religious texts reflected a historical consciousness that viewed time as sacred and divinely planned, with both historical and natural events serving as signs from God. Seventeenth-century Huguenots believed in predestination, and their authors applied that firm understanding to Huguenot history, interpreting God's intent by searching for patterns and aberrations in the stars, in natural history, and in human history. Apocalyptic texts underscored the providential role of the Huguenots as God's chosen people. Those who believed in predestination, that God's overall plan could be glimpsed through the study of the Bible, history, and nature, concurrently held that all processes, large and small, operated according to the same divine will and principles. No matter how small or seemingly insignificant, human events had as much divine meaning and purpose for the ordinary Huguenot as they did for a king or bishop. And because the divine will found expression in operations, both celestial and historical, God's time could be measured.

Giraud's timepiece provided him a daily rendering of his personal world. With it he could determine, and sometimes record, the precise moment when something personally significant occurred. In all likelihood he believed that all things were interconnected. What happened in the greater universe and Heavens, understood as God's plan, whose historical patterns and relationships could be studied, was also reflected in minor incremental matters of Giraud's small world, recorded as daily events. Giraud considered the significance and meaning behind the persecution of the people of La Grave, which he had so meticulously recorded and sought to interpret. Visions of the apocalypse were easily reconciled to early modern mechanical beliefs, and one could render predictions based on a precise reading of the heavens and understanding of the patterns that were routine in God's universe. Anomalies within the measurable, predictable patterns were recognized and noted with wonder or considered miraculous.

Finally, time could be understood and predicted by employing precise measurements, study of the heavens, the stars, and the Bible. Giraud's timepiece represented an undying faith in the measurability and predictability of God's universe. In the same way the Bible served as a compass, so did Giraud's pocket watch mark the moments that had meaning in his life. One's clock or watch, like the Bible and stars, provided direction and a sense of steadiness. Both were sources of guidance that promised security and stability in a world that was ever-changing and frequently turbulent.

A common rhetorical device in Huguenot sermons that portrayed a rational, scientific rendering of the universe was the *machine ronde, grande machine,* or *machine de l'univers*. Huguenot ministers often invoked these expressions when preaching, without defining or explaining their meaning.[46] Two ministers who preached at length on the *machine de l'univers* were Raymond Gaches and Jean Daillé. In his sermon *L'Athéisme confondu* (1655), Gaches preached before the Huguenot congregation at Charenton on the wondrous heavens. He described the universe as a machine of circles moving in rapid, perpetual motions. He also compared the movements of the heavens to the rotational movements of a man-made machine, noting that both consisted of several "wheels" and "circles" and required "a constant hand and readjustment of the pieces," for the universe to "roll" with "rapidity . . . without wearing out . . . without . . . pieces spoiling," and without "circles dismounting." The universe continued "without notice of any change since the beginning of the world up to this hour."[47] Huguenot minister Jean Daillé also preached on the mechanical nature of the universe, designating it a "great machine." Its perfect components required movements that were regular, perpetual, and uniform from the beginning of time: "The Heavens roll always in the same circle, without quitting . . . passing and re-passing continually . . . and also in a perpetual movement, turning and returning without ceasing, but always by the same wheel . . . under the same laws, by virtue of the same causes."[48]

These Huguenot sermons fit nicely within the mainstream of French intellectual life. In the seventeenth century, mechanical philosophy gained momentum among French philosophers, and both Protestants and Catholics challenged the Aristotelianism of previous generations. This was especially the case at the French scientific academies, where support for mechanical philosophy stood in marked contrast to the entrenched scientific propositions of Aristotle followed by the French educational establishment.[49] The new mechanics, inspired by the technological achievements of the age, assumed that the universe functioned like a clock that was consistent and self-perpetuating. This universe operated according to secondary causes, and, for that reason, did not require supernatural oversight or intervention.[50]

The mechanical rhetoric in Huguenot sermons raises questions with regard to the level of popular awareness and support for mechanical philosophy. The frequent use of images like the *machine ronde* or *grande machine,* without definition or explanation, in Huguenot religious texts, suggests the existence of a shared meaning among readers. The word *machine* employed as a metaphor for the universe, implies a confidence in technology. Such language no doubt carried special appeal for Huguenot craftsmen and others whose economic livelihood depended on early machine technology.[51] The image of the universe as consistent, regular, and also predictable would have resonated with additional occupational groups who routinely employed instruments for obtaining precise measurements in their work activities.[52] These sermons revealed an early modern outlook closely connected to the shifting mentality that began in the high Middle Ages, where a focus on quantifiable methods distinctly altered perceptions of space and time. Artisans, merchants, and professionals, relying on empirical approaches in their daily activities and work environment, now saw the universe as predictable, rational, reliable, and measurable.[53]

The intellectual consequences of the mechanical position troubled certain Huguenot ministers. The mechanical philosophy led some to question God's presence, intervention, and even existence. Others disputed this apostasy and argued from a position of intelligent design. For them the beauty and impressiveness of God's universe demonstrated that the world was and remained a product and expression of God's will. Natural processes, regular and consistent, occurred as a consequence of divine forethought and providence.

One Huguenot who was concerned with the currents of atheism and spoke from the position of intelligent design was Raymond Gaches. In his sermon L'Athéisme confondu, Gaches highlighted the self-perpetuating capacity of God's universe, the *machine*, contrasting it to the machines of men, which required constant human intervention. In another example, Gaches discussed atomism, a term associated with mechanical philosophy and embraced classically by Epicurus and, in the seventeenth century, by the French natural philosopher Pierre Gassendi. Gaches considered the natural world to be made up of atoms, which: "compose the animals, fill the earth with riches, and form the earth itself." Unlike Epicurus, Gaches did not believe that atoms combined or collided by chance, but that they possessed design and purpose. In the same way a printer exercised forethought in preparing his characters for creating a book, so did God take great care in planning the universe. He wrote: "A Printer should take all his characters and throw them by chance; who will imagine that they should unite together to form a book which contains great secrets? And this great book of the world, or the wisest learn every day such knowledgeable lessons, would it then have been formed by some atoms which found themselves by chance? Strange thing!"[54] By insisting that the motion of atoms was a matter of supernatural design, Gaches defended the concept that nature by design reflected God's Providence.

While Gaches countered the currents of atheism, the Huguenot minister Pierre Jurieu stood against those who entertained deistic views. Jurieu did so by defending the religious enthusiasm attached to the young prophetess Isabeau Vincent, whose visions and prophesying directly challenged mechanical assumptions. In 1688, French authorities arrested and imprisoned the teenaged shepherdess in the Tower of Crest for prophesying an apocalyptic message of deliverance from the papal antichrist. The fifteen-year-old daughter of a Protestant wool comber, Vincent grew up in Saou, a small town in Dauphiné. Her visions attested to the psychological anxiety that gripped Dauphiné Protestants in the months following the Revocation. In her utterances, Vincent assured her listeners of their divine deliverance. They had endured forty-two months of persecution and, just as the "People of Israel" had survived their trials, they too would persevere. She comforted the persecuted by singing Psalm 42 (Yearning for God in the Midst of Distresses) "without missing a musical note" and stressed the power of the Holy Scripture: "Let the word of God be your fortress." She sang verses of the Commandments in rhyme, leveled threats against the wicked who persecuted the faithful, and recited the Lord's Prayer, Hail Mary, and the Apostles' Creed—all in Latin—without ever "missing one syllable."[55]

Huguenot professionals who encountered Isabeau Vincent found her supernaturalism believable. These included doctors whose examinations found her without illness or any "bodily infirmity."[56] The physician Jacques Massard wrote about Vincent, and Huguenot pastor Pierre Jurieu claimed in his third pastoral letter that her miraculous experiences confirmed his own apocalyptic observations.[57] What eventually won over Huguenot elites, however, was the young woman's seemingly miraculous ability to recite scripture in French. Huguenot witnesses, who journeyed to see for themselves Vincent's trances and visions, were most astonished by the French she spoke in their presence in place of her native *patois*. According to Jurieu, Vincent spoke in a most "correct . . . Dialect" as if "she had been brought up in Paris," in a household where "they speak French best." Equally remarkable was that she spoke without any trained method, "but in a manner very singular, and always full of good Sense." She merely closed her eyes, gracefully elevated her arms, and in a firm voice, cited from Holy Scripture. While in her sleeplike state, she gave warnings, predicted events to come, and condemned Catholic religious practices. After each episode, which usually lasted from three to five hours, Vincent would awaken seemingly completely unaware of what she had said or done.[58]

Though arrested and detained, Vincent had inspired a movement that soon spread to other regions of Dauphiné, where hundreds of young children, some as young as three and six years old, began to prophesy. The anonymous author of *A Relation of Several Hundreds of Children and Others that Prophesie and Preach in Their Sleep &c. First Examined and Admired by Several Ingenious Men, Ministers and Professors of Philosophy at Geneva and Sent from Thence in Two Letters to Roterdam* (1689) details numerous accounts of children, mainly shepherds, preaching and prophesying, usually while they appeared to sleep. In such accounts, onlookers were "not perfectly persuaded of the Miracle, but astonished and amazed at the great many circumstances and proofs, which rendered the things almost altogether unquestionable."[59] This prophetic movement spread across the Rhône to Vivarais and then a few years later resurfaced in the Cévennes, where it gave inspiration to the Camisard Revolt of 1702–10. According to Lionel Laborie, the outbreak of the War of the Spanish Succession in 1701 ignited a wave of "some 8,000 infant prophets" across Languedoc, "inspired by the Holy Spirit announcing the imminent fall of Babylon and the Antichrist—the Roman Catholic Church and the Pope—by the end of the year."[60]

To mechanistically oriented elite Protestant thinkers, Isabeau Vincent represented a significant epistemological problem: though clearly

Protestant in her message, Vincent was disturbingly Catholic in her delivery. One polemicist who defended Vincent was Pierre Jurieu, Huguenot pastor and professor of theology, whose *Lettres pastorales* played a critical role in educating the public about Louis XIV's campaign of religious persecution. In his published work, *The Reflections of the Reverend and Learned Monsieur Jurieu, Upon the Strange and Miraculous Exstasies of Isabel Vincent,* Jurieu challenged critics who doubted the veracity of the young shepherdess's supernatural experiences. Referring to these skeptics as the *Esprits forts* or "strong heads," Jurieu insisted that Vincent's prophesying was neither false nor demonic, as was the typical charge concerning proclaimed Catholic miracles. Jurieu acknowledged the difficulty in differentiating between Catholic and Protestant claims of the miraculous: "How shall we at another time deny our Belief to those numerous Fables, which Popery imposes upon us for Truths; if we once give credit to a Story in all respects like the Fictions rejected by us?"[61]

Yet Jurieu insisted that supposed Catholic miracles—such as a saint turning butter into gold, a friar resurrecting dead birds with the sign of the cross, and a priest healing the sick through recitation of the *Nine Days Prayer*—did not correspond to the supernatural experiences of the Shepherdess of Crest. The Catholic performances were inventions, created for the express purpose of perpetuating faith in Catholic falsehoods and superstitions. Of course, some Catholic claims might be natural remedies, rather than miracles, and some deemed miracles might actually be the work of the Devil, committed to fool others into believing they were the work of God. But for Jurieu, too many eyewitness accounts existed to deny that Isabeau Vincent's experiences were anything but supernatural. In response to critics who maintained humankind no longer lived in an "Age of Miracles"—that such an age had long passed—Jurieu insisted that true miracles still existed to inspire correct belief. Those who firmly adhered to the notion that God was bound by second consequences, or natural laws, what Jurieu referred to as the "machine," were greatly mistaken to dismiss the miraculous even in the seventeenth century.[62]

In order to frame this argument in an epistemologically coherent way that matched the increasing instrumental rationalism of elite Protestants, Jurieu was forced to address the *Esprits forts* directly.[63] He charged that the *Esprits forts*, while not atheists, clearly exercised a wrong understanding of God's actions and Providence. Jurieu argued that God adhered to his established natural laws, to "the Machin [*sic*]," but was not bound by them. He insisted further that God's Providence was truly unknown to humankind. Despite the uniformity and regularity of His laws, God's presence, the "soul of the Machine," was hidden and not always observable: "The Truth is, That God in the most part of his Actions, hides himself (as it were) behind his Creatures; and yet notwithstanding this, he acts both in his Creatures, and by his Creatures . . . so he is in such a manner the Soul of the whole Machine. . . . It is he that determines their Motions, and makes them all to tend to his Ends; He makes the Laws of Nature, but yet sometimes he quits them . . .:"[64] For Pierre Jurieu divine action existed within a providential scheme. Though uniform and regular, God was present and active, guiding natural operations in a mostly consistent but sometimes unpredictable way.

In 1702 the War of the Camisards erupted in the Cévennes. Religious violence had been percolating for years, and, following the assassination of the region's chief cleric, François de Langlade du Chaila, a full-blown guerrilla war began.[65] In the Cévennes, while some 3,000 Protestant rebels organized resistance against 20,000 dragoons, others held secret assemblies in the wilderness, prophesying the end of the papal antichrist.[66] Those officiating over the assemblies were illiterate, self-taught lay preachers known as *prédicant*s. Many of the religious leaders were women, who had stepped in to fill the role of Huguenot ministers who had fled following the Revocation.[67] At their assemblies, many of the children in attendance, known as the *petits prophètes*, would become "ecstatic." They prophesied in French, often reciting lengthy excerpts from scripture, and engaged in glossolalia—speaking in tongues—while falling to the floor in fits and convulsions.

This apocalyptic and prophetic view of the universe existed at all levels of the Huguenot community. Intellectuals, as well as the *petits prophètes*, espoused such beliefs, albeit in more sophisticated forms. One noted author was Jacques Massard, whose volume *Harmonie des prophéties anciennes avec les modernes* appears in the library of Jean Giraud. Massard was a Huguenot physician and iatrochemist, and a firm believer in an apocalyptic explanation for the Huguenot struggle. Giraud may have known or met Massard; his *livre* refers to the *Harmonie des prophéties anciennes avec les modernes* and its author "of La Grave." Massard, in fact, was from Grenoble. Perhaps Giraud associated the writer with La Grave because Massard at one time lived nearby or was known to visit there. The reference remains a mystery.

Massard believed that through biblical exegesis of the books of Daniel and Revelation, other apocalyptic writings, and dream interpretation, he could predict future historical events, including the end of the world. He communicated an understanding of events and time that may have resonated with Giraud. Born to a master apothecary in the 1630s, Jacques Massard grew up Calvinist in Grenoble, France.[68] Little is known of his medical background or training, other than that he was a member of the medical faculty of Grenoble and a practitioner of Paracelsianism.[69] Aligned with this perspective, Massard believed that knowledge concerning the universe was revealed by means of nature, the Holy Bible, and personal revelation. Accordingly, astrological readings and visions illuminated as much as empirically derived knowledge or interpretation of holy text. The correct explication of dreams, natural disasters, and prodigies shed light on the divine timeline, which was further substantiated through biblical text.[70]

Massard followed medical theories that were based on accepted systems of alchemical and astrological belief. Paracelsus and his disciples believed that celestial bodies, particularly the sun and moon, provided the connection between God and human beings on earth. Humans possessed souls and were subject to the stars and planetary motions, which invested the terrestrial world with divine essence. The correct interpretation of celestial signs led to spiritual renewal, and this was closely connected to improved physical health. Paracelsus conceived of the idea that what happened in nature, the macrocosm, was duplicated in the smaller human realm, the microcosm. Paracelsians like Massard interpreted natural operations as a matter of chemical process, and used alchemical techniques for distilling substances to obtain their elemental essence and divine nature, a key to achieving optimum health.[71] Consequently, these studies provided new insights into the smaller vessel of the human microcosm and encouraged the development of empirical science. This, along with Holy Scripture and spiritual revelation, formed the methodological core of Paracelsian medicine.[72]

The resurgence in apocalyptic belief within the Huguenot community in the seventeenth century was likely a consequence of the Revocation. Massard saw himself living in an age in which the world's end was drawing nigh. Seventeenth-century Calvinists, inspired by biblical prophecies, interpreted astronomical anomalies and natural catastrophes as indicators of the end of times. Massard was no different. Guided by his reflections on the books of Daniel and Revelation, Massard perceived the persecution of the Huguenots as an integral part of the prophetic narrative of the Last Judgment and final days. While his apocalyptic worldview followed a longstanding tradition dating back to the Middle Ages, its origins were rooted in the social upheavals and natural calamities of his own day.

Massard's millennialism centered on the story of Huguenot persecution, as delineated in his *Harmonie des prophéties anciennes avec les modernes*. This work, which represented a comprehensive synthesis of biblical, medieval, and early modern apocalyptic thought, joined the list of Huguenot apocalyptic works in circulation since the Revocation of the Edict of Nantes. In the *Harmonie des prophéties anciennes avec les modernes*, Massard delivered an apocalyptic world view based on the writings of both Catholic and Protestant seers, whose predictions, he contended, all aligned. Exact dates were assigned to future events, a practice that occurred with increasing frequency during the late seventeenth century.[73] For Massard, the age of reform began in 1508, the same year King Vladislav II of Hungary began persecuting the Bohemian Brethren, forerunners to later Protestants. The reform would continue until 1759, at which time this world would undergo a cataclysmic end, replaced by Christ's final intervention and His triumphant reign along with the saints. The pope was the millennial beast, destined to mislead those who were locked in a struggle with the forces of the elect, the Huguenots.

Massard provided many examples of conflict and struggle, prophetic references to famine, civil and foreign war, and massacres. Though the struggle commenced in 1508, its deadliest years began only in 1684, with a repeat episode of the notorious St. Bartholomew Day Massacre expected to occur in 1691. The forces of good and evil, embodied by Protestants and Catholics respectively, were bound in conflict with Protestants enduring severe oppression during the reign of Louis XIV. The Christianization of the Ottoman Empire, destruction of the papacy, and conversion of the French monarchy were all to occur within the next sixty years or so, preparing the way for Christ's Second Coming.

Massard backed up his projections by recording and publishing contemporary accounts of people's dreams. The reveries of an anonymous displaced young girl called the Maiden Refugee of Amsterdam were one example. Little was known about her. She was a Protestant refugee who experienced visions while sleeping, a phenomenon Massard referred to as "ecstasies," comparable to those of the "*petits prophètes* of Dauphiné." Along with her mother and sisters, the Maiden Refugee of Amsterdam became a medium for divine premonitions. Massard wrote that the girl often attained her spoken presentiments while "praying aloud, during one half hour or an hour. Sometimes she takes a text of Holy Scripture, which she explains perfectly well, and makes finally a beautiful prayer." Massard carefully captured her dreams as though quoted directly from her tongue, and then provided his own explanations, interpretations that conformed to his apocalyptic narrative. He related one eventful episode, which the young augur described more as a nightmare:

> . . . all the machine of the World is upset and dying . . . I saw
> a strong, great assembly of the world of both sexes, small and
> great, who are arranged in the form of a great circle. . . . Then I
> saw a warrior come of high stature, his hair blond, he was quite
> handsome . . . his eyes sparks of anger . . . he held a whip in his
> right hand and cried out that the timid, the fearful, the cowardly,
> the lazy, the doubtful withdraw because they are not disposed to
> battle against the wicked . . . this man had a very terrible look and
> a voice of thunder.[74]

Massard interpreted this as an account of Christ's return as found in
Revelation. Notable was the reference to what the girl had called "all
the machine of the world." The mechanical reference in the vision,
recorded and published by Massard, a firm believer in the Huguenot
apocalypse, raises questions regarding the meaning behind the imagery.
Massard claimed to have received an account of the dream directly
from the girl herself when in Amsterdam. If true, the account serves
as an example of the degree to which the imagery of the *machine
ronde,* the Huguenot metaphor for the universe, had become common
among Huguenot audiences.

Pierre du Moulin's rendering of the cosmos paralleled Massard's.
Moulin held that planetary forces influenced and directed earthly
activities. "Things elementary are governed by the celestial." He also
mentioned the zodiac as a means to assist those trying to understand
causes and relational interactions. Moulin, like most Renaissance intellectuals, was well read in both early scientific thought and astrology,
as his reference to the zodiac certainly suggests. On more than one
occasion, Moulin employed a clock metaphor as the inspiration for
his mechanical references. In his *Traitté de la conoissance de Dieu,* he
claimed three paths existed by which one could understand God—
by His works (the book of nature), His law, and the gospel. Moulin
compared one's understanding of the clock's internal mechanisms to
understanding God. As one learned the inner workings of the clock,

essentially a metaphor for the universe and its physical mechanisms, one came to understand God and His plans by studying the holy text:

> Just as those who pass before the tower of the public clock, seeing the hour marked by the needle in the dial, but simply not knowing how many minutes remain before the sound of the bell, they cannot see the gears, nor the stop of their turns and movements: but if one gives them access, they see with amazement the wheels, counterweights, turns, and returns up to the hour of the sound: also men see events according to the appearance to their eyes. The Christian admits in the sanctuary of the world of God he marvels to see the coupling of eternal counsel and the weight, the moments of divine providence.[75]

Thus, God's rationality was symbolized by the uniform and consistent operations of the clock. A clock is not just any kind of machine, but one that keeps time, and by applying the metaphor to God's universe, Moulin corroborated God's will and His foreknowledge. The clock metaphor, in essence, was as much about predestination as about God's rationality. Equally important, though God's plan may be revealed, it was immutable. In this sense, like time, divine providence was inevitable. In *Traitté de la conoissance de Dieu,* Moulin stressed the omnipotence of God's will and His immutable nature further. He referred to the "power of malignant spirits, [which] move in the air [creating] terrible storms . . . strange sickness, and transforming men into wolves, frightening the most assured by horrible ghosts, and misleading by ambiguous answers those who inquire of the future . . . wrapping them in error." Moulin acknowledged the existence and power of such supernatural forces and denied that they could defy God's will. Not even "invisible" demons, however disruptive, could obstruct God's plans: "To see all the round machine be shaken, as these demons are not dependent on the goodwill of some sovereign power, which holds their rage in check and encloses them in the barriers of its providence."[76]

Together with the message of Huguenot apocalypse, clock metaphors signified more than rational and consistent universal laws.
Machine-like language that appeared in Huguenot sermons and
other religious works symbolized the Calvinist theological position
of the immutability of divine providence. Huguenot ministers likewise
communicated God's will and purpose with machine metaphors—
in the case of Pierre du Moulin, the clock. The *grande machine* or
machine ronde were symbolic of the Protestant world view in which
daily hardships were interpreted in terms of God's divine plan. From
a theological standpoint, Protestants like Calvin, who emphasized
God's sovereignty, rejected the idea that humans could manipulate
divine grace. All were subject to God's laws and plans, unavoidable
and rational, even if they did not seem to be. Life had purpose and
was not subject to chance. Moulin remarked, "fortune is the mother
of confusion; industry produces order."[77] The Huguenot concept of
the *machine ronde* reflected this perspective, an undying faith in the
rationality and reliability of God's system, as well as God's omnipotence and divine forethought.

Assessment of the Maiden Refugee's visions presented a rare intersection between the social worlds of learned male professionals
and young women. The frequent appearance of mechanical language
without definition or explanation implied the existence of a shared
understanding among readers of these accounts. The use of the word
machine intimated a general confidence in technology. Perhaps more
important, Moulin's clock image offered comfort, especially to dis-
tressed Huguenot refugees and exiles. The early modern era was truly
an age of uncertainty and intellectual crisis, as social and cultural upheaval brought on tragedy, high and unpredictable levels of mortality,
sickness, starvation, and physical discomfort and pain. All this was
exacerbated by the Huguenot political situation, which, after 1685,
resulted in thousands of Huguenots fleeing France to safe refuge. As
a symbol, the Maiden Refugee's "machine of the world" was less a
celebration of technological achievement than it was an index of psychological strain. Giraud's universe might be regarded as an intellectual

vortex in which science, mechanics, prophecy, apocalyptic beliefs, and memories of persecution mixed to produce a pre-Enlightenment and decidedly early modern world view. It was a cosmos that would shortly give way to religion and science inhabiting separate realms, but in this moment a relationship existed that allowed them to operate in tandem as Giraud and other Huguenots made sense of this world and their lives.

Conclusion

Jean Giraud's personal story acquaints the historian with the details of the Huguenots' exodus from La Grave, France, their resettlement in Switzerland, and their efforts to reconstruct a community in a foreign world. His resolution to document these compelling events in his livre de raison was conceived with the desire that the world should know their story, and this book is predicated on that decision.

A variety of archival materials allows the historian to know the essential narrative and to sketch the basic contours of Giraud's community and its relocation. It is Giraud's *livre,* however, that compels and enables us to understand so much more about the refugee experience. Giraud tells about the firsthand experience of being a Protestant in Louis XIV's France, and the harrowing experiences his community endured after the Revocation of the Edict of Nantes. He shares the ordeal of his desperate escape from the world in which he had spent his entire life. We know his personal sorrow at the loss of his children. And we gain a bird's-eye view of how a refugee reconstructed a life for himself and his surviving family, while at the same time caring for his larger religious community. We are also informed by Giraud's account about the larger world of this man and his connections with others. We learn about the lives of Huguenot refugees, how they interacted with each other and with their new community, and the personal impact of larger historical forces and developments. Giraud's testimony instructs us on many subjects: the role of royal power in people's lives, how ordinary Protestants experienced the Counter-Reformation, and the actions taken by individuals for self-preservation.

Giraud documented the diaspora of his community, a microcosm of the greatest exodus in early modern French history. The revelation from his *livre* that the Huguenot members of his community dispersed so widely begs the larger question of how Protestant European nations contended with the mass influx of religious refugees. During this era of international conflict, countries formed alliances based on religion. While Protestant nations welcomed Huguenot refugees officially, their native inhabitants, in competition for jobs and resources, often resented them.

Jean Giraud's livre de raison addresses the problems encountered by French refugees as they adjusted to a new environment. Here Vevey's parish and consistory records also provide valuable information. Though granted financial support, nearly one-half of the refugees arriving in the Pays de Vaud had departed by 1699, strong evidence of the callous, winnowing pragmatism forced on local Swiss governments by higher authorities. Refugees sought acceptance by carefully conforming to Vevey's religious policies, and pursued shrewd social strategies in marriage and godparenthood. Huguenot refugees attempted to secure support from within and outside of refugee households by marriages with both groups. They also promoted social connections with the larger Vevey community by engaging in strategies of vertical integration, with Vevey's social superiors acting as godparents to refugee infants, a practice that created a strong bond in early modern Europe.

Giraud's *livre* conveys the anxiety and social disruption of his time, and portrays the struggle against disorder as communities across Europe imposed measures of social discipline as a bulwark against economic hardship and social disharmony. Vevey relied on its consistory to impose order and to root out aberrant and malevolent behavior that residents believed encouraged social problems and ill will in the community. Religious conformity promoted religious unity, and those who conformed stood a greater chance of securing residency.

Of course, wealth mattered above all else. Those who had escaped

France with the most resources had the best chance of becoming permanent residents in Switzerland. Escaping with easily liquidated assets, Giraud avoided dependency on the largesse of the state, and his abilities as a moneylender and peddler served him well in his new host country. Bern welcomed capitalists and entrepreneurs interested in investing in new manufacturing and other commercial ventures. Jean Giraud's family were forward-thinking investors, and realized the opportunities present in watch manufacturing, a relatively new industry in Switzerland. The family watch business demonstrated an appreciation for new technology, anticipating the technological achievements that the eighteenth century would deliver. An experienced capitalist, Giraud reduced risk through diversification. He continued to peddle and engage in moneylending while selling books and possibly watch parts. Capitalism was the way of the future for the economic growth of nations, and the means by which refugees like Giraud survived.

Death inventories and other legal records reveal much regarding the economy and material life of Giraud's Swiss community. The number of cultural artifacts listed in Giraud's inventory of household goods, together with his book inventories, illustrates the vibrant and cosmopolitan consumption patterns of the age. The seventeenth and eighteenth centuries saw a dramatic upsurge in consumption by an expanding European middle class. People bought and owned more things, including possessions previously affordable only by elites. Buying power spurred on consumption and consumption defined cultural priorities. Both elites and non-elites sought to acquire possessions that were desirable not only because they satisfied essential needs but also because they signified power and social status.

The goods itemized in Giraud's *livre* and found in the inventories of other middle-class Vevey residents reveal new attitudes toward social etiquette and self-presentation. Vevey's residents labored to produce goods for the market, and embraced a material world representative of values consistent with others of their social class and religious temperament. The clothes they wore and the items chosen to furnish their homes connoted appreciation for good manners, proper dress, and a respectable, comfortable lifestyle. Both regional and French fashions inspired local tastes, as evidenced by the assortment of clothes, hats, and accessories for women's hair available to the consumer. Despite sumptuary regulations, the local bourgeoisie, including prosperous refugees, adorned their homes with exotic luxuries and wore the latest fashions. Their style of dress and home furnishings proclaimed a social presence that commanded esteem and respect.

This material world challenges the widely known and contested argument that the Calvinist work ethic encouraged ascetic living. A devout man, Giraud was no ascetic. His livre de raison reveals he enjoyed games, lived comfortably, appreciated the arts, and took pleasure in fine dining. Giraud valued personal appearance and cleanliness and was a man of honor; he projected an aura of sophistication through his books, artwork, and musical instruments. Both intellectual and collector, he was a proud and respectable pillar of his community, who possessed more than mere financial wherewithal. Also a deeply religious and conscientious man, Giraud conveyed through his dress, etiquette and cultivation, orderliness and restraint—traits appropriate for someone of his social standing and strong faith.

Giraud maintained a rapport with other merchants, with whom he discussed and exchanged books. As a merchant, he kept abreast of market trends and international events through his communication networks, corresponding with associates, family, and members of his former church residing in other parts of Switzerland and wider Europe. He was an important channel for the dissemination of information in Vevey, and to the broader international family of Huguenot exiles. His life in France taught him how to keep a low profile, especially when it came to trade in works authorities disapproved or found heretical.

By the early eighteenth century, many Huguenots, unable to leave France, had come to entertain a particular religious enthusiasm that helped them understand and endure their persecution. When some finally managed to leave France, these Huguenot charismatics were not always welcomed abroad, and their dogma was rejected by more conservative Huguenot exiles.[1] Although Giraud did not record his personal views, his inventory of books suggests that he understood well the international political situation, its religious implications, and the Huguenot charismatic influence. Crucial volumes within his collection indicate more than a simple awareness. They suggest rather pointedly that his personal identity as a Protestant incorporated some of these ideas. Certainly, the inventory shows that some Huguenot merchants, who sought reassurance in God's deliverance and final plan like their inspired Huguenot brethren abroad, readily embraced apocalyptic and other supernatural explanations for the Huguenot struggle. For Giraud and other exiles, the Huguenots were a special people, with a divinely ordained role and place in history.

Municipal records show that Jean Giraud died on March 3, 1708.[2] His wife, Magdelaine, followed him in death as she did in life, passing away sixteen years later on April 14, 1724.[3] Giraud's notes indicate that he never gave up hope that the king would grant him amnesty and, with it, the right to return to his beloved La Grave. Amnesty unfortunately never came, and so Giraud and his family made a life in the Pays de Vaud. Without question, Giraud was as resourceful as he was adaptable. Through all, the mainstay of his strength was faith, a force that kept him connected to his community and sustained him through one of the most challenging and darkest human trials of the era.

NOTES

INTRODUCTION

1. Jacques Faucher, Pierre Gravier, Pierre Albert, Jacques Chicot, Jean Gallot, Jean Bouillet, and Jean Monnet are identified as "marchands de la Grave" in church records for neighboring Mizoën. The same individuals are named in Giraud's livre de raison as members of his Church in La Grave. For Mizoën church records, see Archives départementales de l'Isère (ADI), 5 E 238/1, 13 et 14, Mizoën (protestants), baptêmes, mariages, sépultures, (1669–1684); Archives cantonales vaudoises (ACV), PP 713/1 Monnet (famille), Livre de raison de Jean Giraud de La Grave, 1670-1711.

2. Luciani, "Ordering Words," 531.

3. Luciani, "Ordering Words," 530–31.

4. According to historian Laurence Fontaine, only one of four volumes of Jean Giraud's account books survives. Fontaine writes: "The *raizon* (account book) unfortunately covers only some of his business affairs. These are normally inscribed in four volumes: a main book of transactions (*le raizon*), a confidential record of dealings with his business associates (*livre secret*), a log book (*carnets de voyage*), and a book relating to dealings with mountain communities of his region (*livre de la Grave*)." Fontaine and Siddle, "Mobility, Kinship, and Commerce," 61 (footnote 22); Fontaine, *History of Pedlars*, 224 (footnote 28).

5. Fontaine contends that Giraud assumed and managed the family expenses and debts, which included those of his sister, sister's family, uncle, and first and second wives. Fontaine, *The Moral Economy*, 87–88.

6. Debts owed him in his home village of La Grave at the time of his flight totaled 9,145 *livres*. Fontaine, *The Moral Economy*, 87–88.

I. LA GRAVE

1. ACV, PP 713/1, fols. 2v–55r.

2. According to historian Laurence Fontaine, Jean Giraud's father had at one time operated a shop in Lyon. Fontaine, *History of Pedlars*, 13; "Les tribulations d'un huguenot réfugié à Vevey," 47.

3. Hickey, "Innovation and Obstacles," 215–17.

4. Luria, *Territories of Grace,* 24.

5. Hickey, "Innovation and Obstacles," 217.

6. Luria, *Territories of Grace,* 28.

7. Hickey, "Politics and Commerce," 133–51.

8. Fontaine and Siddle, "Mobility, Kinship, and Commerce," 57.

9. Hickey, "Innovation and Obstacles," 215–17.

10. During the fourteenth and fifteenth centuries, small mountain villages in Dauphiné might have had two or three trades; larger villages might have as many as ten, with craftsmen representing from 10 to 30 percent of heads of households. See Belmont, "Les artisans ruraux en Dauphiné," 419–43; For artisans residing in the Hautes-Alpes during the early modern era, see Belmont, *Des ateliers au village.*

11. Fontaine, *History of Pedlars,* 12, 16–18.

12. Farr, *The Work of France,* 115–16.

13. Fontaine, *History of Pedlars,* 15–16.

14. ACV, PP 713/1, fol. 83v.

15. Giraud mentions another Magdelaine Chicot earlier in his notes, to whom he was engaged before marrying his first wife. It does not appear to be the same woman, whom he married later, though both Magdelaines may have been from the same family, Chicot. Giraud contends that the first engagement was broken off by brother Félix Chicot but gives no reason why. ACV, PP 713/1, fol. 84r.

16. According to Laurence Fontaine, Giraud's sister Anne deposited her dowry while her uncle invested 6,000 *livres.* See Fontaine, *History of Pedlars,* 15.

17. Rosenberg, *A Negotiated World,* 27.

18. According to Laurence Fontaine, in addition to her dowry and pension, Giraud's sister also contributed her children's endowment, of which Giraud was the guardian. Fontaine, *History of Pedlars,* 15.

19. Also noted is an item Giraud termed, "L'Art sale." ACV, PP 713/1, fols. 2v–55r, especially fols. 31v–31r, 38v–38r, 44r, and 45v.

20. Archives départementales des Hautes-Alpes (ADH), 1 E 7158, Minutes de Jean Rome (Notaire à La Grave), fols. 33v–35r, January 1, 1678, and fols. 185r–186r, October 23, 1678.

21. It's actually not clear if Marie Giraud was a cousin, aunt, or other relative.

22. Samuel Mours contends 850,000 Protestants lived in France, while Philip Benedict estimates around 800,000. Benedict further estimates 78,000 Protestants were living in Dauphiné prior to the Revocation, with 66,000 residing in rural communities. Another 4,500 lived in cities of 5,000 or more, and 7,000 lived in cities with a population of 2,000 to 5,000. Samuel Mours's statistics have Dauphiné's Protestant minority at 72, 000, with only 40,000 designated as rural. Pierre Bolle contends there were 72,000 Protestants in Dauphiné in the first half of the seventeenth century. Benedict, "The Huguenot Population of France," 8–10; Bolle, *Protestants en Dauphiné,* 15.

23. Bolle, *Protestants en Dauphiné*, 15; Luria, *Territories of Grace*, 51.

24. Luria, *Territories of Grace*, 51.

25. While some historians estimate the number of Protestants living in Besse during the late seventeenth century at around 1,500, relying on Giraud's tally of churchgoers, the best estimate for the membership for Giraud's church in La Grave is 160. According to Laurence Fontaine, Clavans and Besse were "almost equally divided between the two denominations." Fontaine, "Family Cycles, Peddling and Society," 59. Besse, Mizoën, and Bourg d'Oisans also had annex churches. Bolle, *Protestants en Dauphiné*, 16.

26. Giraud leaves behind no remarks regarding his physical church, though his records indicate the destruction of two of his community's Protestant churches in 1682. ACV, PP 713/1, fol. 82v.

27. According to David van der Linden, the king launched a commission in 1656 (in some cases underway in 1661) to determine which Protestant churches satisfied the Edict of Nantes criteria for existing. Protestant consistories were required to supply state authorities with written proof of their temples' existence dating back to 1596 and 1597. van der Linden, *Experiencing Exile*, 204.

28. Archives nationales (AN), TT/272, dossier 7, Archives des consistoires, Terrasses, Chazelet, Ventolon, Hières (Hautes-Alpes, cant. et com. La Grave). Partage d'avis concernant l'exercice de la R. P. R., 1664.

29. Archives départementales de l'Isère (ADI), H+_GRE/E_7, Délibérations du Conseil de direction des pauvres, August 16, 1694, and H+_GRE/B_144, Observations faites sur les états, dressés en 1701, des revenus, biens, charges et dépenses de l'hôpital de Grenoble provenant notamment des legs faits aux pauvres de la religion réformée et aux consistoires de l'ancienne province du Dauphiné, fols. 11r–13v, April 1701.

30. ADI, H+_GRE/B_144, fol. 12r.

31. ADI, 5 E 238/1, 13 et 14, 1669–1684.

32. Parker, "Moral Supervision and Poor Relief," 334–61.

33. Archives départementales de l'Isère (ADI), 4 E 31/64, Archives communales de Mizoën, cultes et assistance publique. Pauvres de la R.P.R.: rôles, comptes des procureurs, etc. (1675-1689). Création et installation de l'hôpital dans la maison Bonnet, ministre de la R.P.R. (1686-1687)

34. ADI, 4 E 31/64, February 13, 1676.

35. Archives départementales des Hautes-Alpes (ADH), 3 E 5125 BB5, Registres des délibérations, fol. 1.

36. Beik, *A Social and Cultural History*, 57. See also ADH, 3 E 5125 BB5.

37. Jean Giraud's uncle, Paul Giraud, represented the Protestants and served as La Grave's village consul in 1657. Archives départementales des Hautes-Alpes (ADH), 3 E 5327 FF5, Pièces de procédures, February 1, 1658.

38. ADH, 3 E 5327 FF5, February 1, 1658 and February 1, 1660.

39. Luria, *Territories of Grace*, 83.

40. Beik, *A Social and Cultural History*, 57.

41. According to Keith Luria, the absence of a seigneur encouraged an autonomous village life. Luria, *Territories of Grace*, 28.

42. At times, a surgeon might be called during a prolonged illness, attesting to Giraud's resources, as surgeons were typically available only to persons of means, and rarely to those living in remote rural areas.

43. ACV, PP 713/1, fols. 82v–86r.

44. "England Marriages, 1538–1973," database, *FamilySearch* (https://familysearch .org/ark:/61903/1:1:NXLQ-2XT: 13 March 2020), Suzanne Chicot in entry for Marc Henry Chabrol, 1690; "England Births and Christenings, 1538–1975," database, *FamilySearch* (https://www.familysearch.org/ark:/61903/1:1:V5LG-4LZ : 5 February 2023), Anne Chicot in entry for Andre Laurent, 1693; "England Births and Christenings, 1538–1975," database, *FamilySearch* (https://www.familysearch.org/ark:/61903/1:1:V5LG-HB9: 5 February 2023), Susanne Chicot in entry for Lucresse Charbrolle, 1696; "England Births and Christenings, 1538–1975," database, *FamilySearch* (https://www.familysearch .org/ark:/61903/1:1:V5LG-N5T: 5 February 2023), Susanne Chicot in entry for Pierre Chabrolle, 1697. See also William A. Minnet and Susan Minnet, eds. *Registers of the Churches of the Tabernacle of Glasshouse Street and Leicester Fields, 1688–1783* (Frome: Butler and Tanner, LTD, 1926), 35, 37, 49, 57, and 63.

45. Gwynn, "Conformity," 30.

46. ACV, PP 713/1, fol. 84v. For information about smallpox at this time see Duncan, Scott, and Duncan, "Smallpox Epidemics," 255–71.

47. Pierre Goubert contends that in 1661 life expectancy was twenty-five years, presumably a consequence of the high infant mortality rates. One-quarter of all children died before their first year, another quarter never reached the age of twenty. Only 10 percent made it to the age of sixty. See Goubert, *Louis XIV*, 21.

48. Jean Giraud noted in his *livre* that his son, Jean Claude, suffered from a cold and high fever for thirty days before his death. His son also underwent chest surgery. ACV, PP 713/1, fols. 84v and 85r.

49. ACV, PP 713/1, fol. 84v.

50. Giraud's inventories list twenty sacks used for storing grain. Giraud also owned sheep, though the extent of his livestock is unknown.

51. Giraud also owned a *garderobe*, furniture used for storing clothes. According to Daniel Roche, cabinets and wardrobes, which were beginning to appear in inventories at this time, illustrate the need for systems of organization that had emerged with increased consumption and ownership of material objects. See Roche, *A History of Everyday Things*.

52. Farm implements included plows (two *araires* and two *socs*), a trident, scraper, saw, and hammers. ACV, PP 713/1, fols. 73v–76v.

53. An eighteenth-century definition of *coquemar* may be found in Furetière, *Dictionnaire*.

54. According to Donna J. Bohanan, "Beds were often the dominant element of a room's furnishings and objects of luxury." Bohanan, *Fashion beyond Versailles*, 61.

55. Giraud identifies four "*cuillères lotton ou fourochettes le tout.*" He also lists sixteen "assiettes," nine "plat (s)" and two "*assiett creuzes.*" ACV, PP 713/1, fols. 73v–76v.

56. For evolving ideas of cleanliness see Vigarello, *Concepts of Cleanliness.*

57. Robert Nye has suggested that the French middle class may have been adopting the aristocratic custom of the duel at this time. Nye, *Masculinity and Male Codes*, 8.

58. Hunter, "The Royal Society's 'Repository'," 162.

59. ACV, PP 713/1, fols. 73v–76v.

60. According to Giraud's livre de raison, members of the Albert family fled to Kassel and Vevey in the wake of the Revocation. ACV, PP 713/1, fol. 82v.

61. The Alberts also sold taffeta, thread, buttons, pins, spurs, soap, musket balls, and gun powder. Other works they sold included the prophecies of Nostradamus, dictionaries, the Meditations of St. Augustine, pharmacology of Bauderon, shepherds' calendars, books of poetry, a work on surgery, and Bertrand Compaigne's *La science des juges criminels, temporels et ecclésiastiques* (1656). Archives cantonales vaudoises (ACV), Bis 562, Documents relatifs à Paul Jullien, marchand de Villar d'Arêne (Dauphiné), 1649–1685.

62. Benoist, *Histoire de l'Édit de Nantes*, 802–803.

63. I'm assuming Giraud is referring to Pierre du Moulin's work, *Anatomie de la Messe*, which went through numerous editions. ACV, PP 713/1, fol. 76v.

64. Fontaine, *History of Pedlars*, 54–58.

65. The Huguenot Jacob Spon died in Vevey, Switzerland, on December 25, 1685, not long after taking refuge there. ACV, PP 713/1, fol. 76v.

66. Bireley, *The Refashioning of Catholicism*, 6.

67. Luria, *Territories of Grace*, 2.

68. Luria, *Territories of Grace*, 27, 39, and 64.

69. Grenoble's Protestants made up only only 3.5 per cent of the city's total population. See Norberg, *Rich and Poor*, 65–69.

70. Arnaud, *Histoire des protestants*, 77.

71. Arnaud, *Histoire des protestants*, 79, 105–106.

72. Arnaud, *Histoire des protestants*, 92–94.

73. The rich merchant I refer to here is Jacques Bérard, who hailed from Mizoën and also had a shop in Lyon. Fontaine, *History of Pedlars*, 105 and 108.

74. Fontaine, *History of Pedlars*, especially pages 106–108.

2. FLIGHT

1. Giraud notes that the homes of the poor, which were pillaged, were abandoned at night—all for liberty. Giraud writes: "*Tout pour leur liberté.*" ACV, 713/1, fol. 76v.

2. Giraud identifies the consuls of La Grave, Félix Gay and Félix Paillas, two *frippons* [*sic*], "rascals or rogues; Paillas less so." ACV, PP 713/1, fol. 76r.

3. ACV, PP 713/1, fol. 78v.

4. Chappell, "Huguenot Memoirs," 323.

5. Whelan, "From the Other Side of Silence," 159.

6. Chappell, "Huguenot Memoires," 325.

7. van der Linden, *Experiencing Exile*, 17–20.

8. van der Linden, *Experiencing Exile*, 163.

9. Whelan, "Marsh's Library," 218, 222, and 224.

10. Yardeni, *Le refuge protestant*, 34.

11. Labrousse, "France, 1598–1685," 295.

12. Wilson, *Beyond Belief*, 24.

13. Geoffrey Treasure contends that one-half of all of Dauphiné's Protestant temples were destroyed in the 1660s. Treasure, *The Huguenots*, 323.

14. Labrousse, *Une foi, une loi, un roi?*, 108.

15. McCullough, *Coercion*, 131, 146, and 150.

16. Lossky, *Louis XIV*, 217.

17. Norberg, *Rich and Poor*, 65–69.

18. van der Linden, *Experiencing Exile*, 198; van der Linden, "Histories of Martyrdom," 349–51 and 361–65; Johnston, "Elie Benoist," 476–82.

19. van der Linden, "Histories of Martyrdom," 349–70.

20. Benoist, *Histoire de l'Édit de Nantes*, 650 and 653.

21. Benoist contends that these were carried out in the parish of Silhac.

22. Benoist lists numerous atrocities. Benoist, *Histoire de l'Édit de Nantes*, 654–55.

23. ACV, PP 713/1, fols. 76r–77v.

24. ACV, PP 713/1, fol. 78v.

25. ACV, PP 713/1, fols. 77v–78v.

26. ACV, PP 713/1, fol. 78v.

27. ACV, PP 713/1, fols. 77r–78v.

28. ACV, PP 713/1, fol. 78v.

29. ACV, PP 713/1, fol. 78r.

30. ACV, PP 713/1, fol. 79v.

31. Manon Chicot's *"fripperie,"* is translated here as old clothes. ACV, PP 713/1, fol. 78r.

32. ACV, PP 713/1, fol. 79v.

33. ACV, PP 713/1, fols. 79v–80v.

34. ACV, PP 713/1, fol. 79r.

35. ACV, PP 713/1, fols. 80v–80r.

36. ACV, PP 713/1, fols. 80r–81v.

37. ACV, PP 713/1, fol. 81r.

38. ACV, PP 713/1, fol. 81r.

39. ACV, PP 713/1, fol. 81v.

40. ACV, PP 713/1, fols. 81v–81r.

41. Giraud also informs the reader that his daughter Suzon contracted smallpox. She thankfully recovered, but 1,200 other children in Geneva died from the disease during their five-week stay in the city. ACV, PP 713/1, fol. 81r.

42. Ruff, *Violence*, 102.

43. Ruff, *Violence*, 109.

44. McCullough, *Coercion*, 250.

45. S. Ougier estimates the number of Protestants fleeing Dauphiné in the wake of the revocation at 20,000. Ougier, "Les réformés," 19–27.

46. Laborie, "Who were the Camisards?," 56.

3. GIRAUD'S COMMUNITY OF EXILES

1. I have found the common use of the word "refugee" in a wide number of communal and cantonal records in the Pays de Vaud in the late seventeen century. Such archival sources included parish, communal, and consistory records, wills, death inventories, and *assignals*.

2. *Habitant* and *bourgeois* were legal terms applied specifically to conditions of residency and citizenship. *Réfugié* was simply a label that came to identify any French Protestant who had fled religious persecution in France. The title *bourgeois* conferred political status and power. The *bourgeoisie* of Vevey served on governing councils, elected magistrates, and benefited from a wide range of economic privileges. By contrast, *habitants* had no political rights and possessed few privileges. Although *habitants* lived in town, their residency could be revoked. *Habitants* also had restricted access to professions and real estate and paid a yearly habitation fee, while pledging their loyalty to civic authorities. By the late seventeenth century, two intermediate statuses had emerged, *petit bourgeois* and *habitant perpétuel*. Their precise distinction is unknown, but both possessed rights of permanent residence. Neither had political rights. See Ducommun and Quadroni, *Le refuge protestant*, 285–93.

3. According to Aaron Spencer Fogleman, the population of Vevey in 1698 was 3,000. His figure of 900 refugees may be a high estimate. Albert de Montet considers the number of refugees at the end of the century, if going by the enumeration of 1696, to be about 700. Marie-Jeanne Ducommun and Dominique Quadroni place the number of Huguenot refugees settling in the bailiwick of Vevey at 262 in 1685, 640 in 1693, and 698 in 1696. Close to 90 percent of refugees in the census of 1693 lived in Vevey's city proper. Fogleman, *Two Troubled Souls*, 19; de Montet, *Vevey à travers les siècles*, 50; Ducommun and Quadroni, *Le Refuge Protestant*, 189 and 191.

4. Terpstra, *Religious Refugees*, 1–2.

5. Ducommun and Quadroni. *Le refuge protestant*, 13.

6. ACV, PP 713/1, fols. 82v–82r.

7. Sautier, "Politique et refuge," 123; Scoville, "Huguenots and the Diffusion of Technology. I," 406.

8. Scoville, "Huguenots and the Diffusion of Technology. II," 407–409.

9. Mottu-Weber, "Marchands et artisans," 383–94.

10. Sautier, "Politique et refuge," 149; Scoville, "Huguenots and the Diffusion of Technology. II," 406.

11. Gwynn, *The Huguenots*, 199 and 203.

12. Scoville, "Huguenots and the Diffusion of Technology. I," 299–304; Gwynn, *Huguenot Heritage*, 74–100.

13. Swindlehurst, "'An Unruly and Presumptuous Rabble,'" 366–74.

14. Laborie, *Enlightening Enthusiasm*, 173 and 175.

15. Barret, "Huguenot Integration," 376.

16. French-speaking Protestants who had fled the Spanish Netherlands founded the Walloon churches in the sixteenth century. van der Linden, *Experiencing Exile*, 2, 37, 41, 48, and 51.

17. Yardeni, "Assimilation," 281.

18. Archives communales de Vevey (AC Vevey), Aa bleu 26, Manual du conseil, fol. 145r, May 12, 1687.

19. AC Vevey, Aa bleu 26, fol. 48v, November 23, 1685.

20. AC Vevey, Aa bleu 26, fol. 98r, August 19, 1686 and fol. 102r, September 13, 1686.

21. AC Vevey, Aa bleu 26, fol. 124r, January 17, 1687 and fol. 134r, March 14, 1687.

22. There were 159 refugee nobles and rentiers living in Vevey from 1696 to 1698, and 47 merchants, most making their living as peddlers or resellers. Most merchants made modest livings as second-hand peddlers or small shop owners. Ducommun and Quadroni highlight this point by quoting a note that appears for the town of Morges from the 1698 census, which reads, "most merchants are of low degree as peddlers or resellers (*La plupart des marchands sont de bas degré, comme colporteurs et revendeurs)."* Ducommun and Quadroni, *Le refuge protestant*, 152, 198–200.

23. Archives communales de Vevey (AC Vevey), Aa bleu 28, Manual du conseil, fol. 353v, April 8, 1695.

24. AC Vevey, Aa bleu 28, fol. 7r, January 25, 1692.

25. AC Vevey, Aa bleu 28, fol. 399r, September 5, 1695.

26. Archives communales de Vevey (AC Vevey), Aa bleu 29, Manual du conseil, fol. 29rv, December 16, 1697.

27. Archives communales de Vevey (AC Vevey), Aa bleu 30, Manual du conseil, fol. 83r (no date) and fol. 84v, November 17, 1698.

28. AC Vevey, Aa bleu 30, fol. 280r, November 27, 1699.

29. AC Vevey, Aa bleu 30, fol. 149r, March 6, 1699.

30. Archives communales de Vevey (AC Vevey), Aa bleu 31, Manual du conseil, fol. 233r, July 18, 1701.

31. Ducommun and Quadroni, *Le refuge protestant*, 48–52.

32. Archives communales de Vevey (AC Vevey), Aa bleu 32, Manual du conseil, fols. 410v–411r, November 14, 1704.

33. AC Vevey, Aa bleu 32, fols. 410v–411r, November 14, 1704.

34. AC Vevey, Aa bleu 32, fols. 410v–411r, November 14, 1704.

35. AC Vevey, Aa bleu 32, fols. 410v–411r, November 14, 1704.

36. AC Vevey, Aa bleu 26, fol. 156r, July 7, 1687 and fol. 184r, November 3, 1687; Archives communales de Vevey (AC Vevey), Aa bleu 28, Manual du conseil, fol. 225v, January 25, 1694; AC Vevey, Aa bleu 32, fol. 214r, July 30, 1703.

37. Ducommun and Quadroni. *Le refuge protestant*, 142. Municipal authorities also addressed women's poverty. The city log indicates municipal authorities subsidized women's lacemaking. In one case, the city furnished the daughter of Jean Daux a spinning wheel and financial support in order for her to learn to spin wool. AC Vevey, Aa bleu 28, fol. 132r, March 20, 1693 and fol. 308r, October 11, 1694; AC Vevey, Aa bleu 32, fol. 463v, February 23, 1705.

38. A fullery is an establishment for processing or "fulling" wool in cloth-making.

39. AC Vevey, Aa bleu 26, fol. 180r, October 20, 1687.

40. Ducommun and Quadroni, *Le refuge protestant*, 142 and 155.

41. AC Vevey, Aa bleu 32, fols. 237v–238r, October 11, 1703.

42. AC Vevey, Aa bleu 28, fol. 212r, December 11, 1693.

43. AC Vevey, Aa bleu 28, fol. 333v, January 3, 1695, and fol. 337v, January 14, 1695.

44. AC Vevey, Aa bleu 28, fol. 343v, February 18, 1695.

45. AC Vevey, Aa bleu 28, fol. 349v, March 14, 1695.

46. AC Vevey, Aa bleu 29, fol. 273v, November 22, 1697.

47. Olivier, *Médecine et santé*, 48–49.

48. Of the 159 requests for work permits that identify occupation, thirteen were for surgeons. Ducommun and Quadroni, *Le refuge protestant*, 213–15.

49. Ducommun and Quadroni, *Le refuge protestant*, 45.

50. According to the minutes of the city log, Vevey, on orders from Bern, took a roll of all men ages fifteen to sixty, additionally specifying those who had left or been engaged outside the country for some time. AC Vevey, Aa bleu 28, fol. 235v, February 26, 1694.

51. AC Vevey, Aa bleu 32, fol. 225v, September 10, 1703.

52. AC Vevey, Aa bleu 32, fol. 226r, September 17, 1703.

53. AC Vevey, Aa bleu 32, fol. 368v, June 26, 1704.

54. AC Vevey, Aa bleu 32, fol. 368v, June 26, 1704.

55. Tosato-Rigo, "Etrangers mais frères," 266; Ducommun and Quadroni, *Le refuge protestant*, 147.

56. AC Vevey, Aa bleu 30, fols. 152v–153r, March 9, 1699.

57. A "Jean Giraut" is also listed though it is not clear if this is a spelling error or is meant to be Jean Giraud.

58. According to Albert de Montet, the category of *petit bourgeois* was established in 1701. The municipal records of Vevey indicate a second class of refugees a year earlier in March of 1699. de Montet, *Vevey à travers*, 118; AC Vevey, Aa bleu 30, fols. 152v–153r, March 9, 1699.

59. The artisan trades represented included shoemakers, tailors, goldsmiths, carpenters, bakers, shirtmakers, glovemakers, an apothecary, surgeon, tanner, weaver, dyer, gardener, locksmith, and bookseller. AC Vevey, Aa bleu 30, fols. 152v–153r, March 9, 1699.

60. Ducommun and Quadroni, *Le refuge protestant*, 241.

61. Ducommun and Quadroni concede that the category of *petit bourgeois* may have been created to meet the needs of refugees, granting them residency while restricting access to full political rights. Ducommun and Quadroni. *Le refuge protestant*, 240–42.

62. Bossy, "Blood and Baptism," 129–31.

63. Farr, *Artisans in Europe*, 245.

64. Fontaine, *History of Pedlars*, 61.

65. Archives cantonales vaudoises (ACV), Eb 132/4, Paroisse réformée de Vevey, fol. 17r, October 25, 1700.

66. Archives cantonales vaudoises (ACV), Eb 132/3, Paroisse réformée de Vevey, fol. 38v, June 12, 1687.

67. ACV, Eb 132/3, fol. 39r, February 8, 1688.

68. ACV, Eb 132/4, fol. 24v, October 15, 1703.

69. The following data is developed from the Vevey's parish records for 1684–1723. More refugee/non-refugee unions occurred in the first decade of immigration from 1685 to 1694, peaking at an average of 2.75 per year. This equaled the rate for marriages in which both parties were refugees. ACV, Eb 132/3, Paroisse réformée de Vevey, 1642–1696, and ACV, Eb 132/4, Paroisse réformée de Vevey, 1696–1723.

70. Berteau, Gourdon, and Robin-Romero, "Godparenthood," 452–55.

71. Mentzer, "Communities of Worship," 33.

72. Conner, *Huguenot Heartland*, 33–36; Mentzer, *Blood and Belief*, 149–52.

73. Alfani and Gourdon, "Spiritual Kinship," 11; Spierling, *Infant Baptism*, 106.

74. ACV, Eb 132/3, fol. 215r, November 29, 1689; ACV, PP 713/1, fol. 85r.

75. ACV, Eb 132/3, fol. 269r, April 1694.

76. Sabean, Teuscher, and Mathieu, *Kinship in Europe*, 2; Farr, *Hands of Honor*, 125–33.

77. Farr, *Hands of Honor*, 129.

78. ACV, Eb 132/3, fol. 240v, December 21, 1691.

79. ACV, Eb 132/4, fol. 18v, February 15, 1697.

80. ACV, Eb 132/3, fol. 260v, July 1693.

81. ACV, Eb 132/3, fol. 189r, January 22, 1687.

82. ACV, Eb 132/3, fol. 193r, August 12, 1687, and folio 262v, September 30, 1693.

83. ACV, Eb 132/3, fol. 293r, February 26, 1696.

84. ACV, Eb 132/3, fol. 231r, January 30, 1691.

85. AC Vevey, Aa bleu 34, Manual du conseil, 1708–1712, no fol.

86. Matzinger-Pfister, "L'Introduction des consistoires," 116.

87. Gordon, *The Swiss Reformation,* 59–60.

88. Larminie, "Life in Ancien Regime Vaud." 45.

89. AC Vevey, Aa bleu 26, fol. 51v, December 15, 1685.

90. AC Vevey, Aa bleu 32, fol. 329r, April 7, 1704; fol. 333r, April 14, 1704; fol. 336v, April 21, 1704; fol. 342v, May 5, 1704.

91. Archives communales de Vevey (AC Vevey), Aa bleu 33, Manual du conseil, fol. 324r, January 3, 1707.

92. AC Vevey, Aa bleu 32, fol. 491v, April 27, 1705.

93. Unfortunately, consistory records for Vevey for the years from January 17, 1691, to February 15, 1698, are missing.

94. Archives cantonales vaudoises (ACV), Bda 132/3, Vevey-La Tour-de-Peilz, April 9, 1689–April 24, 1689.

95. Archives cantonales vaudoises (ACV), Bda 132/4, Vevey-La Tour-de-Peilz, February 24, 1699.

96. ACV, Bda 132/3, July 1, 1689.

97. ACV, Bda 132/4, June 30, 1702

98. ACV, Bda 132/3, December 19, 1690; ACV, Bda 132/4, May 4, 1703, and June 4, 1703.

99. ACV, Bda 132/4, Feb 4, 1701

100. ACV, Bda 132/4, March 31, 1699.

101. ACV, Bda 132/4, June 28, 1700.

102. ACV, Bda 132/4, January 16, 1705

103. Hardwick, *Sex in an Old Regime City,* 6.

104. ACV, Bda 132/4, February 24, 1699.

105. ACV, Bda 132/4, February 9, 1703.

106. ACV, Bda 132/3, May 17, 1688.

107. ACV, Bda 132/4, November 22, 1700.

108. ACV, Bda 132/4, February 10, 1702.

109. ACV, Bda 132/3, November 14, 1690.

110. ACV, Bda 132/4, February 9, 1703.

111. ACV, Bda 132/3, August 8, 1690.

112. ACV, Bda 132/3, December 5, 1690.

113. ACV, Bda 132/3, December 28, 1689, January 6, 1690, and January 8, 1690.

114. ACV, Bda 132/4, August 26, 1698.

115. ACV, Bda 132/4, January 20, 1690, February 18, 1690, and November 11, 1698.

116. ACV, Eb 132/3, fol. 160v, August 10, 1683, and fol. 174v, June 12, 1685.

117. Archives communales de Vevey (AC Vevey), H Noir 1, 1618–1816, Rôles des assistés par l'Hôpital.

118. AC Vevey, Aa bleu 33, fol. 558r, December 31, 1698.

4. ÉMIGRÉ LIVELIHOODS

1. Goubert, *Louis XIV,* 158; Mettam, "Louis XIV and the Huguenots," 17.

2. Refugees founded cloth factories and manufacturers in pottery, pins, hats, cotton, Indian fabrics, ribbons, and silk stockings.

3. Chavannes, "Commerce et industrie à Vevey," 174; Recordon, *Études historiques,* 306 and 315.

4. Kellenbenz, "Technology," 252.

5. Landes, "Watchmaking," 15.

6. Enright, "Organization and Coordination," 128–29; Jequier, "Employment Strategies," 323. According to Catherine Cardinal, at its height in the eighteenth century, the *établissage* system involved approximately thirty different specialized trades. See Catherine Cardinal, *The Watch,* 55–60.

7. Vevey's records on admission to the bourgeoisie identify one Jean Monnet, son of Paul Monnet and grandson of Jean Monnet, accepted into Vevey's bourgeoisie on March 26, 1759. Archives communales de Vevey (AC Vevey), Aa bleu 58, Manual du noble conseil des douze de la Ville de Vevey, fol. 276, March 26, 1759; Piguet, *Les dénombrements,* 16.

8. A total of four refugees worked in metals or watchmaking in Vevey in the late seventeenth century, while Vevey's larger bailliage employed eight. Lausanne and Nyons, by contrast, employed fourteen and thirteen, respectively. The total for the canton was fifty-seven, which was about 3 percent of the total number of refugees listed. Ducommun and Quadroni, *Le refuge protestant,* 199; Archives communales de Vevey (AC Vevey), Documentation horlogers, Archives communales de Vevey to E. Châtelain, December 5, 1972.

9. Paul Monnet received financial assistance from the Bourse Française for several years after arriving in Vevey. In the final years of his life, he was receiving a monthly allowance of 2 *livres.* Paul Monnet died in Vevey on February 4, 1730. Archives communales de Vevey (AC Vevey), Documentation horlogers, E. Châtelain to Greffe Municipal de Vevey, November 27, 1972; AC Vevey, Documentation horlogers, Archives communales de Vevy to E. Châtelain, December 5, 1972.

10. Lavade et Chavannes, *Statistique du district,* 29.

11. Hilfiker, *Vevey,* 75 and 79; Chavannes, "Commerce et industrie," 182–83.

12. The tools listed in Jean Giraud's *livre* included an anvil and several hammers, lathes, screwdrivers, pliers, clockmakers' plates, numerous and varied kinds of files, a blow torch, oil stone, an arbor, watch rods, sliding tweezers, a saw, rivet press, compasses (one designated as a "horloger's compass"), a drive hammer, drill, an engraver, mandrel, and a "watch to place in the front of the boutique." ACV, PP 713/1, fol. 60v.

13. Email Jeanmonod Gilles, archivist of the Archives cantonales vaudoises, to Kristine Wirts, May 16, 2022.

14. Also, a title appears at the top of the list of watchmaker's tools, "Tools of Our Deceased Father," suggesting that the owner of the tools had offspring. Based on the livre de raison and Vevey's municipal records, Giraud had no surviving children. Jean Monnet arrived in Vevey in 1686, followed by his wife Marie, who later moved to Erlangen. Other members of the Monnet household included Marie, Louis, and Jacques Monnet, in all likelihood Monnet's children. According to Giraud's records, two other offspring, Paul Monnet and a younger Jean, settled in Geneva. From there, Paul relocated to Vevey. ACV, PP 713/1, fol. 82v.

15. Piguet, *Les dénombrements*, 16.

16. In French, the title reads: "*Inventaire des linges et autres choses de filles premièrement.*" Due to the placement of this inventory, appearing right before the watch parts and tools inventory in Giraud's livre de raison, it is not clear if it belonged to Giraud or one his Monnet relatives.

17. ACV, PP 713/1, fols. 59v–59r.

18. The notary listed "*une gross fuseau faire de dentelles,*" or large spindle for making lace in Marguerite Moret's shop inventory. Archives cantonales vaudoises (ACV), Bis 113, Livre des inventaires de la Cour de Vevey, January 25, 1692.

19. Piguet, *Les dénombrements*, 21.

20. Archives cantonales vaudoises (ACV), Bis III/II, Cahier d'inventaires et ventes de meubles en matière de tutelle et de succession pour la Cour de Vevey, September 14, 1698.

21. Interestingly, Magdelaine Chicot, Jean Giraud's wife, also bought Marie's lace cushion, some linens, and seven shirts. Another by the surname Monnet bought a small napkin and red dress. ACV, Bis III/II, September 14, 1698.

22. The notary probably meant *coiffes*.

23. According to Michael Kwass, "Many shops were small affairs run by producer-retailers who sold the products that they made. For innumerable tailors, seamstresses, shoemakers, cabinetmakers, watchmakers, silversmiths, or bakers, shops were scarcely more than workshops, storage rooms, or the front room of an otherwise residential home." Kwass, *The Consumer Revolution*, 79.

24. Piguet, *Les dénombrements*, 176.

25. AC Vevey, Aa bleu 29, fol. 21r, February 17, 1696; AC Vevey, Aa bleu 31, fol. 65r, July 18, 1700; AC Vevey, Aa bleu 28, fol. 155v, May 15, 1693.

26. As historian Cissie Fairchilds has noted, "Petty retailing was recognized as 'women's work' and most towns usually granted market stall licenses primarily to women." Fairchilds continues, "In a market in sixteenth-century Munich, for example, there were six male stallholders but forty-seven female ones." Fairchilds, *Women in Early Modern Europe*, 159.

27. ACV, Bis 113, March 11, 1692.

28. Welch, "Sites of Consumption," 233.

29. Archives cantonales vaudoises (ACV), Bis 91, Actes judiciaires et registre d'homologation de testaments, fols. 1r–31r, February 1, 1696.

30. Rochat, *Les régime matrimonial*, 71. For a more thorough discussion of the *assignal* see pages 69–75.

31. Chavannes, "Commerce et industrie," 174; Recordon, *Études historiques*, 315; Piguet, *Les dénombrements*, 16.

32. Hilfiker, *Vevey*, 75; Chavannes, "Commerce et industrie," 82.

33. ACV, Bis 113, July 12, 1693.

34. Ducommun and Quadroni, *Le refuge protestant*, 144.

35. ACV, Bis 113, May 6 (or 16), 1691.

36. Ducommun and Quadroni, *Le refuge protestant*, 145.

37. Hilfiker, *Vevey*, 81.

38. Perret, *Les imprimeries d'Yverdon;* Corsini, *Le livre à Lausanne.*

39. Paul G. Hoftijzer writes: "Publishing houses in Amsterdam, Leiden, Rotterdam, and the Hague produced numerous Latin and later French translations of works that had originally appeared in the English language." See Hoftijzer, "The English Book in the Seventeenth-Century Dutch Republic," 92.

40. Eisenstein, *Grub Street Abroad,* 6 and 53; Hoftijzer, "The Dutch Republic."

41. Houston, *Literacy in Early Modern Europe,* 144 and 158.

42. I am assuming that Giraud was referring to *Le guide d'Amsterdam, enseignant aux voyageurs et aux negocians sa splendeur, son commerce, & la description de ses edifices* (Amsterdam: Daniel de la Feuille, 1701).

43. Giraud's inventory in Vevey lists more than fifty books. ACV, PP 713/1, fols. 57r–58v, June 15, 1702.

44. Giraud's appreciation for historical topics is reexperienced in Vevey. Among the historical works discovered in Giraud's Vevey book inventory are Pierre du Moulin's *La vie et religion de deux bons papes. Léon premier et Grégoire premier*, the anonymous *Relation en abregé de ce qui s'est passé de plus remarquable dans le retour des Vaudois au Piémont*, Lactance's *Histoire de la mort des persécuteurs de l'église primitive* (translated into French from the English version by Gilbert Burnet), and presumably Pierre Jurieu's *Abrégé de l'Histoire Du Concile de Trente*. Works of historical fiction included Marie-Catherine d'Aulnoy's *Histoire de Jean de Bourbon* and Jean de Préchac's *Le Comte Tékély, nouvelle historique.*

Books of controversy Giraud cites include *Un livre de controversé par Philippe de Mornay Seigneur du Plessy contre un jésuite, Un livre de controversé de l'église protestante,* and *Un livre controversé réponse au livre de Monsieur Condon.* Those works not relating to French history, politics, or the Reformed Church included one Catholic version of the New Testament and *Paraphrase des Pseaumes de David* by the Bishop of Grasse, Antoine Godeau.

45. According to historian Geoffrey Adams, "From 1629 until the accession to the throne of Louis XIV . . . the relationship between the Huguenots and the Crown seemed almost idyllic." Adams, *The Huguenots and French Opinion,* 9.

46. Giraud's works on Huguenot apocalyptic themes include Pierre Jurieu's *L'Accomplissement des prophéties ou la délivrance prochaine de l'église,* Pierre du Moulin's *Accomplissement des prophéties: où est montré que les prophéties St. Paul et de l'apocalypse et de Daniel touchant les combats de l'église sont accomplies,* and Jacques Massard's *Harmonie des prophéties anciennes avec les modernes, sur la durée de l'Antéchrist, et les souffrances de l'église.* Giraud also owned the prophecies of Michel Nostradamus.

47. Vevey was home to prominent English regicides Edmund Ludlow, William Cawley, and John Phelps, who took refuge there following the English Restoration. Edmund Ludlow, whose memoirs were published in Vevey in 1689 and 1699, remained in Vevey until his death in 1693. As some of these regicides and their attendant networks were still active at the time Giraud arrived in 1687, it is not inconceivable that Giraud may have entered their social sphere. Taft, "Return of a Regicide," 197–220.

48. Adams, *The Huguenots,* 10.

49. This was at least the case for the Dutch Republic and England. See J. Barnard, "Introduction," 3; McKenzie, "Printing and Publishing," 566–67; Salman, *Pedlars,* 3.

50. Perret, *Les imprimeries d'Yverdon,* 354 and 363.

51. Lányi, " Zwinglian-Calvinist Debate," 106.

52. Schneider, *German Radical Pietism,* 158.

53. ACV, Bda 132/4, July 16, 1701 and July 20, 1701.

54. ACV, Bda 132/4, July 24, 1701.

55. Archives cantonales vaudoises (ACV), Bda 132/5, Vevey-La Tour-de-Peilz, May 9, 1704.

56. ACV, Bda 132/5, June 22, 1704.

57. Shantz, *An Introduction to German Pietism,* 181, 191–95.

58. François Magny was banned from Vevey in 1713 for his religious beliefs. For more on François Magny, see Fogleman, *Two Troubled Souls,* 24–25, and Cranston, *Jean-Jacques,* 70.

59. ACV, Bda 132/4, June 30, 1702.

60. Martin, "Gender and the Suppression," 224–25

61. Ward, *The Protestant Evangelical,* 177; Martin, "Gender and the Suppression," 228.

62. Ward, *The Protestant Evangelical,* 175, 183; Israel, *Radical Enlightenment,* 33–34.

63. Robertson, "The Relations of William III," 144–46.

64. ACV, Bis 113, September 9, 1705.

65. *Le réveil-matin des arithméticiens, soit le comble d'arithmétique.* (1626), *Métaphysique* (n.d.), and *Réponse de Blaise Pascal au Père Noël* (1647).

66. The full title is *Déclaration de Jean de Labadie, cy-devant prêtre, prédicateur et chanoin d'Amiens, contenant les raisons qui l'ont obligé à quitter la communion de l'Église Romaine pour se ranger à celle de l'Église Réformée* (Montauban: P. Braconier, 1650).

67. Pierre du Moulin's *L'Anti-barbare, ou du langage inconnu,* which was among Vassoroz's works, contains a segment on Huguenot prophecy. At the start of Vassoroz's inventory, the notary records Jean Giraud's involvement in assessing the worth of the goods as a friend of the family and in the name of Vassoroz's children. ACV, Bis 113, September 9, 1705.

68. Salman, *Pedlars and the Popular Press,* 122 and 192.

69. It is not surprising that Vassoroz, like Giraud, also owned a trébuchet.

70. Vries, *The Industrious Revolution,* 169.

71. For the connection between peddlers and the consumer revolution, see Salman, *Pedlars and the Popular Press,* 3–4.

72. ACV, Bis 113, February 8, 1688.

73. Bohanan, *Fashion beyond Versailles,* 94.

74. ACV, Bis 113, November 25, 1678.

75. André Save owned works by Laurent Joubert, Félix Plater, John Zwelfer, Giovanni Battista de Monte, Jean Liébault, Lazare Rivière, and Jean François Fernel. ACV, Bis 113, July 8, 1689.

76. Chavannes, "Un prêtre converti," 396–99.

77. Recordon, *Études historiques,* 229, 231, and 235–36.

78. ACV, Bis 113, November 25, 1694

79. ACV, Bis 91, folio 30v–31r, February 20, 1696.

80. ACV, Bis 113, January 25, 1692.

81. Such texts could be found in Huguenot homes and schools in Lyon in the late seventeenth century. See Philip Benedict, *Christ's Churches,* 510.

82. Benedict, *Christ's Churches,* 510.

83. Mentzer, "The Printed Catechism," 94.

84. Carter, *Creating Catholics,* 29.

85. Charbonnier-Burkard, "Doctrine and Liturgy," 53.

86. For the use of the catechism by early modern soldiers, see Vincenzo Lavenia, "Catechism and War."

87. ACV, Bis 91, folio 30v–31r, February 20, 1696.

88. Hamling, "The Household," 37.

89. Vevey's shops sold textiles from Nîmes, Limoges, Holland, London, Spain, Dauphiné, Valence, Vienne, Tuscany, Naples, Geneva, Montpellier, and Rome.

90. ACV, Bis 91, fol. 25r, February 20, 1696.

91. For more concerning dolls as luxury objects in seventeenth-century France, see Rori Bloom, "Playing with Dolls," 9–23.

92. Langalde, *La marchande de modes,* 56–57. There is an English edition of this book, *Rose Bertin: The Creator of Fashion at the Court of Marie Antoinette,* adapted from the French by Angelo S. Rappoport (New York: C. Scribner's Sons, 1913).

93. ACV, Bda 132/5, January 25, 1705.

94. These totals do not include caps (*coiffes*) or other kinds of head covering or ornamentation that were also sold in Vevey's shops during these same years. ACV, Bis 113, January 20, 1688; March 26, 1688; September 13, 1688; March 11, 1700.

95. ACV, Bis 91, fol. 158r, June 22, 1698.

96. With the exception of 1,200 *livres* he left M. F. de la Balme, Seigneur de Vignoles and husband of Angelique Anne de Villeneuve, his grandniece, and 500 *livres* he gave to the Hospital of Vevey, Tallemant willed 3,852 *livres* to the Huguenot refugees of Vevey and 3,852 *livres* to the merchant M. Richard and Vevey's six refugee ministers. Chavannes, *Les réfugiés français,* 207–15.

97. Denominations of money included *écu blancs, louis d'or,* ducats, and silver *cruzados.*

98. The notary identified as *"un coffre à chaise percée pour le nécessité de nature."*

99. ACV, Bis 113, June 11, 1696.

100. ACV, Bis 113, June 11, 1696.

101. For the history of the Matte family in Vevey, see Chavannes, *Les réfugiés français,* 235–47.

102. Another cover is described as consisting of red Spanish wool with gold thread.

103. ACV, Bis 113, March 1, 1697; Matte's inventory actually lists five family paintings and nine others, large and small, with two small gold frames.

104. In Matte's kitchen there were three coffee makers, three *rechauds* (heaters/warmers), a *coquemar,* silver tobacco box, sugar holder, a spit for roasting meat, four silver salt holders, and six bottles for placing in ice.

105. Listed among Matte's effects were two gold medals, one copper medal, and four silver medals. The notary identified the last as silver medals of "Roy G."—possibly Roy Guillaume, translated in English as King William. ACV, Bis 113, March 1, 1697.

106. This slave, who went by the name Jean Pierre Matte, later converted to Christianity.

107. Archives cantonales vaudoises (ACV), Bis 114, Livre des inventaires de la Cour de Vevey, September 19, 1724.

108. Archives cantonales vaudoises (ACV), Bis 101, Comptes de Tutelles, September 19, 1724.

109. ACV, Bis 114, September 19, 1724.

110. ACV, PP 713/1.

111. Kittel, "Early Modern Merchant's Marks," 208–27; Walsh, "The Medieval Merchant's Mark," 2; Holman, "Holbein's Portraits," 143.

112. Walsh, "The Medieval Merchant's Mark," 1.

113. Parés, *Las marcas,* 30–33.

114. Walsh, "The Medieval Merchant's Mark," 2; Holman, "Holbein's Portraits," 143.

115. Greiner, "Merchant Marks," 167–68; Parés, *Las marcas,* 28–29; Kittel, "Early Modern Merchant's Marks," 208–27; Burghart, "Signata de mea marcha," 141–158.

5. A PEDDLER'S COSMOS

1. Cipolla, *Clocks and Culture,* 53; Vial and Cote, *Les horlogers lyonnais.*

2. Fillet, "Les horloges publiques," 101–19.

3. Similarly, John Styles explores the question of why eighteenth-century working men owned pocket watches in "Time Piece," 44–50.

4. Racevskis, *Time and Ways of Knowing,* 26.

5. Landes, *Revolution in Time,* 88; Sherman, *Telling Time,* 21.

6. For a description of the *oignon* watch, see Racevskis, *Time and Ways,* 38.

7. Adas, *Machines as the Measure,* 60–61.

8. ACV, PP 713/1, fol. 76v.

9. Arguably, Catholics dated events by holy and feast days. See Walsh, "Holy Time," 79–95.

10. ACV, PP 713/1, fols. 79v, 81r, 85v, and 79r.

11. Minute hands were not introduced to watches until 1680. Until 1680, watches told the time according to a single hour hand. Landes, "Watchmaking," 4.

12. ACV, PP 713/1, fols. 77v, 84r–85r.

13. Gerson, *Nostradamus,* 36; Thomas, *Religion and the Decline of Magic,* 351–52; Harley, *Moon Lore,* 191–94.

14. ACV, PP 713/1, fol. 81v.

15. Giraud's notes and inventories indicate that the night's darkness was a challenge. Giraud owned torches, a lamp, and candlesticks, all probably to provide light during the night.

16. Landes, "Watchmaking," 3.

17. Catherine Cardinal attributes France's decline in the watchmaking industry in the second half of the seventeenth century to the emigration of Huguenot watchmakers to England, Switzerland, and the Dutch Republic. See Cardinal, *The Watch,* 40.

18. Boorstin, *The Discoverers,* 68; Landes, "Watchmaking," 7–8.

19. Racevskis, *Time and Ways,* 40; Cipolla, *Clocks and Culture,* 73.

20. Boorstin, *The Discoverers,* 68–69; Cipolla, *Clocks and Culture,* 69–70, 73; Cardinal, The Watch, 38–46.

21. ACV, PP 713/1, fol. 60v.

22. Interestingly, Michael J. Sauter explores the connection between early modern science and public timekeeping in Berlin during the eighteenth century in Sauter, "Clockwatchers and Stargazers," 685–709.

23. Other noteworthy inventions included von Guericke's air pump (later improved by Robert Boyle), Savery's steam engine, and Huygens's pendulum clock, and later much improved pocket watch.

24. Bouteroue, *La réponse,* 61.

25. Armstrong, *Bibliographia,* viii; Disdrelle, "Protestant Polemic," 4.

26. Charbonneau, "Huguenot Prophetism," 27.

27. Moulin was a firm adherent of Aristotelianism. Armstrong, *Bibliographia,* viii.

28. Moulin, *Physique,* 45.

29. Moulin, *Première décade* (1653), 238.

30. It is not clear what Moulin meant by a "forty-hour eclipse." Moulin, *Septième décade,* 84.

31. Moulin, *Deuxième décade,* 214–15.

32. Moulin, *Traitté de la conoissance,* 66.

33. Advances were made first by Dutch spectacle makers and then by the noted Italian astronomer and mathematician Galileo Galilee.

34. Moulin, *Sixième décade,* 216; Moulin, *Sermons sur quelques textes,* 35.

35. Moulin, *Première décade* (1643), 217: "La Parole de Dieu sert comme de lunettes pour lire plus clairement au livre de Nature."

36. An early modern definition for *lunettes hollandaises* may be found in W. Maigne's *Dictionnaire classique,* 405.

37. Moulin, *Sixième décade de sermons* (1647), (épître).

38. Moulin, *Troisième decade de sermons,* 105.

39. Moulin, *Sermons sur quelques textes,* 6.

40. Moulin, *Sermons sur quelques textes,* 173.

41. Chapuis, *Les corporations,* 3.

42. AC Vevey, Aa bleu 28, fols. 31v–32r, April 18, 1692.

43. For a description of the conflicting Calvinist views of sacred time and space, see Walsh, "Holy Time," 79–95.

44. The history books Giraud left behind at La Grave included a history of Alexander the Great, a history of Lyon, three volumes of the history of Geneva, three volumes of the history of the Reformed Church, and Jacob Spon's *Voyage d'Italie, de Dalmatie, de Grèce, et du Levant.* History books listed in the Vevey inventory include two historical novels: Catherine d'Aulnoy's *History of Jean de Bourbon* and Jean de Préchac's *Le Comte Tékély. nouvelle historique.* Other political-historical texts named in the Vevey inventory include a history of the Council of Trent, *Relation en abregé de ce qui s'est passé de plus remarquable dans le retour des Vaudois,* and Pierre du Moulin's *La vie et religion de deux bons papes.*

45. Giraud's works on Huguenot apocalyptic themes include Pierre Jurieu's *L'Accomplissement des prophéties ou la délivrance prochaine de l'église,* Pierre du Moulin's *Accomplissement des prophéties: où est montré que les prophéties St. Paul et de l'apocalypse et de Daniel touchant les combats de l'Église sont accomplies,* and Jacques Massard's *Harmonie des prophéties anciennes avec les modernes.* Giraud also owned the prophecies of Michel Nostradamus. ACV, PP 713/1, fols. 57r–58v, June 15, 1702.

46. Brisac, *Le souhait,* 22–23; Daillé, *Vint sermons,* 6, 15; Moulin, *Traitté de la conoissance,* 8–13; Moulin, *Sixième decade,* 70, 117; Gaches, *Seize sermons,* 45, 310; Gaches, *Quatre,* 14; Gaches, *Le triomphe,* 43.

47. Gaches, *L'Athésme confondu,* 15–18.

48. Daillé, *Vint sermons,* 2–4.

49. Brockliss, "The Scientific Revolution," 55–89.

50. Shapin, *The Scientific Revolution,* 30–46.

51. Examples of Huguenot occupations involved with early machine technology include the following: textile workers, inventors, printers, instrument makers, watch and clock makers, furniture makers, paper makers, gun and silver smiths, miners, and book binders.

52. This category of occupational groups would have included individuals involved in textiles, knife and scissor making, cabinet making, printing, silver smithing, and gun smithing, to name a few.

53. For the shift towards greater quantification, see Crosby, *The Measure of Reality.*

54. Gaches, *L'Athéisme confondu,* 16 and 34.

55. Jurieu, *The Reflections,* 53, 57–61.

56. Jurieu, *The Reflections,* 5.

57. Massard, *Remarks Upon the Dream* and in his *Harmonie des prophéties;* Monahan, *Let God Arise,* 36.

58. Jurieu, *The Reflections,* 3.

59. *A Relation of Several Hundreds of Children,* 2–3, 5.

60. Laborie, "Huguenot Propaganda," 647.

61. Jurieu, *The Reflections,* 8, 45.

62. Jurieu, *The Reflections,* 25.

63. It is worth noting that Pierre Bayle, Jurieu's polemical arch-nemesis, identified the *Esprits forts* as free thinkers or early deists. Flynn, *New Encyclopedia,* 343. Renowned deist Anthony Collins referred to the new "secte" of *Esprits forts* in the title to one of his work's on deism. See Anthony Collins, *Discours sur la liberté de penser.*

64. Jurieu, *The Reflections,* 8, 15, and 16.

65. For a description of François de Langlade du Chaila's murder, see Monahan, *Let God Arise,* 62–63.

66. Laborie, "Huguenot Propaganda," 642.

67. Nearly two-thirds of those arrested for prophesying or attending assemblies in 1701 and 1702 were women. Monahan, *Let God Arise*, 3, 55, and 55–56.

68. Little is known of Massard other than he was the son of a Calvinist Grenoblois and the father of seven children. He worked as an apothecary and was a member of Grenoble's medical faculty. For Massard's biography, see Wirts and Tuttle, "Jacques Massard," 84–132; Charbonneau, "Huguenot Prophetism," 23.

69. Massard was also a disciple Jan Baptiste Van Helmont, a leading Paracelsian and originator of seed theory.

70. For reading on Paracelsus and the intellectual connections between early modern magic and medicine, see Webster, *Paracelsus: Medicine, Magic, and Mission*.

71. Moran, *Distilling Knowledge*, 69, 72 and 76.

72. Debus, *The French Paracelsians*, 8.

73. Baumgartner, *Longing for the End*, 134.

74. Massard, *Explication*, 96, 106–107.

75. Moulin, *Traitté de la conoissance*, 16 and 39.

76. Moulin, *Traitté de la conoissance*, 10.

77. Moulin, *Traitté de la conoissance*, 9.

CONCLUSION

1. Laborie, *Enlightening Enthusiasm*, 172.

2. Archives communales de Vevey (AC Vevey), D orange 30, Registre des décès, fol. 9r, March 3, 1708.

3. AC Vevey, D orange 30, fol. 36v, April 14, 1724.

BIBLIOGRAPHY

ARCHIVES

France

Archives départementales des Hautes-Alpes (ADH)
Sous-série 3 E: Archives communales: Commune de La Grave
   3 E 5125 BB5, Registres des délibérations, 1666–1673.
   3 E 5327 FF5, Pièces de procédures, 1651–1668.

Sous-série 1 E: Notaires
   1 E 7158, Minutes de Jean Rome (Notaire à La Grave), 1678.

Archives départementales de l'Isère (ADI)
Sous-série 4 E: Archives communales déposées
   4 E 31/64, Archives communales de Mizoën, cultes et assistance
   publique. Pauvres de la R.P.R.: rôles, comptes des procureurs, etc.
   (1675–1689). Création et installation de l'hôpital dans la maison
   Bonnet, ministre de la R.P.R. (1686–1687).

Série H Dépôt: Archives hospitalières déposées, dont Hôpital de Grenoble
   H+_GRE/E_7, Délibérations du Conseil de direction des pauvres
   (1683–1711).
   H+_GRE/B_144, Observations faites sur les états, dressés en 1701, des
   revenus, biens, charges et dépenses de l'hôpital de Grenoble provenant notamment des legs faits aux pauvres de la religion réformée et
   aux consistoires de l'ancienne province du Dauphiné (1702).

Sous-série 5 E: Registres paroissiaux et d'état civil, collection départementale
   5 E 238/1, 13 et 14: Mizoën (protestants), baptêmes, mariages et sépultures (1669–1684).

Archives nationales (AN)

Série TT 230–276: Archives des consistoires, 1566–1740

TT/272 (1587–1697), dossier 7, Terrasses, Chazelet, Ventolon, Hières (Hautes-Alpes, cant. et com. La Grave). Partage d'avis concernant l'exercice de la R. P. R., 1664.

Archives cantonales vaudoises (ACV)

Série Bda: Registres des consistoires, 1574–1798

Bda 132/3, Vevey-La Tour-de-Peilz, 1687–1691.
Bda 132/4, Vevey-La Tour-de-Peilz, 1698–1703.
Bda 132/5, Vevey-La Tour-de-Peilz, 1703–1706.

Bis 1–345: Cours de justice du district de Vevey, 1555–1845 (Sous-fonds)

Bis 91, Actes judiciaires (1691–1718) et registre d'homologation de testaments (1698–1700),
Bis 101, Comptes de Tutelles, 1726–1746.
Bis 111/11, Cahier d'inventaires et ventes de meubles en matière de tutelle et de succession pour la Cour de Vevey, 1696–1709.
Bis 113, Livre des inventaires de la Cour de Vevey, 1688–1719.
Bis 114, Livre des inventaires de la Cour de Vevey, 1719–1726.

Bis 346–622: Cours de justice du district de Vevey, 1501–1844 (Sous-fonds)

Bis 562, Documents relatifs à Paul Jullien, marchand de Villar d'Arêne (Dauphiné), 1649–1685.

Eb: Registres paroissiaux, 1562–1989

Eb 132/3, Paroisse réformée de Vevey, 1642–1696.
Eb 132/4, Paroisse réformée de Vevey, 1696–1723.

PP numérique: Archives privées entrées dès 1979

PP 713/1, Monnet (famille), 1670–1759, Livre de raison de Jean Giraud de La Grave, 1670–1711.

Archives communales de Vevey (AC Vevey)

Aa bleu 1–170: Administration générale. Manuaux du Conseil (Ancien régime), puis procès verbaux de la Municipalité et du Conseil de Régie

Aa bleu 26, Manual du conseil, 1685–1688.

Aa bleu 27, Manual du conseil, 1689–1691.

Aa bleu 28, Manual du conseil, 1692–1695.

Aa bleu 29, Manual du conseil, 1696–1698.

Aa bleu 30, Manual du conseil, 1698–1700.

Aa bleu 31, Manual du conseil, 1700–1702.

Aa bleu 32, Manual du conseil, 1702–1704.

Aa bleu 33, Manual du conseil, 1705–1708.

Aa bleu 34, Manual du conseil, 1708–1712.

Aa bleu 58, Manual du noble conseil des douze de la ville de Vevey, 1757–1761.

D orange 30–31: Population. Etat civil. Décès., 1704–1881.

D orange 30, Registre des décès, 1704–1863.

Documentation horlogers

H Noir 1, 1680–1816, Rôles des assistés par l'Hôpital

PRINTED PRIMARY SOURCES

Benoist, Elie. *Histoire de l'Édit de Nantes: contenant les choses les plus remarquables qui se sont passées en France avant & après sa publication, à l'ocasion de la diversité des religions, et principalement les contraventions, inexecutions, chicanes, artifices, violences, & autres injustices, que les reformez se plaignent d'y avoir souffertes, jusques à l'édit de revocation, en octobre 1685; avec ce qui a suivi ce nouvel édit jusques à présent.* Volume 5. Delft: Adrien Beman, 1695.

Bouteroue, Denis de. *La réponse des bons anges aux voix angéliques des mauvais, ou Réfutation d'un escrit publié sous le nom de Jean d'Auric touchant les motifs de son apostasie, le 30 janvier 1627.* n.p., 1627.

Brisac, Alexandre. *Le souhait de l'église ou sermon sur le Chap. LXIV d'Essaie, V. 1.2.3.4.* Charenton, 1649.

Collins, Anthony. *Discours sur la liberté de penser, et de raisonner sur les matières les plus importantes, écrit à l'ocasion de l'acroissement d'une nouvelle secte d'Esprits Forts. Ou de gens qui present librement.* Traduit de l'anglois. London, 1717.

Daillé, Jean. *Jean Daillé: pronocés à Charenton sur certains jours et certains temps de l'année.* Genève: P. Chouët, 1658.

d'Aulnoy, Marie-Catherine. *Histoire de Jean de Bourbon, Prince de Carency*. La Haye: A. Moetjens, 1704.

Furetière, Antoine. *Dictionnaire universel, contenant généralement tous les mots françois tant vieux que modernes, et les termes des sciences et des arts*. Tome Premier. A – D. Rotterdam: Reinier Leers, 1718.

Gaches, Raymond. *L'Athéisme confondu, ou, sermon sur ces paroles l'insensé dit en son coeur il n'y a point de Dieu, prononcé à Charenton*. Charenton: Samuel Perier, 1655.

———. *Quatre sermons le premier chap. de la seconde Épistre de Saint Pierre*. Charenton: Louis Vendosme, 1655.

———. *Seize sermons sur divers textes de l'Écriture Sainte*. Genève: I. Antoine & S. de Tournes, 1660.

———. *Le triomphe de l'Evangile, ou sermon sur la II Épitre de Saint Paul aux Corinithians*. Charenton: Louis Vendosme, 1654.

Godeau, Antoine. *Paraphrase des Pseaumes de David, en vers françois*. Paris: Pierre le Petit, 1659.

Le guide d'Amsterdam, enseignant aux voyageurs et aux negocians sa splendeur, son commerce, & la description de ses edifices. Amsterdam: Daniel de La Feuille, 1701.

Jurieu, Pierre. *Abrégé de l'histoire Concile de Trente, avec un discours contentant les réflexions historiques sur les conciles, & particulièrement sur la conduite de celuy de Trente, pour prouver que les Protestans ne sont pas obligéz à se soûmettre à ce dernier concile*. Amsterdam: Henri Desbordes, 1683.

———. *L'Accomplissement des prophéties ou la délivrance prochaine de l'église*. Rotterdam: Abraham Archer, 1686.

———. *The Reflections of the Reverend and Learned Monsieur Jurieu, Upon the Strange and Miraculous Exstasies of Isabel Vincent, the Shepardess of Saou in Dauphiné*. London: Printed for Richard Baldwin, 1689.

Labadie, Jean de. *Déclaration de Jean de Labadie, cy-devant prêtre, prédicateur et chanoine d'Amiens, contenant les raisons qui l'ont obligé à quitter la communion de l'Église Romaine pour se ranger à celle de l'église réformée*. Montauban: P. Braconier, 1650.

Massard, Jacques. *Explication d'un songe divin de Louis XIV. Et de deux autres songes divins d'une personne de qualité, et de merité de La Haye. Avec sept revelations de la Dem. Refugiée à Amsterdam*. Amsterdam: Jean & Gilllis Janssons à Waesberge, 1690.

———. *Harmonie des prophéties anciennes avec les modernes, sur la durée de l'Antéchrist, et les souffrances de l'église*. Cologne: Pierre Marteau, 1687.

————. *Remarks Upon the Dream of the Late Abdicated Queen of England Upon that of Madam the Dutchess of La Valiere, Late Mistress to the French King, and Now Nun of the Order of Bare-Footed Carmelites at Paris*. London: Printed for Tho. Salusbury, 1690.

Mollenc, Michel. *Le réveil-matin des arithméticiens, soit le comble d'arithmétique*. Celerier: Genève, 1626.

Moulin, Pierre du. *Accomplissement des prophéties: où est montré que les prophéties St. Paul et de l'apocalypse et de Daniel touchant les combats de l'église sont accomplies*. Genève: Pierre Chouët, 1660.

————. *L'Anti-barbare, ou du langage inconnu: tant es prières des particuliers qu'au service public: où sont aussi représentées les clauses principales de la messe*. Genève: Pierre Chouët, 1660.

————. *Deuxième décade de sermons*. Genève: Pierre Chouët, 1653.

————. *Physique ou science naturelle avec une table des matières et chapitres*. Rouen: Jean et David Berthelin, 1655.

————. *Première décade de sermons*. Genève: Jacques Chouët, 1643.

————. *Première décade de sermons*. Genève: Pierre Chouët, 1653.

————. *Septième décade de sermons*. Genève: Jacques et Pierre Chouët, 1648.

————. *Sermons sur quelques textes de l'Écriture Sainte*. Genève: Pierre Aubert, 1625.

————. *Sixième décade de sermons*. Genève: Jacques & Pierre Chouët, 1647.

————. *Traitté de la conoissance de Dieu*. Genève: Pierre Aubert, 1637.

————. *Troisième décade de sermons*. Genève: Jacques Chouët, 1643.

————. *La vie et religion de deux bons papes. Léon premier et Grégoire premier*. Genève: Pierre Chouët, 1649.

Préchac, Jean de. *Le Comte Tékély, nouvelle historique*. La Haye: H. de Bulderen, 1686.

Relation en abregé de ce qui s'est passé de plus remarquable dans le retour des Vaudois au Piémont, depuis le 16 août 1689, jusqu'au 15 juillet 1690. La Haye: Olivier Le Franc, 1690.

A Relation of Several Hundreds of Children and Others that Prophesie and Preach in Their Sleep &c. First Examined and Admired by Several Ingenious Men, Ministers and Professors of Philosophy at Geneva and Sent from Thence in Two Letters to Roterdam. London: Richard Baldwin, 1689.

Réponse de Blaise Pascal au Père Noël. 1647.

Spon, Jacob. *Voyage d'Italie, de Dalmatie, de Grèce, et du Levant*. Lyon: Cellier, 1678.

SECONDARY SOURCES

Adams, Geoffrey. *The Huguenots and French Opinion, 1685–1787: The Enlightenment Debate on Toleration*. Waterloo: Wilfrid Laurier Press, 1991.

Adas, Michael. *Machines as the Measure of Men: Science, Technology, and Ideologies of Western Dominance*. Ithaca: Cornell University Press, 1989.

Alfani, Guido, and Vincent Gourdon. "Spiritual Kinship and Godparenthood: An Introduction." In *Spiritual Kinship in Europe, 1500–1900*, edited by Guido Alfani and Vincent Gourdon, 1–43. Houndmills Basingstoke Hampshire: Palgrave Macmillan, 2012.

Armstrong, Brian G. *Bibliographia Molinaei: An Alphabetical, Chronological and Descriptive Bibliography of the Works of Pierre Du Moulin (1568–1658)*. Genève: Librairie Droz, 1997.

Arnaud, Eugène. *Histoire des protestants du Dauphiné aux XVIe, XVIIe, and XVIIIe siècles, Volume II*. Paris: Grassart, 1884.

Barnard, John. "Introduction." In *The Cambridge History of the Book in Britain*. Volume IV: 1557–1695, edited by John Barnard, D. F. McKenzie, and Maureen Bell, 1–25. Cambridge: Cambridge University Press, 2002.

Barrett, Eileen. "Huguenot Integration in Late 17th- and 18th-Century London: Insights from Records of the French Church and Some Relief Agencies." In *From Strangers to Citizens: The Integration of Immigrant Communities in Britain, Ireland and Colonial America, 1550–1750*, edited by Randolph Vigne and Charles Littleton, 375–82. Brighton: Sussex Academic Press, 2001.

Baumgartner, Frederic J. *Longing for the End: A History of Millennialism in Western Civilization*. New York: St. Martin's Press, 1999.

Beam, Sara. *The Trial of Jeanne Catherine: Infanticide in Early Modern Geneva*. Toronto: University of Toronto Press, 2021.

Beik, William, *A Social and Cultural History of Early Modern France*. Cambridge: Cambridge University Press, 2009.

Belmont, Alain. "Les artisans ruraux en Dauphiné aux XIVe et XVe siècles d'après les rôles de taille et les révisions de feux." *Histoire, Économie et Société* (1993): 419–43.

———. *Des ateliers au village. Les artisans ruraux en Dauphiné sous l'Ancien Régime*, Tomes 1 & 2. Grenoble: Presses Universitaires de Grenoble, 1998.

Benedict, Philip. *Christ's Churches Purely Reformed: A Social History of Calvinism*. New Haven: Yale University Press, 2002.

———. "The Huguenot Population of France, 1600–1685: The Demographic Fate and Customs of a Religious Minority." *Transactions of the American Philosophical Society* 81, no. 5 (1991): i–164.

Bernat, Chrystel, and David van der Linden. "Rethinking the Refuge: A Systematic Approach to Huguenot Communities in the Dutch Republic." *Church History and Religious Culture* 100, 4 (2020): 439–45.

Berteau, Camille, Vincent Gourdon, and Isabelle Robin-Romero. "Godparenthood: Driving Local Solidarity in Northern France in the Early Modern Era. The Example of Aubervilliers Families in the Sixteenth–Eighteenth Centuries." *The History of the Family* 17, no. 4 (2012): 452–67.

Bireley, Robert. *The Refashioning of Catholicism, 1450–1700: A Reassessment of the Counter-Reformation.* Washington D.C: The Catholic University of America Press, 1999.

Bloom, Rori. "Playing with Dolls in Old Regime Fairy Tales." In *Modes of Play in Eighteenth-Century France,* edited by Fayçal Falaky and Reginald McGinnis, 9 – 23. Lewisburg, PA: Bucknell University Press, 2022.

Bohanan, Donna J. *Fashion beyond Versailles: Consumption and Design in Seventeenth-Century France.* Baton Rouge: Louisiana State University Press, 2012.

Bolle, Pierre. *Protestants en Dauphiné: L'aventure de la Réforme.* Veurey: Éd. Le Dauphiné, 2001.

Boorstin, Daniel. *The Discoverers: A History of Man's Search to Know His World and Himself.* New York: Random House, 1983.

Bossy, John. "Blood and Baptism: Kinship Community and Christianity in Western Europe from the Fourteenth to the Seventeenth Centuries." *Sanctity and Secularity: The Church and the World* 10 (1973): 129–43.

Brockliss, L. W. B. "The Scientific Revolution in France." In *The Scientific Revolution in National Context,* edited by Roy Porter and Makuláš Teich, 55–89. Cambridge: Cambridge University Press, 1992.

Burghart, Marjorie. "Signata de mea marcha: les marques de marchands dans les comptes du péage de Chambéry (XVe siècle)." *Médiévales. Langues, Textes, Histoire* 66 (2014): 141–58.

Cardinal, Catherine. *The Watch: From its Origins to the XIX Century.* Translated by Jacques Pages. New York: Tabard Press, 1989.

Carter, Karen E. *Creating Catholics: Catechism and Primary Education in Early Modern France.* Notre Dame, IN: University of Notre Dame Press, 2011.

Chappell, Carolyn Lougee. "Emigration and Memory: after 1685; after 1789." *In Egodocuments and History: Autobiographical Writing in its Social Context since the Middle Ages*, edited by Rudolf Dekker, 89–106. Hilversum, Rotterdam: Verloren. Published in cooperation with the Faculty of History and Art Studies of Erasmus University, 2002

———. *Facing the Revocation: Huguenot Families, Faith, and the King's Will.* New York: Oxford University Press, 2017.

———. "Family Bonds across the Refuge." In *Memory and Identity: The Huguenots in France and the Atlantic Diaspora*, edited by Bertrand Van Ruymbeke and Randy J. Sparks, 172–93. Columbia, SC: University of South Carolina, 2003.

———. "Huguenot Memoirs," In *A Companion to the Huguenots*, edited by Raymond A. Mentzer and Bertrand Van Ruymbeke, 323–47. Leiden: Brill, 2016.

———. "'The Pains I took to Save My/His Family:' Escape Accounts by a Huguenot Mother and Daughter after the Revocation of the Edict of Nantes." *French Historical Studies* 22 (1999): 1–64.

Chapuis, Alfred. *Les corporations d'horlogers vaudois au XVIIIe siècle*: Vevey, Lausanne, etc. La Chaux-de-Fonds: Arts Graphiques Haefeli et Co., 1946.

Charbonneau, Jason. "Huguenot Prophetism, Clerical Authority, and the Disenchantment of the World, 1685–1710." M.A. Thesis, Carleton University, 2012.

Charbonnier-Burkard, Marianne. "Doctrine and Liturgy of the Reformed Churches of France." In *A Companion to the Huguenots*, edited by Raymond A. Mentzer and Bertrand Van Ruymbeke, 43–65. Leiden: Brill, 2016.

Chavannes, Jules. "Commerce et industrie à Vevey au XVIIme et au XVIIIme siècle." *Revue historique vaudoise* 51 (1943): 172–84.

———. "Un prêtre converti par un martyr: le missionnaire Philippe Aiguisier." *Bulletin de la société de l'histoire du protestantisme français*. (Paris: Agence Centrale de la Société, 1861): 396–99.

———. *Les réfugiés français dans le pays de Vaud, et particulièrement à Vevey.* Lausanne: Georges Bridel, 1874.

Cipolla, Carlo. *Clocks and Culture: 1300–1700.* New York: W.W. Norton & Company, 2003.

———, ed. *The Fontana Economic History of Europe: The Sixteenth and Seventeenth Centuries.* London: Collins/Fontana, 1974.

Clark, Mary. "Foreigners and Freedom: the Huguenot Refuge in Dublin City, 1660–1700." *Proceedings of the Huguenot Society of Great Britain and Ireland* 27, no. 3 (2000): 382–91.

Conner, Philip. *Huguenot Heartland: Montauban and Southern French Calvinism during the Wars of Religion.* Aldershot: Ashgate, 2002.

Corsini, Silvio. *Le livre à Lausanne: Cinq siècles d'édition et d'imprimerie 1493–1993.* Lausanne: Payot, 1993.

Cosmos, Georgia. *Huguenot Prophecy and Clandestine Worship in the Eighteenth Century: 'The Sacred Theatre of the Cévennes.'* Aldershot: Ashgate, 2005.

Cranston, Maurice. *Jean-Jacques: The Early Life and Work of Jean-Jaqcues Rousseau, 1712– 1754.* Chicago: University of Chicago Press, 1991.

Crosby, Alfred W. *The Measure of Reality: Quantification and Western Society, 1250–1600.* Cambridge: Cambridge University Press, 1997.

Debus, Allen G. *The French Paracelsians : the Chemical Challenge to Medical and Scientific Tradition in Early Modern France.* Cambridge: Cambridge University Press, 2002.

Disdrelle, Nicole M. "Protestant Polemic in Post-Edict France: Pierre du Moulin and the Seventeenth-Century Huguenot World, 1598–1625." M.A. Thesis, University of Guelph, 2010.

Ducommun, Marie-Jeanne, and Dominique Quadroni. *Le refuge protestant dans le Pays de Vaud (fin XVIIe–début XVIIIe s.). Aspects d'une migration.* Genève: Droz, 1991.

Duncan, Stephen R., Susan Scott, and Christopher J. Duncan, "Smallpox Epidemics in Cities in Britain." *The Journal of Interdisciplinary History* 25, no.2 (Autumn 1994): 255–71.

DuPlessis, Robert S. *Transitions to Capitalism in Early Modern Europe: Economies in the Era of Globalization, c. 1450–1820.* Cambridge: Cambridge University Press, 2019.

Eisenstein, Elizabeth L. *Grub Street Abroad: Aspects of the French Cosmopolitan Press from the Age of Louis XIV to the French Revolution.* Oxford: Clarendon Press, 1992.

Enright, Michael J. "Organization and Coordination in Geographically Concentrated Industries." In *Coordination and Information: Historical Perspectives on the Organization of Enterprise,* edited by Naomi R. Lamoreaux and Daniel M. G. Raff, 103–46. Chicago: University of Chicago Press, 1995.

Fairchilds, Cissie C. *Women in Early Modern Europe, 1500–1700.* Harlow: Pearson Longman, 2007.

FamilySearch. "England Births and Christenings, 1538–1975." Anne Chicot in entry for Andre Laurent, 1693. Accessed March 20, 2023. https://www.familysearch.org/ark:/61903/1:1:V5LG-4LZ.

———. "England Births and Christenings, 1538–1975. Susanne Chicot in entry for Lucresse Charbrolle, 1696. Accessed March 20, 2023. https://www.familysearch.org/ark:/61903/1:1:V5LG-HB9.

———. "England Births and Christenings, 1538–1975. Susanne Chicot in entry for Pierre Chabrolle, 1697. Accessed March 20, 2023. https://www.familysearch.org/ark:/61903/1:1:V5LG-N5T.

———. "England Marriages, 1538–1973." Suzanne Chicot in entry for Marc Henry Chabrol, 1690. Accessed March 20, 2023. https://familysearch.org/ark:/61903/1:1:NXLQ-2XT.

Farr, James R., *Artisans in Europe, 1300–1914.* Cambridge: Cambridge University Press, 2000.

———. *Hands of Honor: Artisans and Their World in Dijon, 1550–1650.* Ithaca: Cornell University Press, 1988.

———. *The Work of France: Labor and Culture in Early Modern Times, 1350–1800.* Lanham: Rowman and Littlefield, 2008.

Fillet, M. Le Chanoine. "Les horloges publiques dans le sud-est de la France depuis le XVe jusqu'au XVIIIe siècle," *Bulletin archéologique du comité des travaux historiques et scientifiques* (1902): 101–19.

Flynn, Tom. *New Encyclopedia of Unbelief.* Amhurst, NY: Prometheus Books, 2007.

Fogleman, Aaron. *Two Troubled Souls: An Eighteenth-Century Couple's Spiritual Journey in the Atlantic World.* Chapel Hill: University of North Carolina Press, 2013.

Fontaine, Laurence. "Family Cycles, Peddling and Society in Upper Alpine Valleys in the Eighteenth Century." In *Domestic Strategies: Work and Family in France and Italy, 1600–1800,* edited by Stuart Woolf, 43–68. Cambridge: Cambridge University Press, 1991.

———. *History of Pedlars in Europe.* Translated by Vicki Whittaker. Durham: Duke University Press, 1996.

———. *The Moral Economy: Poverty, Credit, and Trust in Early Modern Europe.* Cambridge: Cambridge University Press, 2014.

Fontaine, Laurence, and David Siddle, "Mobility, Kinship, and Commerce in the Alpes, 1500–1800." In *Migration, Mobility, and Modernization,* edited by David Siddle, 47–69. Liverpool: Liverpool University Press, 2000.

Gerson, Stéphane. *Nostradamus: How an Obscure Renaissance Astrologer Became the Modern Prophet of Doom*. New York: St. Martin's Press, 2012.

Gordon, Bruce. *The Swiss Reformation*. Manchester: Manchester University Press, 2002.

Goubert, Pierre. *Louis XIV and Twenty Million Frenchmen*. Translated by Anne Carter. New York: Vintage, 1972.

Greiner, Grace Catherine. "Merchant Marks and Marginal Evidence for the Late-Sixteenth-Century Circulation of Cambridge, Trinity College, MS R. 4.20." *Journal of the Early Book Society for the Study of Manuscripts and Printing History* 24 (2021):159–89.

Gwynn, Robin. "Conformity, Non-conformity and Huguenot Settlement in England in the Later Seventeenth Century." In *Religious Culture of the Huguenots, 1660–1750*, edited by Anne Dunan-Page, 23–41. London: Routledge, 2006.

———. *Huguenot Heritage: The History and Contribution of the Huguenots in Britain*. Brighton: Sussex Academic Press, 2001.

———. *The Huguenots in Later Stuart Britain: Volume II—Settlement, Churches, and the Role of London*. Brighton: Sussex Academic Press, 2018.

Hamling, Tara. "The Household." In *Early Modern Childhood: An Introduction*, edited by Anna French, 33–54. London: Routledge, 2019.

Hardwick, Julie. *Sex in an Old Regime City: Young Workers and Intimacy in France, 1660–1789*. Oxford: Oxford University Press, 2020.

Harley, Timothy. *Moon Lore*. Rutland, VT: C. E. Tuttle, 1970.

Hickey, Daniel. *The Coming of French Absolutism: The Struggle for Tax Reform in the Province of Dauphiné, 1540–1640*. Toronto: University of Toronto Press, 1986.

———. "Innovation and Obstacles to Growth in the Agriculture of Early Modern France: The Example of Dauphiné." *French Historical Studies* 15, no. 2 (Autumn 1987): 208–40.

———. "Politics and Commerce in Renaissance France: The Evolution of Trade along the Routes of Dauphiné." *Canadian Journal of History* 6, no. 2 (1971): 133–51.

Hilfiker, André. *Vevey, centre économique régional*. Lausanne: Impr. Vaudoise, 1966.

Hoftijzer, Paul G. "The Dutch Republic: Centre of the European Book Trade in the 17th Century." European History Online, published by the Leibniz Institute of European History, Mainz, November 23, 2015. http://www.ieg-ego.eu/hoftijzerp-2015-en.

———. "The English Book in the Seventeenth-Century Dutch Republic." In *The Bookshop of the World: the Role of the Low Countries in the Book-Trade, 1473–1941,* edited by Lotte Hellinga, Alastair Duke, Jacob Harskamp, and Theo Hermans, 89–107. Leiden: Brill, 2001.

Holman, Thomas S. "Holbein's Portraits of the Steelyard Merchants: An Investigation." *Metropolitan Museum Journal* 14 (1979): 139–58.

Holt, Mack. *The French Wars of Religion, 1562–1629.* Cambridge: Cambridge University Press, 1995.

Houston, R. A. *Literacy in Early Modern Europe: Culture and Education, 1500–1800.* Harlow: Pearson Education Limited, 2002.

Hunter, Michael. "The Royal Society's 'Repository' and Its Background." In *The Origins of Museums: The Cabinet of Curiosities in Sixteenth- and Seventeenth-Century Europe,* edited by Oliver Impey and Arthur Mac-Gregor, 160–168. Oxford: Clarendon Press, 1985.

Hylton, Raymond. "Dublin's Huguenot Refuge: 1662–1817." *Dublin Historical Record* 40, no. 1 (1986): 15–25.

———. *Ireland's Huguenots and Their Refuge, 1662–1745: An Unlikely Haven.* Brighton: Sussex Academic Press, 2005.

Israel, Jonathan I. *Radical Enlightenment: Philosophy and the Making of Modernity, 1650–1750.* Oxford: Oxford University Press, 2001.

Jequier, François. "Employment Strategies and Production Structures in the Swiss Watchmaking Industry." In *Favorites of Fortune: Technology, Growth and Economic Development since the Industrial Revolution,* edited by Patrice Higonnet, Henry Rosovsky, David S. Landes, 322–36. Cambridge: Harvard University Press, 1991.

Johnston, Charles. "Elie Benoist, Historian of the Edict of Nantes." *Church History* 55, no. 4 (Dec. 1986): 468–88.

Kellenbenz, Hermann. "Technology in the Age of the Scientific Revolution, 1500–1700." In *The Fontana Economic History of Europe: The Sixteenth and Seventeenth Centuries,* edited by Carlo Cipolla, 177–272. London: Collins/Fontana, 1974.

Kittel, Thomas. "Early Modern Merchant's Marks in Medieval Manuscripts." *Renaissance Studies* 34, no. 2 (April 2020): 208–27.

Kwass, Michael. *The Consumer Revolution, 1650–1800.* Cambridge: Cambridge University Press, 2022.

Laborie, Lionel. *Enlightening Enthusiasm: Prophecy and Religious Experience in Early Eighteenth-Century England.* Manchester: Manchester University Press, 2015.

———. "Huguenot Propaganda and the Millenarian Legacy of the Désert in the Refuge (1702–1730)." *Proceedings of the Huguenot Society of Great Britain and Ireland* XXIX, no. 5 (2012) 640–54.

———. "Who were the Camisards?" *French Studies Bulletin* 32, no. 120 (2011): 54–57.

Labrousse, Elisabeth. "France, 1598–1685." In *International Calvinism, 1541–1715,* edited by Menna Prestwich, 285–314. Oxford: Clarendon Press, 1985.

———. *"Une foi, une loi, un roi?": La Révocation de l'Édit de Nantes.* Genève: Labor et Fides, 1985.

Landes, David S. *Revolution in Time: Clocks and the Making of the Modern World.* Cambridge: Harvard University Press, 1983.

———. "Watchmaking: A Case Study in Enterprise and Change." *The Business History Review* 53, no. 1, (Spring 1979): 1–39.

Langlade, Émile. *La marchande de modes de Marie Antoinette: Rose Bertin.* Paris: A. Michel, 1911.

———. *Rose Bertin: The Creator of Fashion at the Court of Marie Antoinette.* Translated by Angelo S. Rappoport. New York: C. Scribner's Sons, 1913.

Lányi, Gábor János. "Zwinglian-Calvinist Debate on Church Discipline in the Pays de Vaud." *Studia Universitatis Babeş-Bolyai Theologia Reformata Transylvanica* 62, no. 2 (2017): 94–119.

Larminie, Vivienne. "Exile, Integration and European Perspectives: Huguenots in the Pays de Vaud." In *The Huguenots: History and Memory in Transnational Context: Essays in Honour and Memory of Walter C. Utt,* edited by David J. B. Trim, 241–62. Leiden: Brill, 2011.

———. "Life in Ancien Regime Vaud." *History Today* 48, no. 4 (1998): 44–50.

———, ed. *Huguenot Networks: 1560–1780: The Interactions and Impact of a Protestant Minority in Europe.* New York: Routledge, 2017.

Lavade, Louis, and Daniel-Alexandre Chavannes. *Statistique du district de Vevey.* Lausanne: Impr. A Fischer et Luc Vincet, 1806.

Lavenia, Vincenzo. "Catechism and War." Routledge. Accessed May 20, 2023. https://doi.org/10.4324/9780367347093-RERW15-1.

Lemaître, Nicole. "Les livres de raison en France (fin XIIIe–XIXe siècles)." *Testo E Senso* 7 (2006): 1–18.

Lossky, Andrew. *Louis XIV and the French Monarchy*. New Brunswick, NJ: Rutgers University Press, 1994.

Luciani, Isabelle. "Ordering Words, Ordering the Self: Keeping a *Livre de Raison* in Early Modern Provence, Sixteenth through Eighteenth Centuries." *French Historical Studies* 38, no. 4 (October 2015): 529–48.

Luria, Keith P. *Territories of Grace: Cultural Change in the Seventeenth-Century Diocese of Grenoble*. Berkeley: University of California Press, 1991.

Maigne, W. *Dictionnaire classique des origins, inventions et découvertes dans les arts les arts, les sciences, et les lettres*. Paris: Larousse et Boyer, 1864.

Major, J. Russell. *From Renaissance Monarchy to Absolute Monarchy: French Kings, Nobles, and Estates*. Baltimore: John Hopkins University Press, 1994.

Martin, Lucinda. "Gender and the Suppression of 'Anabaptist Pietists' in Bern." In *Sisters: Myth and Reality of Anabaptist, Mennonite, and Doopsgezind Women*, ca. 1525–1900, edited by P. Visser, 211–28. Leiden: Brill, 2014.

Matzinger-Pfister, Regula. "L'introduction des consistoires dans le Pays de Vaud." In *Sous l'œil du consistoire. Sources consistoriales et histoire du contrôle social sous l'Ancien Régime*, edited by Nicole Staremberg Goy and Danièle Tosato-Rigo, 113–23. Lausanne: Études de Lettres, 2004.

McCullough, Roy L. *Coercion, Conversion and Countersinsurgency in Louis XIV's France*. Leiden: Brill, 2007.

McKenzie, D. F. "Printing and Publishing 1557–1700: Constraints on the London Book Trades." In *The Cambridge History of the Book in Britain*, 4, edited by John Barnard, D. F. McKenzie, and Maureen Bell, 553–67. Cambridge: Cambridge University Press, 2014.

Mentzer, Raymond. *Blood and Belief: Family Survival and Confessional Identity Among the Provincial Huguenot Nobility*. West Lafayette, IN: Purdue University Press, 1994.

———. "Communities of Worship and the Reformed Churches of France." In *Defining Community in Early Modern Europe*, edited by Michael J. Halvorson and Karen E. Spierling, 25–42. London: Routledge, 2008.

———. "The Printed Catechism and Religious Instruction in the French Reformed Churches." In *Books Have Their Own Destiny: Essays in Honor of Robert V. Schnucker*, edited by Robin Bruce Barnes, Robert Kolb, and Paula L. Presley, 93–101. Kirksville, MO: Thomas Jefferson University Press, 1998.

Mettam, Roger. "Louis XIV and the Huguenots." *History Today* 35, no. 5 (May, 1985): 15–21.

Minnet William A., and Susan Minnet, eds. *Registers of the Churches of the Tabernacle of Glasshouse Street and Leicester Fields, 1688–1783.* Frome: Butler and Tanner, LTD, 1926.

Monahan, W. Gregory, *Let God Arise: The War and Rebellion of the Camisards.* Oxford: Oxford University Press, 2014.

de Montet, Albert. *Vevey à travers les siècles: recueil de notes.* Vevey: Commune de Vevey, Service des Intérêts Généraux, 1978.

Moran, Bruce T. *Distilling Knowledge: Alchemy, Chemistry, and the Scientific Revolution.* Cambridge: Harvard University Press, 2005.

Mottu-Weber, Liliane. "Marchands et artisans du second refuge à Genève." In *Genève au temps de la Révocation de l'Édit de Nantes,* 1680–1705, edited by Olivier Reverdin et al., 315–97. Genève: Librarie Droz, 1985.

Mouysset, Sylvie. *Papiers de Famille: Introduction à l'étude des livres de raison (France, XVe– XIX siècle).* Rennes: Presses Universitaires de Rennes, 2007.

Musgrave, Peter. *The Early Modern European Economy.* New York: St. Martin's Press, 1999.

Norberg, Kathryn. *Rich and Poor in Grenoble, 1600–1814.* Berkeley: University of California Press, 1985.

Nye, Robert A. *Masculinity and Male Codes of Honor in Modern France.* Berkeley: University of California Press, 1998.

Olivier, Eugène. *Médecine et santé dans le Pays de Vaud au XVIIIe siècle (1675–1798), Partie 2, Tome 1.* Lausanne: Payot, 1962.

Orcibal, Jean. *Louis XIV et les protestants. La cabale des accommodeurs de religion. La caisse des conversions. La révocation de l'Édit de Nantes.* Paris: J. Vrin, 1951.

Ougier, S. "Les réformés de l'Oisans." *Bulletins de la société dauphinoise d'ethnologie et d'anthropologie* 3, no. 1 (January 1896): 19–27.

Parés, Iban Redondo. *Las marcas de mercader en Castilla y Europa (siglos XV y XVI).* Medina del Campo, Valladolid: Fundación Museo de las Ferias, D.L., 2020.

Parker, Charles H. "Moral Supervision and Poor Relief in the Reformed Church of Delft, 1579–1609." *Archiv für Reformationsgeschichte-Archive for Reformation History* 87, No. jg (1996): 334–61.

Perret, Jean-Pierre. *Les imprimeries d'Yverdon au XVIIe et au XVIIIe siècle.* Lausanne: F. Roth, 1945.

Phillips, Henry. *Church and Culture in Seventeenth-Century France.* Cambridge: Cambridge University Press. 1997.

Piguet, Émile. *Les dénombrements généraux de réfugiés huguenots au Pays de Vaud et à Berne à la fin du XVIIe siècle* (second partie). Lausanne: Éditions La Concorde : Impr. de Corbière et Jugain, 1939.

Racevskis, Roland. *Time and Ways of Knowing under Louis XIV: Molière, Sévigné, Lafayette.* Lewisburg: Bucknell University Press, 2003.

Recordon, Édouard. *Études historiques sur le passé de Vevey.* Vevey: Imprimerie Säuberlin et Pfeiffer S.A., 1970.

Robertson, L.A. "The Relations of William III with the Swiss Protestants, 1689–1697." *Transactions of the Royal Historical Society* 12 (1929): 137–62.

Rochat, Antoine. *Le régime matrimonial du pays de Vaud à la fin de l'Ancien Régime et sous le code civil vaudois.* Lausanne: Bibliothèque historique vaudoise, 1987.

Roche, Daniel. *A History of Everyday Things: The Birth of Consumption in France, 1600–1800.* Cambridge: Cambridge University Press, 2000.

Rosenberg, Harriet G. *A Negotiated World: Three Centuries of Change in a French Alpine Community.* Toronto: University of Toronto Press, 1988.

Ruff, Julius R. *Violence in Early Modern Europe, 1500–1800.* Cambridge: Cambridge University Press, 2001.

Sabean, David Warren, Simon Teuscher, and Jon Mathieu, eds. *Kinship in Europe: Approaches to Long-Term Development (1300–1900).* New York: Berghahn Books, 2007.

Salman, Jeroen. *Pedlars and the Popular Press: Itinerant Distribution Networks in England and the Netherlands 1600–1850.* Leiden: Brill, 2013.

Sauter, Michael J. "Clockwatchers and Stargazers: Time Discipline in Early Modern Berlin." *American Historical Review* 112, no. 3 (2007): 685–709.

Sautier, Jérôme. "Politique et refuge. Genève face à la Révocation de l'Édit de Nantes." In *Genève et au temps de la Révocation de l'Édit de Nantes, 1680–1705*, edited by Olivier Reverdin et al., 3–158. Genève: Libraire Droz, 1985.

Schneider, Hans. *German Radical Pietism.* Translated by Gerald T. MacDonald. Lanham, MD: Scarecrow Press, 2007.

Schwartz, Hillel. *The French Prophets: The History of a Millenarian Group in Eighteenth-Century England.* Berkeley: University of California Press, 1980.

Scoville, Warren C. "Huguenots and the Diffusion of Technology. I." *Journal of Political Economy* 60, no. 4 (Aug. 1952): 294–311.

———. "Huguenots and the Diffusion of Technology. II." *Journal of Political Economy* 60, no. 5 (Oct. 1952): 392–411.

———. *The Persecution of Huguenots and French Economic Development, 1680–1720.* Berkeley: University of California Press. 1960.

Shantz, Douglas H. *An Introduction to German Pietism: Protestant Renewal at the Dawn of Modern Europe.* Baltimore: Johns Hopkins University Press, 2013.

Shapin, Steven. *The Scientific Revolution.* Chicago: University of Chicago Press, 1996.

Sherman, Stuart. *Telling Time: Clocks, Diaries, and English Diurnal Form, 1660–1785.* Chicago: University of Chicago Press, 1996.

Spierling, Karen E. *Infant Baptism in Reformation Geneva: The Shaping of a Community, 1536–1564.* London: Routledge, 2016.

Spufford, Margaret. *The Great Reclothing of Rural England: Petty Chapmen and their Wares in the Seventeenth Century.* London: Hambledon Press, 1984.

Stanwood, Owen. *The Global Refuge: Huguenots in an Age of Empire.* Oxford: Oxford University Press, 2020.

Styles, John. "Time Piece: Working Men and Watches," *History Today,* 58 (2008): 44–50.

Swindlehurst, Catherine. " 'An Unruly and Presumptuous Rabble': The Reaction of the Spitalfields Weaving Community to the Settlement of the Huguenots, 1660–90." In *From Strangers to Citizens: The Integration of Immigrant Communities in Britain, Ireland, and Colonial America, 1550–1750,* edited by Randolph Vigne and Charles Littleton, 366–74. Brighton: Sussex Academic Press, 2001.

Taft, Barbara. "Return of a Regicide: Edmund Ludlow and the Glorious Revolution." *History* 76, no. 247 (June 1991): 197–220.

Terpstra, Nicholas. *Religious Refugees in the Early Modern World: An Alternative History of the Reformation.* Cambridge: Cambridge University Press, 2015.

Thomas, Keith. *Religion and the Decline of Magic: Studies in the Popular Beliefs of Sixteenth- and Seventeenth-Century England.* London: Penguin Books, 1991.

Tosato-Rigo, Danièle. "Étrangers mais frères: les réfugiés huguenots." In *Berns mächtige Zeit. Das 16. und 17. Jahrhundert neu entdeckt,* edited by André Holenstein, 266–69. Bern: Schulverlag: Stämpfli, 2006.

Treasure, Geoffrey. *The Huguenots.* New Haven: Yale University Press, 2013.

"Les tribulations d'un huguenot réfugié à Vevey." *Revue historique vaudoise* 37, Issue 2 (Février, 1929): 46–58.

van der Linden, David. *Experiencing Exile: Huguenot Refugees in the Dutch Republic, 1680–1700.* Aldershot, Hamps: Ashgate, 2015.

———. "Histories of Martyrdom and Suffering in the Huguenot Diaspora." In *A Companion to the Huguenots,* edited by Raymond A. Mentzer and Bertrand Van Ruymbeke, 348–70. Leiden: Brill, 2016.

Van Ruymbeke, Bertrand, (introduction), David van der Linden, (review), Eric Schnakenbourg, (review), Bryan Banks, (review), and Owen Stanwood, (response). "The Global Refuge: The Huguenot Diaspora in a Global and Imperial Perspective : A Discussion of Owen Stanwood's The Global Refuge: Huguenots in an Age of Empire." *Journal of Early American History* II, 2–3 (2021):193–234. doi: https://doi.org/10.1163/18770703-11020014.

Vial, E., and C. Côte. *Les horlogers lyonnais de 1550 à 1650*. Paris: Georges Rapilly, 1927.

Vigarello, Georges. *Concepts of Cleanliness: Changing Attitudes in France since the Middle Ages*. Translated by Jean Birrell. Cambridge: Cambridge University Press, 1988.

Vries, Jan de. *The Industrious Revolution: Consumer Behavior and the Household Economy, 1650 to the Present*. Cambridge: Cambridge University Press, 2008.

Walsh, James P. "Holy Time and Sacred Space in Puritan New England." *American Quarterly* 32, no. 1 (Spring 1980): 79–95.

Walsh, Paul. "The Medieval Merchant's Mark and Its Survival in Galway." *Journal of the Galway Archaeological and Historical Society* 45 (1993): 1–28.

Ward, W. R. *The Protestant Evangelical Awakening*. Cambridge: Cambridge University Press, 1992.

Webster, Charles. *Paracelsus: Medicine, Magic, and Mission at the End of Time*. New Haven: Yale University Press, 2008.

Welch, Evelyn. "Sites of Consumption in Early Modern Europe." In *The Oxford Handbook of the History of Consumption*, edited by Frank Trentmann, 228–50. Oxford: Oxford University Press, 2012.

Whelan, Ruth. "From the Other Side of Silence: Huguenot Life-Writing, a Dialogic Art of Narrating the Self." In *Narrating the Self in Early Modern Europe*, edited by Bruno Tribout and Ruth Whelan, 139–60. Oxford: Peter Lang, 2007.

———. "The Huguenots and the Imaginative Geography of Ireland: A Planned Immigration Scheme in the 1680s." *Irish Historical Studies* 35, no. 140 (Nov. 2007): 477–95.

———. "Marsh's Library and the French Calvinist Tradition: the Manuscript Diary of Élie Bouhéreau (1643–1719)." In *The Making of Marsh's Library: Learning, Politics and Religion in Ireland, 1650–1750*, edited by Muriel McCarthy and Ann Simmons, 209–34. Dublin and Portland: Four Courts Press, 2004.

———. "Persecution and Toleration: The Changing Identities of Ireland's Huguenot Refugees." *Proceedings of the Huguenot Society of Great Britain and Ireland* 27, no 1. (1998): 20–35.

———. "Promised Land: Selling Ireland to French Protestants in 1681." *Proceedings of the Huguenot Society of Great Britain and Ireland* 29, no. 1 (2008): 37–50.

———. "Writing the Self: Huguenot Autobiography and the Process of Assimilation." In *From Strangers to Citizens: The Integration of Immigrant Communities in Britain, Ireland, and Colonial America, 1550–1750*, edited by Randolph Vigne and Charles Littleton, 463–77. Brighton: Sussex Academic Press, 2001.

Wilson, Christie Sample. *Beyond Belief: Surviving the Revocation of the Edict of Nantes in France.* Bethlehem: Lehigh University Press, 2011.

Wirts, Kristine, and Leslie Tuttle, "Jacques Massard: Prophecy and the Harmony of Knowledge." In Volume 1 of *Early Modern Prophecies in Transnational, National, and Regional Contexts,* edited by Lionel Laborie and Ariel Hessayon, 84–132. Leiden: Brill, 2021.

Yardeni, Myriam. "Assimilation and Integration." In *A Companion to the Huguenots,* edited by Raymond A. Mentor and Bertrand Van Ruymbeke, 273–90. Leiden: Brill, 2016.

———. *Le refuge protestant.* Paris: Presses Universitaires de France, 1985.

INDEX